D0148862

PLAY AND LITERACY
IN EARLY CHILDHOOD

Research From Multiple Perspectives

Second Edition

The Library
St. Mary's College of Maryland
St. Mary's City, Maryland 20686

PLAY AND LITERACY
IN EARLY CHILDHOOD

Research From Multiple Perspectives

Second Edition

Edited by

KATHLEEN A. ROSKOS
John Carroll University

and

JAMES F. CHRISTIE
Arizona State University

LEA Lawrence Erlbaum Associates
Taylor & Francis Group

New York   London

Cover design by Tomai Maridou.

Lawrence Erlbaum Associates
Taylor & Francis Group
270 Madison Avenue
New York, NY 10016

Lawrence Erlbaum Associates
Taylor & Francis Group
2 Park Square
Milton Park, Abingdon
Oxon OX14 4RN

© 2007 by Taylor & Francis Group, LLC
Lawrence Erlbaum Associates is an imprint of Taylor & Francis Group, an Informa business

Printed in the United States of America on acid-free paper
10 9 8 7 6 5 4 3 2 1

International Standard Book Number-13: 978-0-8058-5640-8 (Softcover) 978-0-8058-5639-2 (Hardcover)

No part of this book may be reprinted, reproduced, transmitted, or utilized in any form by any electronic, mechanical, or other means, now known or hereafter invented, including photocopying, microfilming, and recording, or in any information storage or retrieval system, without written permission from the publishers.

Trademark Notice: Product or corporate names may be trademarks or registered trademarks, and are used only for identification and explanation without intent to infringe.

Library of Congress Cataloging-in-Publication Data

Play and literacy in early childhood : research from multiple perspectives / edited by
    Kathleen A. Roskos and James F. Christie. -- 2nd ed.
        p. cm.
    Includes bibliographical references and index.
    ISBN-13: 978-0-8058-5639-2 (c : alk. paper)
    ISBN-10: 0-8058-5639-0 (c : alk. paper)
    ISBN-13: 978-0-8058-5640-8 (p : alk. paper)
    ISBN-10: 0-8058-5640-4 (p : alk. paper)
    1. Play. 2. Language arts (Early childhood). I. Roskos, Kathy. II. Christie, James F.

LB1140.35.P55P557 2007
372.6--dc22   2006036803

Visit the Taylor & Francis Web site at
http://www.taylorandfrancis.com

and the LEA Web site at
http://www.erlbaum.com

Contents

Preface

Kathleen A. Roskos and James F. Christie

We embark on the 2nd edition of this volume in turbulent times. Children's play is under serious attack in a brave new world dominated by early learning standards and achievement outcomes (Wood & Attfield, 2005; Zigler & Bishop-Josef, 2004). Nowhere is this more pronounced than in early literacy education, although other areas of early learning, such as mathematics and science, are rapidly coming under critical scrutiny. Age-old beliefs about play as a recess from work have marginalized it as a context for learning school readiness skills, increasingly seen as essential for academic and life success.

Since our first edition almost a decade ago, much has happened to put play in this precarious position. It is not that the "play problem" is suddenly new and pressing. The role, purposes, and value of play have long been debated in early childhood education around this central question: What does it do for learning? Play can be engaging, serious, and deep; but it can also be silly, dangerous, naughty, and downright nasty (Sutton-Smith, 1998). How play, a gigantic category of activity, is harnessed to promote academic learning and child well-being has perplexed the early childhood field for some time (e.g., Glickman, 1984). Still, play's potential in early learning remains a persistent hope among early educators, and this idea is well-rooted in curricular thought. Not without cause, to be sure, as the power of play is seen in the advancing combinatorial activity of young children, which pulls forward their problem-solving and symbolic thinking abilities (Bruner, 1972; Siegler, 2000; Vygotsky, 1966).

At the turn of the 21st century, however, the very idea of play's educational potential came under attack, brought on by some new harder edged realities. Scientific gains in early development and learning engendered a new vision of early childhood education. Powerful research syntheses of how people learn (Bransford, Brown & Cocking, 2000), how young children develop and grow (Shonkoff & Phillips, 2000), and how to prevent reading difficulties (Snow,

Burns, & Griffin, 1998) converged on the significance of the early years in human learning. Starting earlier, science showed, is not only beneficial to human intelligence, but essential to children's life chances as educated persons.

The new scientifically-based idea that children should start earlier was met with considerable consensus among educators, policymakers, program developers, economists, parents, and even news commentators. All agreed that all children deserve the chance to learn early and to start school ready to learn more. What starting earlier meant in a practical sense (i.e., what young children should be doing) proved far less clear and harder to solve, however.

Standards helped to address this problem (in a practical sense) by outlining what children should know and be able to do before school entry. By 2005, most states had developed early learning standards for preschoolers (Neuman & Roskos, 2005). Many states coupled early learning standards with their broader K–12 educational reform efforts, resulting in assessments and standards-based curriculum models as part of the early learning standards package (Roskos, in press; Roskos & Vukelich, 2006). This gave rise to a new standards-based architecture in early childhood education, decidedly more academic than traditional child-centered curriculum approaches. Play's role in this new architecture quickly became a source of contention between defenders of play-based approaches and those pushing for more defined teaching intentions, learning outcomes, and goals in early education (Wood & Attfield, 2005; Zigler, Singer, & Bishop-Josef, 2004). At issue is how play contributes to school readiness, that complex of starting earlier from a scientific perspective.

Federal policy in the United States also offered up ideas about what young children should be doing to get started earlier. (It is also noteworthy that national curriculum policies in the United Kingdom paralleled this trend in the United States.) The Good Start, Grow Smart policy (U.S. Department of Education, 2000), for example, mapped out a three-pronged plan to strengthen Head Start: (a) a reporting system that assesses standards of learning in early literacy, language, and numeracy skills; (b) "voluntary" guidelines to help states set quality criteria for early childhood education (e.g., early learning standards); and (c) a plan to provide information to the early childhood community about research-based curriculum. Play did not enter into this high-level discussion, however, despite the recent advances in cognitive neuroscience that pointed to fundamental play–learning links (e.g., in self-regulation; Blair, 2002; Shonkoff & Phillips, 2000).

The No Child Left Behind Act (2001) established the Early Reading First program to fund the development of model programs to support the school readiness of preschool-aged children, particularly those from low-income families. This program lays out a well-defined early literacy program that for the most part emphasizes direct instruction in essential early literacy skills and deemphasizes play-based approaches. Play centers are encouraged, but only if they are geared to early literacy activities, such as games, puzzles, and word play.

Clearly, the turn into the 21st century was not business as usual in early childhood education; not for early literacy, not for play. Together, scientific advances, standards, and national policies seriously challenged play's stronghold in the early childhood curriculum and questioned its value in helping children acquire the new preschool basics of language, prereading, and mathematics. Like David, play faced a mighty Goliath.

However, play is resilient and its defenders steadfast. Even as current events threaten play's role in early childhood education (as we have known it), they also open up new possibilities for understanding and promoting the play–literacy interface. Recent curriculum guidance in the United Kingdom, for example, sets out a *pedagogy of play*, broadly defined as providing play-based activities, designing play–learning environments, and using play-supportive teaching techniques (Wood & Attfield, 2005). Following from a Play = Learning conference held at Yale University in 2005, Singer, Golinkoff, and Hirsh-Pasek (2006) argued convincingly for play–learning links at home and school. Play-based techniques, such as play planning (Bodrova & Leong, 1996) and complex sociodramatic play (Elias & Berk, 2002) are also gaining empirical ground as best practices in developing children's school readiness skills (Hornbeck, Bodrova, & Leong, 2006).

That recent history creates a new future for exploring, probing, challenging, and reenvisioning the play–literacy interface goes to the core of this second edition. More than ever, new inquiry and old research seen with new eyes are needed to describe and explain play's role in preparing young children for the rigors of learning to read and write in school. If, as Vygotsky (1966) argued, play is the "leading source of development in the preschool years" (p. 62), then Goliath-like challenges of today create yet another opportunity for that "profound internal analysis" needed to understand play's significance in early learning.

In this volume, we look back and look ahead, revisiting studies reported before and also introducing new inquiries into play's role in early literacy development and learning, especially as these shed light on school readiness. Studies that directly focus on play–literacy links are few and far between, so within this volume we attempt to mine those we have plus some new studies and syntheses that take these links in new directions. Our commentators, as well, have tried to knit together the known with new insights and to take what we are learning to new starting places for research.

OVERVIEW OF THE CONTENTS

This second edition of *Play and Literacy in Early Childhood* builds on two generations of play–literacy research and lays the groundwork for a third. In 1991, Jim Christie edited the first volume on play–literacy research, gathering together several key studies that existed on play as a process and a context for early literacy experiences (Christie, 1991). A sampler of first-generation play–literacy research, the book consolidated a small but growing body of inquiry and also provided practitioners with a knowledge base on literacy in play.

Building on this collection in 2000, we examined a second generation of unpublished studies and research syntheses organized around three perspectives on the role of play activity in literacy development and learning (Roskos & Christie, 2000). Studies from a cognitive perspective focused on the mental processes that appear to link play and literacy activity (e.g., negotiating meanings, thinking symbolically, and using language to make sense of experience). Those taking an ecological stance emphasized environmental factors, examining issues of access and the affordances of specific environments. Studies from a sociocultural perspective stressed cultural influences and the interface between the literacy and play cultures of home and those of the school. Commentators who critiqued the collection from these different perspectives applauded a growing body of multitheoretical evidence at the play–literacy interface (e.g., situational and critical literacies), but also lamented persistent methodological problems (e.g., definitions of play). So, a few steps forward, as the second-generation sample showed, but also a few steps back from where a strong play–literacy line of inquiry should be.

This volume samples a third generation of studies, and in light of the paradigm shift we described earlier, we have organized this collection around a different set of perspectives on the play–literacy interface. Research is evolving on this interface between the play environment, replete with complexities, and the literacy environment, equally dense with interactions. It is increasingly concerned with the convergence of systems and processes on this boundary and the transformational links that reach across it to adapt one way of sense-making (play) to another (literacy).

THE PLAYFUL MIND

Is play biological or cultural in origin? About this issue, there is long-standing debate, and no clear answer in sight, although neuroscience is unearthing new data relevant to the debate. The young brain is amazingly versatile and a "jungle of potentials" waiting for "its evolutionary moments." Here, play may serve as a biology-serving agent that compels and actualizes synaptic connections (Sutton-Smith, 1999, p. 246). Play (in early childhood) may be necessary because it supplies the brain with what it needs to grow: exploring, testing ideas and skills, combining materials and actions, repeating actions to automaticity, inventing, and pretending. It also—by way of pretense—cultivates a *theory of mind* where it becomes possible to understand one's own mind and that of others, including deception, which may be an adaptive response. This playful mind perspective opens up new avenues of thought about the play–literacy interface.

The Play–Literacy Instructional Environment

Are playful early experiences with print and books beneficial? That question has been asked often in the play–literacy research—and the answer is "yes."

Literacy-enriched play environments encourage more play with print, support book reading, develop language skills, and motivate children to read and write. What remains unanswered, however, is whether or not playful experiences with literacy result in meaningful improvements in children's later academic achievement. If so, how? How do language and literacy-rich play experiences help shape literacy development in different ways at different times? How do environmental influences affect the individual expression of emerging literacy concepts and skills? The ecology of play has a long research tradition, but the combination of child development research, science-based early literacy instruction, and neuroscience generate new research questions form this perspective.

The Play–Literacy Social Context

Can social relationships and local literacy-in-play practices shape literacy development? We have only scratched the surface on this question, which shifts the focus of attention from what's going on in there (inside the head) to what's going on out there (outside the head in the social milieu). Fundamentally, the sociocultural perspective seeks to understand the influences of social participation and human relationships, whether in peer-led or adult-led situations. It attempts to describe children's participation in local literacy events, their position or role in these events, the ideological assumptions that literacy events hold, and the literacy objects and spaces used to engage in literacy activity (Rowe, 2006). A sociocultural focus expands the agenda for play–literacy research by broadening the scope of the who, what, when, and where of investigation. It widens the lens on literacy development, attempting to trace change from its earliest roots, and urges new prospective theoretical models to capture this dynamic, such as microgenetic studies (Yaden, 2006). Making headway on the play–literacy interface from this perspective is moving forward, but in many ways it is a "slow go" due to methodological challenges of documenting multiple, interacting systems.

Taking a look at the play–literacy research sample through these lenses opens up new possibilities for theory, for research, and for practice. As in the first edition, play scholars provide critical commentary on each set of studies and offer thoughtful comments on the scientific quality of the work. We deeply appreciate their commitment to this role, and the insights they offer that help us to move the play–literacy research agenda forward.

Part I of the book consists of three chapters that consider play–literacy relationships as a matter of mind, moving from the inside to the outside, so to speak. Peter K. Smith starts off with a crisp review of what we know about play's connection with cognitive development in general and what this knowledge might imply for early literacy development. He also makes recommendations on types of research designs that are needed to tease out the connections between play and cognition. Certain elements relevant to this chapter (e.g., longitudinal play–literacy research) are extended in the Pellegrini and Van Ryzin commentary. Chapter 2, by R. Keith Sawyer and

Stacy DeZutter, introduces a new topic, and one rarely addressed in the play–literacy field: the improvisational nature of collaborative sociodramatic play and its relevance to foundational literacy skills. They pose a theory of *collaborative emergence* that attempts to explain the formation of narrative elements in the minds of individual players from jointly improvised play dialogue. Sense of narrative, in short, is first "collaboratively emergent," then individually constructed as a mental tool for organizing and expressing experience. Engaged in collaborative sociodramatic play, children develop a theory of mind as they negotiate with others to create the play story, and appropriate jointly shared narrative elements that help them to understand their own and the minds of others.

Deborah Wells Rowe's chapter carries this theme into another context, that of book-related dramatic play among 2- and 3-year-old children. She observed several patterns that suggest play's role in the sense-making of book experiences, which may be at the root of in-the-head comprehension monitoring strategies, such as imaging, anticipating, recalling, and retelling. Anthony D. Pellegrini and Mark J. Van Ryzin discuss (once again) the persistent definitional and methodologcial issues that plague play–literacy studies, and call for more imagination in research designs, especially longitudinal designs that employ modern techniques, such as hierarchical linear modeling, that help address critical developmental questions (e.g., in the development of narrative competence).

In Part II, the set of studies shifts from matters of mind to the learning environment, and what it has to offer the playful mind. The set begins with our own recent work focused on the concept of *educational play* and its role in developing the new pre-K basics: language, literacy, and mathematics. We describe the potential of a blended curriculum for incorporating early literacy concepts and skills into play activity linked to curricular goals. Based on her dissertation, in chapter 7, Myae Han reports on individual differences in accessing what the play environment has to offer and the implications for individual literacy development. Widening the lens on the environment to the early childhood program, Loraine Dunn and Sara Ann Beach update their chapter from the first edition with new research findings that show classroom literacy environments and provisions for literacy-related play are still far from ideal in many early childhood classrooms. They report on a recent long-term intervention project, Early Steps to Literacy, that used varying degrees of professional development to increase preschool teachers' knowledge of literacy learning and teaching. Results showed that teachers who received sustained professional development and ongoing support from a mentor showed the largest improvements in their beliefs and practices relating to teaching early literacy.

In his commentary, James E. Johnson notes all three chapters in this section reflect a fundamental shift in early education, away from traditional notions of play-based education that educates the "whole child" toward a view that emphasizes school readiness. He expresses support for the notion of blended curriculum in which play activities are linked with academic goals and standards. However, he also cautions against letting academic standards lead to a neglect of the complex cognitive-affective processes that underlie all learning.

Part III of the book includes three chapters that look at play–literacy relationships through the sociocultural lens. The chapters by Susan B. Neuman and Nigel Hall remain intact from the earlier edition as rich descriptions of play–literacy links in family and classroom settings. Chapter 11 by Bodrova and Leong provides a thorough explanation of the play–literacy connection from a Vygotskian perspective. Focusing on play and writing, the pair describe their research with a play-planning procedure that integrates the development of mature play and writing. They report that the play-planning intervention helps at-risk preschoolers and kindergarteners to meet early literacy developmental benchmarks needed for beginning reading instruction. The commentary by Peter Hannon is organized around three reflections that take us into deep thought about the nature of literacy in play, the role of the home setting, and what adults are doing in the name of play (which looks a lot like teaching).

This collection of research studies and critiques shows once again the potential of play in helping children gain the concepts and skills that are the building blocks of full-blown literacy. Engaging in book play, improvising with peers, taking advantage of the play environment, participating in social events are ways of playing that can benefit the young child's literacy development. The collection, however, also gets us to thinking new thoughts about the playful mind, the playful environment, and the playful context. It challenges play–literacy researchers to use their imaginations to overcome persistent methodological problems, to break from the past into new territories of study (e.g., neurosciences), to work harder for multidisciplinary perspectives in examining the play–literacy interface, and to push harder for the incorporation of play into the early literacy education of young children.

REFERENCES

Blair, C. (2002). School readiness. *American Psychologist, 57,* 111–127.

Bodrova, E., & Leong, D. (1996). *Tools of the mind: The Vygotskian approach to early childhood education.* Columbus, OH: Merrill.

Bransford, J., Brown, A., & Cocking, R. (2000). *How people learn: Brain, mind, experience and school.* Washington, DC: National Academy Press.

Bruner, J. (1972). *Beyond the information given: Studies in the psychology of knowing.* New York: Norton.

Christie, J. F. (1991). *Play and early literacy development.* Albany, NY: SUNY Press.

Eckler, J. A., & Weininger, O. (1989). Structural parallels between pretend play and narratives. *Developmental Psychology, 25,* 736–743.

Elias, C. L., & Berk, L. E. (2002). Self-regulation in young children: Is there a role for dramatic play? *Early Childhood Research Quarterly, 17,* 216–238.

Glickman, C. (1984). Play in public school settings: A philosophical question. In T. Yawkey & A. Pellegrini (Eds.), *Child's play: Developmental and applied* (pp. 255–271). Hillsdale, NJ: Lawrence Erlbaum Associates.

Hornbeck, A., Bodrova, E., & Leong, D. (2006, April). *Make-believe play and drawing as the roots of emergent writing in preschool: The Vygotskian approach.* Paper presented at the annual meeting of the American Educational Research Association, San Francisco.

Neuman, S. B., & Roskos, K. (2005). The state of state pre-kindergarten standards. *Early Childhood Research Quarterly, 20,* 125–145.

No Child Left Behind: Reauthorization of the Elementary and Secondary Education Act Legislation and Policies. (2001). Retrieved November 18, 2005, from http://www.ed.gov/about/offices/list/oese/legislation.html#leg

Roskos, K. (in press). Policy shaping early literacy education and practice: potentials for difference and change. In M. Pressley, A. Billmon, K. Levy, K. Reffitt, & J. Reynolds (Eds.), *The literacy achievement we have, the literacy achievement research we need.* New York: Guilford.

Roskos, K., & Christie, J. (Eds.). (2000). *Play and literacy in early childhood: Research from multiple perspectives.* Mahwah, NJ: Lawrence Erlbaum Associates.

Roskos, K., & Vukelich, C. (2006). Early literacy policy and pedagogy. In D. K. Dickinson & S. B. Neuman (Eds.), *Handbook of early literacy* (Vol. 2, pp. 295–310). New York: Guilford.

Rowe, D. (2006, April). *A social practice perspective on two year-olds' learning about writing.* Paper presented at the annual meeting of the American Educational Research Association, San Francisco.

Shonkoff, J., & Phillips, D. (2000). *From neurons to neighborhoods: The science of early childhood development.* Washington, DC: National Academy Press.

Siegler, R. (2000). The rebirth of children's learning. *Child Development, 71,* 26–35.

Singer, D., Golinkoff, R., & Hirsh-Pasek, K. (Eds.). (2006). *Play = learning.* Oxford, UK: Oxford University Press.

Snow, C., Burns, M. S., & Griffin, P. (1998). *Preventing reading difficulties in young children.* Washington, DC: National Academy Press.

Sutton-Smith, B. (1998). *The ambiguity of play.* Cambridge, MA: Harvard University Press.

Sutton-Smith, B. (1999). Evolving a consilience of play definitions: Playfully. In S. Reifel (Ed.), *Play and culture studies* (Vol. 2, pp. 239–256). Stamford, CT: Ablex.

U.S. Department of Education. (2002, April). *Good start, grow smart.* Washington, DC: Author.

Vygotsky, L. (1966). Play and its role in the mental development of the child. *Soviet Psychology, 12*(6), 62–76.

Wood, E., & Attfield, J. (2005). *Play, learning and the early childhood curriculum* (2nd ed.). Thousand Oaks, CA: Sage.

Yaden, D. (2006, April). *Developing a prospective, developmental theory of early writing ability: Applications from dynamic skill theory, indeterministic constraints modeling, and probabilistic epigenesis.* Paper presented at the annual meeting of American Educational Research Association, San Francisco.

Zigler, E. F., & Bishop-Josef, S. J. (2004). Play under siege: A historical overview. In E. F. Zigler, D. G. Singer, & S. J. Bishop-Josef (Eds.), *Children's play: The roots of reading* (pp. 1–14). Washington, DC: Zero to Three Press.

Zigler, E. F., Singer, D. G., & Bishop-Josef, S. J. (Eds.). (2004). Children's play: The roots of reading. Washington, DC: Zero to Three Press

About the Authors

Sara Ann (Sally) **Beach** is Professor of Literacy Education at the University of Oklahoma. She previously taught children in the primary grades and as a reading specialist. Her research interests include exploring literate identity in learners of all ages, critical literacy, and teacher education.

Elena Bodrova is a senior researcher at Mid-continent Research for Education and Learning (McREL) in Denver, Colorado. Prior to coming to the United States, she was a senior researcher at the Russian Center for Educational Innovations and the Russian Institute for Preschool Education. She received her PhD from the Academy of Pedagogical Sciences, Moscow, and her MA from Moscow State University.

James F. Christie is a Professor of Curriculum and Instruction at Arizona State University, where he teaches courses in language, literacy, and early childhood education. His research interests include early literacy development and children's play. His publications include the co-authored books *Play, Development, and Early Education*; *Building a Foundation for Preschool Literacy*; *Teaching Language and Literacy* (2nd ed.); and *Play and Literacy in Early Education*. He is a member of the Early Literacy Development Commission of the International Reading Association and past president of the Association for the Study of Play. He is currently project co-director for the Arizona Centers of Excellence in Early Education (ACE[3]) Early Reading First project.

Stacy DeZutter is a doctoral student in the Department of Education at Washington University in St. Louis, Missouri, where she studies sociocultural perspectives on cognitive development. Stacy holds a master's degree in Theatre and Performance Studies from the University of Pittsburgh, and has been teaching creative dramatics and improvisation for more than 17 years.

Loraine Dunn is an Early Childhood Education (ECE) faculty member at the University of Oklahoma, where she serves as ECE program coordinator, teaches graduate and undergraduate classes, and oversees the child development laboratory and student teaching placements. She was part of a team that developed the Early Steps to Literacy project funded by an Early Childhood

Educator Professional Development grant from the U.S. Department of Education. Her research focuses on child care program quality, developmentally appropriate practice, and children's learning and development. She and a colleague recently completed a longitudinal study of the quality of child care programs in the context of Oklahoma's tiered reimbursement system. She began her career in child care and Head Start before moving on to university laboratory preschool programs. She earned bachelor's and master's degrees in Child Development from Iowa State University and a PhD in Child Development and Family Studies from Purdue University.

Nigel Hall is Professor of Literacy Education at Manchester Metropolitan University in the United Kingdom. His specialist area is literacy in early childhood, with a particular interest in play, interactive writing, and learning to punctuate. He is an editor of the *Journal of Early Childhood Literacy* and has recently co-edited the *Handbook of Early Childhood Literacy*.

Myae Han is an Assistant Professor of Individual and Family Studies at the University of Delaware, where she teaches courses in early childhood education and early literacy. Her research interests are children's play and early literacy development. She is currently a co-director of the Delaware Early Reading First project.

Peter Hannon is Professor of Education at the University of Sheffield, England. He has researched in the areas of early childhood education and literacy, including preschool intervention programs. He is the author of *Literacy, Home and School* (1995) and *Reflecting on Literacy in Education* (2000).

James E. Johnson is Professor-in-Charge of Early Childhood Education at the Pennsylvania State University. His area of scholarship focuses on children's play, culture, teacher education, and curriculum. Recent publications include *Play, Development and Early Education,* and *Approaches to Early Childhood Education* (4th ed.).

Deborah J. Leong is a professor of psychology and the director of the Center for Improving Early Learning at Metropolitan State College of Denver. She received her PhD from Stanford University and her MEd from Harvard University. With Elena Bodrova, she has co-authored numerous books, articles, and videos on the Vygotskian approach, including *Tools of the Mind: The Vygotskian Approach to Early Childhood Education*.

Susan B. Neuman is a Professor in Educational Studies at the University of Michigan, specializing in early literacy development. She returned to this position in 2004 after a 2-year hiatus, during which she served as the U.S. Assistant Secretary for Elementary and Secondary Education. Her research and teaching interests include early childhood policy, curriculum, and early reading instruction, pre-K through Grade 3. Her publications include *Handbook for Early Literacy Research: Volume II* (2005); *Access for All: Closing the Book Gap for Children in Early Education* (2001); *Handbook on Early Literacy Research* (2001); and *Learning to Read and Write: Developmentally Appropriate Practice* (NAEYC, 2000), among others.

Anthony D. Pellegrini is a Professor of Psychological Foundations of Education in the Department of Educational Psychology at the University of Minnesota, Twin Cities Campus. He has research interests in methodological issues in the general area of human development, with specific interests in direct observations. His substantive interests are in the development of play and dominance. He is a Fellow of the American Psychological Association and has been awarded a Fellowship from the British Psychological Society.

Kathleen A. Roskos teaches courses in reading instruction and reading diagnosis at John Carroll University. Formerly an elementary classroom teacher, she has served in a variety of educational administration roles, including director of federal programs in the public schools and department chair in higher education. For 2 years she directed the Ohio Literacy Initiative at the Ohio Department of Education, providing leadership in P–12 literacy policy and programs. She studies early literacy development and learning, teacher cognition, and the design of professional education for teachers, and has published research articles on these topics in leading journals. She is currently a member of the e-Learning Committee and the Early Childhood Commission of the International Reading Association and President of the Literacy Development for Young Children special interest group of that organization.

Deborah Wells Rowe is Associate Professor of Early Childhood Education and works in the Language, Literacy, and Culture Program at Vanderbilt University. Her research explores the ways preschoolers and primary-grade children connect writing, reading, dramatic play, and other sign systems. She teaches undergraduate and graduate courses related to literacy and qualitative methods.

R. Keith Sawyer is Associate Professor of Education at Washington University in St. Louis, Missouri. He is the author or editor of nine books, including *Pretend Play as Improvisation* (1997) and *The Cambridge Handbook of the Learning Sciences* (2006). His research focuses on creativity, collaboration, and learning.

Peter K. Smith is Professor of Psychology and Head of the Unit for School and Family Studies at Goldsmiths College, University of London. He is also a Fellow of the British Psychological Society. He received his BSc at the University of Oxford and his PhD from the University of Sheffield. His research interests are in social development, play, school bullying, grandparenting, and evolutionary theory. He is co-author of *Understanding Children's Development* (1988, 1991, 1998, 2003), and co-editor of the *Blackwell Handbook of Childhood Social Development* (2002) and of *The Nature of Play: Great Apes and Humans* (2005). He has written widely on children's play, especially pretend play training, and rough-and-tumble play.

Mark J. Van Ryzin is a PhD student in Educational Psychology at the University of Minnesota, Twin Cities Campus. His research interests include educational innovation, teacher education and professional development, and educational policy. For his PhD dissertation, he is investigating the formation of teacher–student relationships and how these relationships influence student outcomes in school.

THE PLAYFUL MIND

1

Pretend Play and Children's Cognitive and Literacy Development: Sources of Evidence and Some Lessons From the Past

Peter K. Smith
Goldsmiths College, University of London

The role of play in children's development is not only controversial scientifically; it has also led to extreme positions at times in regards to policies regarding early education. On the one hand, advocates of the play ethos (to which I return later) have seen play as preeminently the child's way of learning; free play was seen as most beneficial for children well into infant school, and direct instruction methods were seen as inappropriate. More recently, notably in the United States (Zigler & Bishop-Josef, 2004) and the United Kingdom (Hall, 2005), a desire to improve cognitive and literacy skills in young children, including those from disadvantaged backgrounds, has led to the opposite viewpoint, an emphasis on direct instruction and a neglect of play opportunities. In fact, many researchers, myself included, see both as extreme positions and would argue for a blended program (Christie & Roskos, 2006) in the early years.

However, what is the evidence to support this or any other position, regarding play and development? In this chapter I review the sources of evidence. After an initial broad overview, I focus mainly on pretend play and on cognitive and literacy development. I look at some main theories, including evolutionary perspectives, cross-cultural evidence, arguments by design, correlational evidence, and experimental evidence. In general I am not trying to review relevant studies in detail (this has been done in other reviews; e.g., Christie & Roskos, 2006; Smith, 2005; other chapters in this volume), but rather discussing the nature of the evidence and principles of study. Some important pitfalls in experimental studies were exposed during the 1970s and 1980s, and I revisit these. I end with some suggestions for further research in this area.

THE ROLE OF PLAY IN DEVELOPMENT

There is a range of legitimate views about the role of play in development. On the one hand, play has been held up as the child's way of learning, and as essential to development. At the other extreme, play has been regarded as simply letting off excess energy, a time-wasting activity when there is nothing better to do. There is, of course, a range of intermediate positions.

The Play Ethos, and Other Metaphors of Play

I have earlier (Smith, 1988) described the *play ethos* as an uncritical and extreme assertion of the functional importance of play that has been very influential from around the 1920s to at least the 1980s if not the present day. The following quotes illustrate this point of view:

> Play is indeed the child' work, and the means whereby he grows and develops. Active play can be looked upon as a sign of mental health; and its absence, either of some inborn defect, or of mental illness. (Isaacs, 1929, p. 9)

> The realisation that play is essential for normal development has slowly but surely permeated our cultural heritage. (Department of the Environment, 1973, p. 1)

> Play is the elemental learning process by which humankind has developed … It is the very process of learning and development, and as such all that is learnt through it is of benefit to the child. (Welsh Assembly, 2002)

These quotes are from U.K. sources, but similar quotes can be found from the United States and from other Western sources. In a similar vein, Sutton-Smith (1997) described the play as progress rhetoric about play, which idealizes play and ignores any possible negative aspects of it.

This somewhat extreme view of the benefits of play may have come about as an overreaction to the alternative view that play is a largely superfluous activity. Although Spencer's excess energy view of play has little scientific credibility these days, there are certainly views in many educational and government circles that instruction in cognitive and language skills are most important, even in the preschool and early school years. As a result, play has been rather marginalized in many preschool curricula, and play times have a lower priority in schools, with playgrounds being sold off and school recess breaks decreased or eliminated (Pellegrini & Blatchford, 2000; Zigler & Bishop-Josef, 2005).

A more balanced view is that play is indeed important for learning in early childhood, but it is not the only route to do so (Smith, 1982). The ubiquity of play in children and indeed most mammals; the rebound effects found after deprivation of play; and the design characteristics of play, whereby it provides many opportunities for learning, all argue for the developmental value of play experiences. It is very likely that play evolved precisely for this reason—as a relatively safe means of getting useful learning experiences in cognitive, social, and other domains.

However, play is obviously not the only way of learning. Children can learn through observation, trial and error, and direct instruction. Direct instruction or teaching is something particular to humans (compared to other species, apart from a few specialized examples; Galef, Whiskin, & Dewar, 2005), and can be a very efficient way of learning compared to the more haphazard experiences that play provides.

In this respect, play has perhaps two advantages and one major disadvantage, as far as human learning is concerned. One advantage of play is the intrinsic motivation and fun of playing; this is part of all usual definitions of play. Children enter into play voluntarily, and enjoy it—they do not (normally) have to be coerced into playing. As young children also do not normally have the conscious intrinsic desire to learn specific skills (e.g., that which might motivate an adult to learn a new language, for travel or for their work), the fun of play is most important. Too much forced instruction at a young age can lead to boredom and apathy. This links to the second advantage of play, its creativity. As Bruner (1972) eloquently argued, in play children can try out new combinations, new behaviors that might not be in any syllabus. Most of the time, of course, this does not lead to any great inventions! However, in smaller but more pervasive ways, it is arguable that free play helps inculcate a mindset in which a child feels free to explore, try new ideas, and not be limited too much by conventional constraints. In comparison, rote learning, for example, even if effective in imparting a fixed body of knowledge, such as a number system, or the words of a song or religious text, will lead to a different mindset, in which knowledge is prescribed and not to be questioned. Needless to say, there are important cultural differences and value judgments in contrasting these positions, but advocates of play would argue that creative thought is at a premium in the contemporary world.

The disadvantage of play is the other side of the coin to what we have discussed, its unplanned and haphazard nature. It can be seen as rather a shotgun approach to learning: An active child exposed to the environment will learn more than an inactive one, through whatever he or she encounters. In our earlier evolutionary history (and that of other mammals and playing species), direct instruction was rare or absent, and play was a necessary mechanism for learning. Mammals and especially humans need flexible behavior patterns, of which learning is an essential part, so play provided a vital general-purpose mechanism for facilitating such learning. However, as humans evolved, the cultural means of direct instruction—first through apprenticeship and observation of skilled activity, and then through writing, textbooks, face-to-face teaching—then play may be seen as a rather inefficient means of learning.

Thus, if we know what we need to learn, and want to learn it, direct instruction may well be the most effective method. However, remember the two provisos favoring play: (a) How certain are we that we know precisely what should be learned, and (b) are we motivated to learn? These provisos retain a notable place for play, most especially for younger children, where the motivational aspects are especially important.

It then becomes an empirical question whether some form of play or some form of instruction is more effective, for particular kinds of learning, at particular ages, and in particular cultures. Learning can be achieved by different routes, what some authors call *equifinality*. However, some routes may be more effective than others. The picture is complicated by the need to consider both free play (chosen by children, unconstrained by adults) and structured play (deliberately channeled by adults toward educational ends). First, however, let us look at the types of evidence available.

Types of Evidence

There are various types of evidence we might look at to ascertain the extent to which play experiences could be useful for learning (e.g., in cognitive development, or literacy development). Some types of evidence simply make a plausible case for play being helpful in learning. Some types of evidence are empirically based, either correlating play with learning outcomes, or directly contrasting play with other kinds of experience for their effectiveness in learning.

Making a Plausible Case for the Importance of Play in Learning

The Evolution of Play.   A first source of evidence is the evolutionary history of play (Burghardt, 2005; Fagen, 1981; Power, 2000; Smith, 1982). We have already discussed how this makes a case for play as a general-purpose learning mechanism, for learning about the social and physical environment, and also for physical coordination and muscular strength, as much mammalian play is physical exercise play and play fighting and chasing. Children also play fight and chase, and may well develop some physical and social skills in doing so (Pellegrini, 2002), but readers of this book are probably more interested in object and pretend play, much more characteristic of human children, and much more likely to be involved in cognitive and literacy skills.

The Cross-Cultural Evidence of Play.   A second source of evidence is how play varies in different societies, and in relation to children's needs and outcomes. Focusing on pretend play, it is clear that this is very widely observed and in all kinds of societies (Eibl-Eibesfeldt, 1989). In hunter-gatherer people such as the Kalahari San, Konner (1972) observed children using sticks and pebbles to represent village huts and herding cows. In the Hadza of Tanzania, children make dolls out of rags and play at being predators (Blurton Jones, 1993). In a review, Gosso, Otta, Salum e Morais, Ribeiro, and Bussab (2005) not only describe pretend and fantasy play among South American Indian communities such as the Parakana, but state that "children of all forager groups studied exhibit fantasy play" (p. 233). Such play is generally tolerated by adults rather than encouraged, and is generally imitative of adult roles in such societies.

Among settled agricultural communities, pretend play is again generally present, but some reports at least suggest it can be at low frequency. Gaskins (1999) observed children up to 5 years of age in a Mayan village community in the Yucatan, Mexico, and found that although pretend play happened, it was rare. Not only was it not encouraged by adults, but adults often placed early work demands on children. Even young children may be asked to help in looking after even younger siblings, running errands, scaring birds away from crops, preparing food, selling food, and so on. Play in Kpelle children in Liberia has been described by Lancy (1996). Again such play is imitative of adult roles. For example, make-believe play at being a blacksmith involves the kinds of social roles (blacksmith, apprentice, client) and behavioral routines (fetching tools, lighting fire, hammering) that, in more complex forms, are seen in the adult behavior. Lancy believes that "make-believe play can provide opportunities for children to acquire adult work habits and to rehearse social scenes" (p. 89); this is a commonly held view in the anthropological literature.

However there is going to be a developmental trade-off between skills gained through play, with skills learned and contributions to subsistence actually made, through helping in the activity itself; in other words, between practicing for the future and contributing now. As children get older, the balance shifts. Bock's (1995, 2005) work with mixed-economy communities in the Okavango Delta, Botswana, detail with precision the competing payoffs (for adults) of allowing children to gain some skills through play, and actually requiring them to help in subsistence activities. His most detailed analyses relate to play pounding of grain, an activity engaged in (in pretend context) by young girls. Parents may tolerate or encourage such play, or require girls to take part in actual subsistence activities, such as actually pounding grain, sifting it, and so on. From his data, the developmental crossover for girls' play pounding is at 9 to 10 years.

An interesting cross-cultural comparison of play in four communities was reported by Morelli, Rogoff, and Angelillo (2003). They observed children aged around 2 to 3 years in the Efe of the Democratic Republic of the Congo, a traditionally hunter-gatherer (foraging) people, although they are now also doing some farming work; a Mayan agricultural town in San Pedro, Guatemala where people worked either at home (weaving, trading, carpentry) or as laborers or farmers; and two middle-class White American communities (in Massachusetts and Utah) where parents had a lot of formal schooling, and a majority were employed away from home.

The main differences found were between the Efe and San Pedro community children on the one hand, and the U.S. children on the other hand. Both the Efe and San Pedro children were seen some three to five times more often in emulation of work in play, imitative of adult work activities as discussed earlier (e.g., playing store, pretending to cut firewood, making tortillas out of dirt, pretending to shoot animals with a bow and arrow, or comforting a doll). Indeed, they had much more opportunity to observe adult work activities than children in the two U.S. communities. By contrast, the U.S. children were seen four to five times more often in play with an adult. They were also seen some-times in scholastic play (literacy- or numeracy-related activity for fun; e.g., singing alphabet songs, reading a story), and some 10 times more often in con-versations with adults on child-related topics (e.g., "Did you have a nice time playing on the swings?").

In sum, the cross-cultural evidence points to several conclusions. First, pre-tend play is ubiquitous and thus is probably useful for children. This is consis-tent with the evolutionary view as mentioned earlier. Indeed Slaughter and Dombrowski (1989) suggested that "children's social and pretend play appear to be biologically based, sustained as an evolutionary contribution to human psychological growth and development. Cultural factors regulate the amount and type of expression of these play forms" (p. 290). Second, there is some ten-sion between skills children may acquire through play (mainly through imitat-ing adult subsistence activities) and contributions they might actually make directly to subsistence. This tension seems less in foraging societies, but more pronounced in agricultural communities, where pretend play may be less val-ued (see also Smilansky, 1968). Finally, in contemporary societies, we have a situation where (apart from housework) adult subsistence activities are both less visible to children and also much more complex. Whereas a child play pounding grain may actually develop some useful skills for real pounding, it is unlikely that a child playing a doctor develops useful skills for being a real doc-tor to any similar extent.

However, in contemporary societies adults enter much more into chil-dren's play. They encourage certain kinds of play, including pretend play; talk about play; and generally channel, structure, or coopt play toward more edu-cational ends. These are examples of what MacDonald (1993) calls parental investment. This can be seen in a positive light, as increasing the skills divi-dends that pretend and sociodramatic play might provide. However, it is worth bearing in mind that parents' interests are not identical with children's inter-ests, and when parents attempt to channel children into more educational forms of play, this may or may not be in the child's own interests. Parents them-selves may be manipulated by media, commercial, and manufacturing inter-ests to purchase and consume toys, backed up by the prevalent play ethos (Smith, 1994; Sutton-Smith, 1986).

Arguments From Design. A quite different set of arguments about the im-portance of play for learning come from seeing to what extent is play designed to provide certain kinds of learning opportunities. Relevant here are play changes in relation to age, sex, and other characteristics; and examining ex-actly what experiences children get through play.

- *Age.* In terms of frequency, pretend play begins during the second year of life, peaks during the preschool years (3, 4, and 5 years), and declines during the primary school years (Fein, 1981). In the preschool years it oc-cupies up to some 15% of free time. Harris (1994) argues that "The stable timing of its onset in different cultures strongly suggests a neuropsychological timetable and a biological basis" (p. 256). This would tie in with the evolutionary arguments to suggest that pretend play has some definite benefits during the preschool years.

- *Sex.* There do not seem to be substantial differences in frequency of engaging in pretend play during the preschool period. Some studies find that girls engage in more frequent and more sophisticated pretend play than boys, but findings are inconsistent (Göncü, Patt, & Kouba, 2002) and dependent on the play environment, toys available, and the kinds of activities measured. Whereas girls' pretend play often involves domestic themes, boys' pretend play is often more physically vigorous, rough-and-tumble type activity, perhaps with superhero themes (Holland, 2003; Smith, 1977). Girls do seem to use their more mature language abilities in pretend play (Göncü et al., 2002). In general, however, the evidence suggests that any benefits of pretend play apply rather equally to girls and boys.

- *Other characteristics.* Pretend play, like other kinds of play, does seem to be affected by adverse circumstances. Play is less likely in malnourished children (Cullumbine, 1950), and pretend play is less frequent and more repetitive in very anxious and insecure children (Bretherton, 1989). It also may be less frequent and sophisticated in children from poorer socioeconomic backgrounds (Smilansky, 1968). This latter finding has been disputed (McLoyd, 1982) because the observations are mainly limited to nursery schools rather than other play environments such as streets or playgrounds; but in so far as they can be generalized, they may be due to differing levels of encouragement from adults (typically greater in better off families). This evidence suggests a sensitivity of levels of pretend play to context and adult encouragement, and a balancing of energy and time costs of play against other priorities (e.g., conserving energy if malnourished).

- *What happens in play.* It is clear that in pretend play, and especially in sociodramatic play, children are engaging in quite a lot of high-level cognitive and social activities, compatible with it aiding various developmental competences in the preschool years. Howes and Matheson (1992) described stages in the development of social pretense with mothers and peers. At first, the mother (or older partner, perhaps a sibling) has a scaffolding role, supporting the play by suggesting and demonstrating actions. The mother might give teddy a bath and then hand the teddy to the infant. Thus early pretend play is largely imitative, following well-established scripts or story lines, such as feeding the baby, and sustained by realistic props like dolls. However, by 3 or 4 years children take a more active role in initiating pretend play, and adapt less realistic objects or even just imagine the object completely. Two particular areas of cognitive development suggested by studying the nature of pretend play are theory of mind and narrative skills.

Theory of mind abilities involve understanding (representing) the knowledge and beliefs of others. Possession of theory of mind is usually measured by the understanding that another person may hold a false belief, by means of tasks such as the unexpected transfer task and the unexpected object task (Mitchell, 1997). Because knowledge and beliefs are representations of reality, theory of mind involves a representation of a representation, a second-order or metarepresentation.

Adapting objects for pretend purposes (e.g., a wooden block might become a baby) suggests some cognitive metarepresentational skills (an object is represented as something else, in the mind). Howes, Unger, and Matheson (1992) describe how by 37 to 48 months "children adopt relational roles, are willing to accept identity transformations and generate or accept instruction for appropriate role performance. Children negotiate scripts and dominant roles and use metacommunication to establish the play script and clarify role enactment" (p. 68). Information may be exchanged about real-life activities ("Doctors don't do that, silly!").

Language is thus used in quite complicated ways in pretend play. de Lorimier, Doyle, and Tessier (1995) found children more intensely involved in negotiations in pretense than in nonpretense contexts. Howe, Petrakos, and Rinaldi (1998) found that at 5 to 6 years, siblings who did a lot of pretend play were more likely to use internal state terms, especially in high-level negotiations about play. All these could be relevant to theory of mind skills.

Another skill that is being practiced in pretend and especially sociodramatic play is the development of narrative skills. Early pretend play has a simple story line (e.g., feeding baby), but soon becomes both more complex (i.e., a sequence of feeding, bathing baby, and putting baby to bed). In sociodramatic play, the narrative line being followed can be quite sustained (Smilansky, 1968, incorporated a criterion of a play sequence lasting at least 10 minutes to be counted as sociodramatic play) and can be less dependent on routine scripts (i.e., more innovative elements such as putting out a fire, fighting monsters, traveling to a foreign country, are incorporated).

As pretend play becomes decontextualized (freer from lifelike props such as dolls), many children develop an imaginary companion (Taylor, 1999). This is especially common in the 3- to 8-year-old period. Imaginary companions engage in a lot of imaginary activities with the child, and complex narrative sequences and histories may be involved. Although some parents worry about this, most evidence suggests that children with imaginary companions are generally strong in pretend play orientation, but are not confused about the status of their imaginary companions and are aware they are different from real friends.

Thus sociodramatic play and imaginary companions provide natural opportunities for narrative competence in children; although opportunities for related prereading or literacy skills can be enhanced by structuring such play in various ways, for example, by providing print materials, introducing message sending into the story line, and so on.

Empirical Evidence for the Importance of Play in Learning

Correlational Evidence.   Probably the majority of empirical studies are correlational, as they are easier to carry out than experimental studies. In a correlational study, a reasonably large number of children are assessed both for some characteristics of play, and also for some learning outcomes, at one point in time. A positive correlation is taken to support the influence of play on learning.

Let us look at one example. Taylor and Carlson (1997) studied 152 children aged 3 to 4 years. They measured pretend and fantasy play (including level of pretend play, impersonation, imaginary companions), and derived a principal fantasy component. They correlated scores on this with performance on theory of mind tasks. They controlled for verbal intelligence. They found no relationship for 3-year-olds, but a significant relationship for 4-year-olds ($r = .27$, or $r = .20$ when controlled for verbal intelligence) and a modest correlation for the whole sample of $r = .16$, $p < .04$, significant, although accounting for only 2.6% of the variance. Taylor and Carlson stated "the results of this study provide strong evidence that there is a relation between theory of mind and pretend play development in 4-year-old children" (p. 451), while admitting that inferences about causality are not warranted.

This example is typical of quite a large number of studies, and the conclusion quoted is a fair one, if we read *relation* simply to mean *correlation*. However, let us review some of the limitations of correlational studies. One is very well known: A positive (or indeed negative) correlation found could be due to one or more third factors. For example, verbal intelligence could both help children in complex pretend play, and separately help their performance on theory of mind tasks. Thus, Taylor and Carlson (1997) did well to control for this. Similarly, chronological age, or developmental status measured in other ways, or experiences such as having older siblings, or having a lot of adult conversations, might be third factors in this domain. Taylor and Carlson separated their two main age groups, which is in some ways better than just partialing out age from the correlations; it showed that the correlation was absent at 3 years and present at 4 years. Nevertheless, any study is limited in the number of aspects it can partial out or control for, and of course some crucial one may be omitted. Most correlational studies simply control for either age or verbal intelligence (a few do neither, and thus their results are of little value).

Correlational studies can be strengthened by introducing a longitudinal component, obtaining the correlations at two (or more) points in time from the same children, and then examining the cross-lagged correlations. Astington and Jenkins (1999) did this for language skills and theory of mind; controlling for age and earlier abilities, earlier language ability predicted later theory of mind, but earlier theory of mind did not predict later language ability, suggesting that skill in language development might be an underlying factor that explains theory of mind skills. A similar methodology could productively be used in pretend play studies.

Another set of issues about correlational studies address what measures are actually correlated. For example, there are many possible measures of pretend play: frequency, complexity, use of role play or impersonation, transformations, diversity of themes, and so on. In fact Taylor and Carlson (1997) had nine measures of pretend play, in addition to their overall measure. Most such studies have fewer measures. If you have a lot of measures, you get more useful information, but there can be a danger then of cherry-picking the perhaps one or two significant findings, without applying appropriate (e.g., Bonferroni) corrections for multiple statistical tests.

However many measures you have, you may be missing out on the aspect of play that is important; for example, maybe it is language use in pretend play that is important, not just overall amount of time spent in it. The measures also need to be age appropriate. Indeed Taylor and Carlson (1997) invoked this kind of argument: "We are not certain why this relation between fantasy and theory of mind was not found for the 3-year-olds. Perhaps our methods for assessing individual differences in fantasy were not as appropriate for younger children as for the older ones" (p. 451).

Altogether a considerable number of correlational studies were carried out in the 1970s and 1980s, linking pretend and sociodramatic play to a range of outcomes, including language skills, conservation abilities, creativity, role-taking ability, and perspective-taking ability. The correlational studies generally produced positive findings, but not always partialing for age, and not always consistent. Smith (2005) reviewed in detail studies that had correlated pretend play with theory of mind. Some studies reported positive correlations between measures of pretend play and theory of mind, others did not. Most, but not all, partialed for age or equivalent (IQ, language ability). The overall pattern of correlations was found to be very patchy. No single correlation reached the $r = .5$ level. The majority were nonsignificant. Smith concluded that although this was consistent with pretend play being one kind of experience useful for theory of mind skills, it was not consistent with it being a very important or essential factor; if pretend play had a strong causal role in theory of mind one would expect a stronger and more consistent pattern of high positive correlations.

Experimental Evidence.   Although longitudinal correlational studies can potentially provide stronger evidence for causal links than can conventional (single time point) correlational studies, they are still open to the third factor objection. Controlled experimental studies have been seen as the best answer to this, and the best way to establish a causal link. If participants are randomly assigned to experimental and control groups, and the experimental group receives (say) an enhanced pretend play experience, then any beneficial outcomes should be due to this difference between the experiences of the two groups; third factors are controlled for so long as the experimental and control groups are genuinely randomly assigned, and (better still) are shown to be equivalent on such measures (e.g., age, verbal intelligence).

A number of experimental studies on pretend and sociodramatic play have been carried out since the 1970s. One spur for this was the work of Smilansky (1968), who had observed that immigrant children in Israeli preschools did not show much sociodramatic play, and that they were also behind in language and cognitive skills. She argued forcefully that sociodramatic play was essential for normal development in preschool children, and that if a child was deficient in it, intervention should be carried out to encourage and enhance it. Smilansky and others found that it is quite possible to get children to do more and better sociodramatic play by having preschool teachers and staff model such play, encourage it, take children on visits (e.g., to hospitals or zoos), and provide suitable props and equipment, what was called *play tutoring*.

A number of intervention studies used play tutoring to test Smilansky's hypothesis about the importance of sociodramatic play. Equivalent groups of children (e.g., classes from the same school) either experienced play training or acted as a control group to allow for effects of age and general preschool experience. Differences between pre- and posttest performance on various developmental tasks were compared; if the play tutored children improved more, this was felt to be strong evidence that sociodramatic play really was important. Through the 1970s and 1980s, a number of studies of this kind all got positive results; it seemed that whatever outcome tests the researchers used, play tutored children improved more.

Some experimental studies were also carried out on individual pretend play, in relation to cognitive abilities. The main series were by Dansky and colleagues (e.g., Dansky, 1980), who suggested that pretend play helps associative fluency (a measure of creativity), and Golomb and colleagues (e.g., Golomb, Gowing, & Friedman, 1982), who argued that pretense assists conservation learning. Again, the results of all these experimental studies were supportive.

However, experimental studies also have problems, and a more critical evaluation of this body of work appeared by the 1980s (Christie & Johnsen, 1985; Smith, 1988). Smith (1988) argued that the play ethos (referred to earlier) had actually distorted the design and interpretation of many of these studies. Three main problems were identified:

- *Selective interpretation of results.* A number of studies carried out many statistical tests—for example on different measures, different age groups, and so on—but only highlighted significant findings. This is problematic, as we would expect one $p < .05$ result just by chance, in every 20 tests made. A variant of this problem was to report trends (even at just the $p < .10$ level) that went the expected way. Characteristically, methodological excuses were given to explain away nonsignificant findings.
- *Effects of experimental bias.* Many studies did not take precautions about experimenter effects. Quite unconsciously, an experimenter might favor the experimental group during testing, or scoring, if her or she believes they should be doing better. Testing and scoring of results should be

done blind to whether children are in the experimental or control condition, as routine precautions (just as is done in medical research).

• *Use of inappropriate control groups.* Some studies did not employ control group(s) that only differed on the measure (e.g., pretend play experience) about which inferences were being made. For example, in many play tutoring studies following Smilansky's (1968) work, a pretend play enhanced group was compared with a control group that not only had no pretense enhancement, but also less verbal stimulation or adult involvement generally. Thus it was not clear whether improvements in the experimental group were due to pretend play or verbal stimulation.

When further experiments were run to control for these difficulties, the specific benefits of play tutoring were generally not found. In some cases, experimenter effects were directly indicated (Smith & Whitney, 1987). When control groups were equated for verbal stimulation (skills tutoring), then both play and control groups improved with time and age (Christie & Johnson, 1985; Hutt, Tyler, Hutt, & Christopherson, 1989; Smith, Dalgleish, & Herzmark, 1981; Smith & Syddall, 1978); it seemed that the general adult stimulation was important, rather than specifically the pretend play. Indeed Hutt et al. (1989) commented, "We would seriously question the importance placed upon fantasy play as an aid to cognitive development" (p. 116). In my view, these findings are again consistent with pretend or sociodramatic play being one way to gain skills, but no more so necessarily than other ways of actively engaging with the social and physical environment.

Subsequent to this critical debate in the 1980s, some experimental studies have been made of pretend play in relation to theory of mind. Unfortunately, these studies formed a separate tradition and did not refer to the earlier work just reviewed. For example, Dias and Harris (1988, 1990) looked at effects of make-believe play on deductive reasoning. They produced experimental evidence that setting current reality aside and imagining a fictive alternative may be important in understanding false beliefs, and thus in theory of mind development. However their studies suffered some of the limitations of the earlier studies of the 1970s and 1980s. In the 1988 study, there was no blind testing (although scoring was done blind). In the 1990 study, there was neither blind testing nor, apparently, blind scoring. Also in all studies, a "let's pretend" instruction was actually present in all conditions. Leevers and Harris (1999) reported further studies within this paradigm, leading them to reinterpret the earlier work. They now argue that it is not the fantasy or pretend component, but simply any instruction that prompts an analytic, logical approach to the premises, which helps at these syllogistic tasks.

A direct training study on pretend play and theory of mind by S. Dockett (1998; personal communication) in an Australian preschool center compared two groups of children who attended morning and afternoon sessions. All children were pre- and posttested on measures of shared pretense and on theory of mind ability. One group of children received play training for 3 weeks, focusing on sociodramatic play around a pizza shop theme. The control group experienced the normal curriculum. The play training group significantly increased in frequency and complexity of group pretense, relative to the control group; and also improved significantly more on the theory of mind tests, both at posttest and at follow-up 3 weeks later. This study provides the best evidence yet for a causal link from pretend play to theory of mind, but the testing was not done blind to condition.

SUMMARY

There are good reasons to expect that, in young children at least, pretend play can have an important role in learning. This is supported by evolutionary considerations for play in general, and by the ubiquity of play, including pretend play, cross-culturally. It is supported by the design features of pretend play, including the kinds of opportunities and experiences children encounter during such play episodes. It is also fair to say that none of these sources of evidence suggest that pretend play has an essential role in learning. They do not support the play ethos. They do suggest that pretend play is one way of acquiring cognitive (and literacy) skills, and indeed a natural and enjoyable way. However, skills can also be acquired by observation, by exploration and trial and error, and by instruction.

The many correlational studies on pretend play do not take us much further than this. Even when controlling for age, verbal intelligence, or both, positive correlations are still open to alternative third factor explanations (e.g., number of siblings). There are two ways to make correlational studies more useful. One is to embed them in a longitudinal design, and examine cross-lagged correlations. Another is to look at the overall pattern of correlations across a large number of studies. The latter was attempted by Smith (2005) in relation to pretend play and theory of mind, with the conclusion—supporting that earlier—that pretend play may well facilitate theory of mind but is unlikely to be the most important or essential factor.

Both examining what goes on in pretend play and carrying out correlational studies may be useful in the early stages of a research phase. For example, theory of mind was developed conceptually in the 1980s, and it was important to make a case that pretend play could be an important factor in theory of mind development. However, experimental studies are really necessary to make a more convincing case. Returning to design features may then be useful again in understanding how any substantiated outcome, or benefit, of play actually comes about.

However, we have seen that experimental studies also need to be designed with care. One important consideration is the nature of experimental and control groups; control groups need to control for possible third factors such as verbal stimulation. It may also be useful to have more than one kind of experimental group. For example, the learning benefits of unconstrained, freely chosen pretend play may differ from the learning outcomes of more structured pretend play (which may differ again from, e.g., forms of direct instruction). Even then, structuring pretend play can be done in various ways—less intrusively, just by providing special props and equipment (this may be difficult to distinguish from unstructured play, at least in a nursery or preschool setting), through to encouraging certain play themes, and then through to actually leading the themes or getting children to follow specific stories, as in thematic fantasy play (Saltz & Johnson, 1974).

As far as possible, anyone involved in testing children and scoring outcomes should be blind to the condition that they are in (and preferably, blind to the purpose of the study). In addition, if large numbers of tests are made, these should be fully reported and appropriate corrections made to significance levels. Negative findings must be given as much weight as positive ones. These kinds of issues are, of course, true absolutely generally in psychological and education experiments, but it is arguable that the prevalent play ethos has tended to make these shortcomings particularly noticeable in experimental play research.

A combination of research strategies, including well-informed experimental studies, will hopefully move our understanding forward in the future, but future investigators are well advised to consider play in a broad evolutionary and cross-cultural context, and to look at the history of play research over the last several decades, so that we build on the lessons of the past and do not repeat previous mistakes.

REFERENCES

Astington, J. W., & Jenkins, J. M. (1999). A longitudinal study of the relationship between language and theory of mind development. *Developmental Psychology, 35,* 1311–1320.

Blurton Jones, N. (1993). The lives of hunter-gatherer children: Effects of parental behavior and parental reproductive strategy. In M. E. Pereira & L. A. Fairbanks (Eds.), *Juvenile primates: Life history, development, and behaviors* (pp. 309–326). New York: Oxford University Press.

Bock, J. (1995). *The determinants of variation in children's activities in a southern African community.* Unpublished doctoral dissertation, University of New Mexico, Department of Anthropology.

Bock, J. (2005). Farming, foraging, and children's play in the Okavango Delta, Botswana. In A. D. Pellegrini & P. K. Smith (Eds.), *The nature of play: Great apes and humans* (pp. 254–281). New York: Guilford.

Bretherton, I. (1989). Pretense: The form and function of make-believe play. *Developmental Review, 9,* 383–401.

Bruner, J. S. (1972). The nature and uses of immaturity. *American Psychologist, 27,* 687–708.

Burghardt, G. M. (2005). *The genesis of animal play: Testing the limits.* Cambridge, MA: Harvard University Press.

Christie, J. F., & Johnsen, E. P. (1985). Questioning the results of play training research. *Educational Psychologist, 20,* 7–11.

Christie, J. F., & Roskos, K. A. (2006). Standards, science, and the role of play in early literacy education. In D. Singer, R. Golinkoff, & K. Hirsh-Pasek (Eds.), *Play = learning.* Oxford, UK: Oxford University Press.

Christie, J. F., & Johnsen, E. P. (1985). Questioning the results of play training research. *Educational Psychology, 20*, 7–11.

Cullumbine, H. (1950). Heat production and energy requirements of tropical people. *Journal of Applied Physiology, 2*, 201–210.

de Lorimier, S., Doyle, A-B., & Tessier, O. (1995). Social coordination during pretend play: Comparisons with nonpretend play and effects on expressive content. *Merrill-Palmer Quarterly, 41*, 497–516.

Dansky, J. L. (1980). Make-believe: A mediator of the relationship between play and associative fluency. *Child Development, 51*, 576–579.

Department of the Environment. (1973). *Children at play* (Design Bulletin No. 27). London: HMSO.

Dias, M., & Harris, P. L. (1988). The effect of make-believe play on deductive reasoning. *British Journal of Developmental Psychology, 6*, 207–221.

Dias, M., & Harris, P. L. (1990). The influence of the imagination on reasoning by young children. *British Journal of Developmental Psychology, 8*, 305–318.

Dockett, S. (1998). Constructing understandings through play in the early years. *International Journal of Early Years Education, 6*, 105–116.

Eibl-Eibesfeldt, I. (1989). *Human ethology.* New York: Aldine de Gruyter.

Fagen, R. M. (1981). *Animal play behavior.* New York: Oxford University Press.

Fein, G. (1981). Pretend play: An integrative review. *Child Development, 52*, 1095–1118.

Galef, B. G., Whiskin, E. E., & Dewar, G. (2005). A new way to study teaching in animals: Despite demonstrable benefits, rat dams do not teach their young what to eat. *Animal Behaviour, 70*, 91–96.

Gaskins, S. (1999). Children's lives in a Mayan village: A case of culturally constructed roles and activities. In A. Göncü (Ed.), *Children's engagement in the world: Sociocultural perspectives* (pp. 25–61). New York: Cambridge University Press.

Golomb, C., Gowing, E. D., & Friedman, L. (1982). Play and cognition: Studies of pretense play and conservation of quantity. *Journal of Experimental Child Psychology, 33*, 257–279.

Göncü, A., Patt, M. B., & Kouba, E. (2002). Understanding young children's pretend play in context. In P. K. Smith & C. H. Hart (Eds.), *Blackwell handbook of childhood social development* (pp. 418–437). Oxford, UK: Blackwell.

Gosso, Y., Otta, E., Salum e Morais, M. de L., Ribeiro, F. J. L., & Bussab, V. S. R. (2005). Play in hunter-gatherer society. In A. D. Pellegrini & P. K. Smith (Eds.), *The nature of play: Great apes and humans* (pp. 213–253). New York: Guilford.

Hall, N. (2005). Play, literacy, and situated learning. In J. Moyles (Ed.), *The excellence of play* (2nd ed., pp. 86–97). Maidenhead, UK: Open University Press.

Harris, P. L. (1994). Understanding pretence. In C. Lewis & P. Mitchell (Eds.), *Children's early understanding of mind* (pp. 235–259). Hove, UK: Lawrence Erlbaum Associates, Ltd.

Holland, P. (2003). *We don't play with guns here.* Maidenhead, UK: Open University Press.

Howe, N., Petrakos, H., & Rinaldi, C. M. (1998). "All the sheeps are dead. He murdered them.": Sibling pretense, negotiation, internal state language, and relationship quality. *Child Development, 69*, 182–191.

Howes, C., & Matheson, C. C. (1992). Sequences in the development of competent play with peers: Social and pretend play. *Developmental Psychology, 28*, 961–974.

Howes, C., Unger, O., & Matheson, C. C. (1992). *The collaborative construction of pretend.* Albany: State University of New York Press.

Hutt, S. J., Tyler, S., Hutt, C., & Christopherson, H. (1989). *Play, exploration and learning: A natural history of the preschool.* London: Routledge.

Isaacs, S. (1929). *The nursery years.* London: Routledge & Kegan Paul.

Konner, M. (1972). Aspects of the developmental ethology of a foraging people. In N. Blurton Jones (Ed.), *Ethological studies of child behaviour* (pp. 285–304). Cambridge, UK: Cambridge University Press.

Lancy, D. F. (1996). *Playing on the mother-ground.* New York: Guilford.

Leevers, H. J., & Harris, P. L. (1999). Persisting effects of instruction on young children's syllogistic reasoning with incongruent and abstract premises. *Thinking and Reasoning, 5,* 145–173.

MacDonald, K. (1993). Parent–child play: An evolutionary perspective. In K. MacDonald (Ed.), *Parent–child play* (pp. 113–143). Albany: State University of New York Press.

McLoyd, V. C. (1982). Social class differences in sociodramatic play: A critical review. *Developmental Review, 2,* 1–30.

Mitchell, P. (1997). *Introduction to theory of mind: Children, autism and apes.* London: Edward Arnold.

Morelli, G. A., Rogoff, B., & Angelillo, C. (2003). Cultural variation in young children's access to work or involvement in specialized child-focused activities. *International Journal of Behavioral Development, 27,* 264–274.

Pellegrini, A. D. (2002). Rough-and-tumble play from childhood through adolescence: Development and possible functions. In P. K. Smith & C. Hart (Eds.), *Blackwell handbook of social development* (pp. 438–453). Oxford, UK: Blackwell.

Pellegrini, A. D., & Blatchford, P. (2000). *The child at school: Interactions with peers and teachers.* London: Arnold.

Power, T. G. (2000). *Play and exploration in children and animals.* Mahwah, NJ: Lawrence Erlbaum Associates.

Saltz, E., & Johnnson, J. ((1974). Training for thematic fantasy in culturally disadvantaged children: Preliminary results. *Journal of Educational Psychology, 66,* 623–630.

Slaughter, D., & Dombrowski, J. (1989). Cultural continuities and discontinuities: Impact on social and pretend play. In M. N. Block & A. D. Pellegrini (Eds.), *The ecological content of children's play* (pp. 282–310). Norwood, NJ: Ablex.

Smilansky, S. (1968). *The effects of sociodramatic play on disadvantaged preschool children.* New York: Wiley.

Smith, P. K. (1977). Social and fantasy play in young children. In B. Tizard & D. Harvey (Eds.), *Biology of play* (pp. 123–145). London: SIMP/Heinemann.

Smith, P. K. (1982). Does play matter? Functional and evolutionary aspects of animal and human play. *Behavioral and Brain Sciences, 5,* 139–155.

Smith, P. K. (1988). Children's play and its role in early development: A re-evaluation of the "play ethos". In A. D. Pellegrini (Ed.), *Psychological bases for early education* (pp. 207–226). Chichester, UK: Wiley.

Smith, P. K. (1994). Play training: An overview. In J. Hellendoorn, R. van der Kooij, & B. Sutton-Smith (Eds.), *Play and intervention* (pp. 185–194). Albany: State University of New York Press.

Smith, P. K. (2005). Social and pretend play in children. In A. D. Pellegrini & P. K. Smith (Eds.), *The nature of play: Great apes and humans* (pp. 173–209). New York: Guilford.

Smith, P. K., Dalgleish, M., & Herzmark, G. (1981). A comparison of the effects of fantasy play tutoring and skills tutoring in nursery classes. *International Journal of Behavioral Development, 4,* 421–441.

Smith, P. K., & Syddall, S. (1978). Play and nonplay tutoring in preschool children: Is it play or tutoring which matters? *British Journal of Educational Psychology, 48,* 315–325.

Smith, P. K., & Whitney, S. (1987). Play and associative fluency: Experimenter effects may be responsible for previous findings. *Developmental Psychology, 23,* 49–53.

Sutton-Smith, B. (1986). *Toys as culture.* New York: Gardner.

Sutton-Smith, B. (1997). *The ambiguity of play.* Cambridge, MA: Harvard University Press.

Taylor, M. (1999). *Imaginary companions and the children who create them.* New York: Oxford University Press.

Taylor, M., & Carlson, S. M. (1997). The relation between individual differences in fantasy and theory of mind. *Child Development, 68,* 436–455.

Welsh Assembly. (2002). *Welsh Assembly government play policy.* Cardiff, Wales: Author.

Zigler, E. F., & Bishop-Josef, S. J. (2004). Play under siege. In E. F. Zigler, D. G. Singer, & S. J. Bishop-Josef (Eds.), *Children's play: The roots of reading* (pp. 1–13). Washington, DC: Zero to Three Press.

2

Improvisation: A Lens for Play and Literacy Research

R. Keith Sawyer and Stacy DeZutter
Washington University

The word *improvisation* conjures up images of a jazz quartet performing late at night. Sometimes the word is used more broadly, to describe situations in which something unexpected happens and the advance plan has to be modified. In the middle of preparing a new recipe, for example, the cook discovers that he or she is out of a key ingredient, and has to think of a substitute or switch to a different recipe in midcourse. Almost all teachers improvise every day, responding to the unique demands of each class as students encounter new subject matter for the first time (Sawyer, 2004).

These three examples show what is most interesting about improvisation—it involves a complex and ever-changing tension between structure and freedom, between fixity and play. Of course, improvisation by definition is not scripted or structured in advance; it is impromptu and spontaneous. However, it is not complete chaos in which anything goes. Improvisation includes structured elements, along with change and modification.

It is in this sense that children's social play is improvisational (Sawyer, 1997). Sociodramatic play is a collaborative group improvisation, where each of the participants in the group contributes, and everyone's actions build on those of the others. In this chapter, we suggest that the improvisational dimension of children's play is what makes it an important contributor to emergent literacy. We begin by summarizing research that connects children's play to literacy acquisition. We emphasize one thread in this research: the identification of parallels between play and narrative competence. Play is a situated social practice, and the relation between play and literacy can be described using the lens of improvisation.

EMERGENT LITERACY AND PLAY CONNECTIONS

Research on emergent literacy suggests that certain early childhood activities contribute to how readily a child will learn to read and write. By characterizing

21

literacy in young children as emergent, researchers working in this area emphasize that literacy does not have a clearly definable starting point. Children who cannot yet decode or produce written texts nevertheless engage in literate behaviors, and these behaviors foster skills that assist the development of conventional reading and writing (Mason & Allen, 1986; Teale & Sulzby, 1986). Activities such as parent–child storybook reading and social pretend play are thought to foster literacy acquisition by providing opportunities for children to interact with texts and engage in literacy-related behaviors with adults and other children (Yaden, Rowe, & MacGillivray, 2000).

There is a wide body of literature that considers the relationship of children's pretend play to emergent literacy. Some of this research has focused on identifying the elements of children's spontaneous sociodramatic play that might contribute to later abilities to read and write, and other work has explored how deliberate interventions might enhance the literacy-bolstering effects of children's play (Glaubman, Kashi, & Koresh, 2001; Groth & Darling, 2001; Pellegrini, 1985; Rowe, 1998, 2000; Yaden et al., 2000). Research of the latter type has included such approaches as play training (Christie, 1991) and literacy-enriched play environments (Neuman & Roskos, 1990, 1991, 1997).

In brief, the role of play in literacy acquisition is exercised in three key areas: symbolic transformations, metaplay language, and narrative competence. Research surrounding children's use of symbolic transformations in play notes that during play, children frequently let one object stand in for another, and transform their own identities as they take on make-believe roles. These symbolic transformational processes are thought to strengthen children's general representational skills and prepare them to engage in the symbolic representation involved in writing (Hall, 1991; Neuman & Roskos, 1993; Pellegrini, 1985; Pellegrini, Galda, Dresden, & Cox, 1991; Rowe, 1998). Research on metaplay examines the role that children's talk with each other about their play may serve in the development of literacy skills such as metalinguistic awareness (Fein, 1981). Both symbolic transformation and metaplay involve narrative competence thought to be another strong link between play and literacy. Improvisation is most closely associated with narrative competence, serving as a means of creating the play experience as a kind of on-the-spot story.

Scholars have identified several connections between sociodramatic play and narrative competence (Branscombe & Taylor, 2000; Eckler & Weininger, 1989; Galda, 1984; Glaubman et al., 2001; Kavanaugh & Engel, 1998; Pellegrini, 1985; Pellegrini & Galda, 2000; Sachs, Goldman, & Chaille, 1984; Silvern et al., 1986).

Both are framed as *alternative worlds*, separate from the everyday world of the child. To understand pretend play, children must realize that the actions that they enact are not "real" and do not mean what they would if they had been enacted in the real world; the play world is framed as separate and distinct from everyday life (Bateson, 1955/1972; Leslie, 1987). Similarly, when reading a story, children need to understand that the world of the story is also framed—the characters and events in the story world are fictional, and do not necessarily exist in the real world.

Both have *fictional characters.* When children participate in social play, they enact characters—spacemen, mothers, and dinosaurs—speaking and acting as those characters would in the framed world of play, thus assuming roles. Children need to acknowledge when another child speaks to them in the voice of a play character, and they have to be able to engage in conversational interactions between fantasy characters. Relatedly, children need to understand the role of characters in a story, and their interactions with one another and story events.

Both involve the production and comprehension of *decontextualized language.* One of the linguistic features of the narrative genre, at least in mainstream U.S. society (Michaels, 1981), is that narrative language can be decontextualized—a narrative can be told anytime, to anyone, and understanding it does not require prior shared knowledge on the part of the speaker and audience. Young children have difficulty developing this ability to generate decontextualizable stories (Michaels, 1981). The fantasy conversations of social play are not as decontextualized as well-formed stories, but they are an intermediate form of language—partially narrative in genre, and more decontextualized than much of children's speech (Sawyer, 2002).

Both have *plot elements* such as motivating events, tensions, and release. Some of the most difficult elements of narrative for children to grasp are the relations between elements. Some researchers have shown that an understanding of the relation between a character's goal and the character's actions does not develop until after age 5 (Trabasso, Stein, Rodkin, Munger, & Baughn, 1992). In social play, children enact characters with goals, and they create fantasy scenarios in which those characters take actions to achieve their goals.

FROM NARRATIVE COMPETENCE TO NARRATIVE PRACTICE

Because of the shared characteristics of sociodramatic play and narrative elements, many scholars have hypothesized that play contributes to narrative competence, which then leads to greater receptivity to literacy instruction when children start school, as beginning reading instruction is heavily dependent on stories. However, simply observing these parallels does not adequately attend to an important difference between play and narrative: Play is open ended and improvisational, whereas narrative, as conceptualized in much of this research, is stable and structured. Examples of such narrative structures include the goal–action–outcome maps proposed by Trabasso et al. (1992). Nicolopoulou (1997) referred to these approaches as *formalist,* focusing on the formal structure of narratives, and neglecting the ways that children use narratives in rich social situations. We argue that many of the benefits of play for literacy stem from its improvisational nature, both because play involves engagement with narrative as a practice rather than as a static structure, and because this practice involves continuous negotiation among collaborating players.

There are two ways that contemporary scholarship has begun to address the relation between play and narrative. One has been to explore *narrative practice* rather than narrative competence per se (Daiute, 1989; Dyson, 1991; Heath, 1983; Nicolopoulou, 1997; Paley, 1984, 1988). Narrative is viewed as a form of social practice. Children do not simply possess a decontextualized competence about narrative structures; instead, they learn how to participate in situated narrative practices—such as a youngster telling a story about what happened at Granddad's house to his mother with Granddad providing hints and filling in details throughout the child's storytelling—a form of scaffolding (Falk, 1980).

Several researchers and educators have experimented with different scaffolds in an attempt to enhance the developmental benefits of improvisational group play for narrative development. In *thematic fantasy play* (Saltz, Dixon, & Johnson, 1977), children hear a story read to them, select or are assigned roles from the story, and enact the story with teachers prompting, narrating, and at times taking roles and joining in the enactment. Paley (1988) encouraged her preschool students to share their stories with the class, and enact them with other children in a play-like fashion (cf. Fein, Ardila-Rey, & Groth, 2000). Trawick-Smith (2001) recommends that teachers spontaneously scaffold children's play by interjecting appropriate leading questions related to character and plot development, although this must be done carefully as Pellegrini and Galda (1993) found that adult intervention may inhibit the sophistication of children's play language. Daiute (1989) studied third through fifth graders' collaboratively generated stories. She concluded that these children generated effective collaborative narratives with the support of a "general narrative structure" (p. 20); that is, explicit instructions from the teacher (e.g., "Tell a story about a child who gets lost in Boston").

Thinking about play as improvisation highlights certain of children's literacy behaviors in play that are less evident when narrative is analyzed in terms of structure. For example, Wolf and Hicks (1989) found that children use three different kinds of talk during play—namely narrative, character dialogue, and "stage managing"—and that children as young as 3 demonstrated an awareness of the difference in these types of speech. By focusing on narrative as processual and contingent, Wolf and Hicks were able to observe young children's deliberate use of intertextuality in their play, as they moved among the three different types of narrative voice. Wolf and Hicks's findings reveal children engaging in sophisticated, subtle literacy-related behaviors during play that may go unnoticed in a narrow focus on the structural components of play narrative.

Dyson (1991) presented the following example from her study of children's jointly constructed play narratives:

> "Bombs away!" shouts 5-year-old Chiel, in the midst of a World War II sea battle. Brandon, a classmate, is intrigued and joins in the play, adding more sound effects: "Lalalalalalala." Chiel responds by setting the current scene and narrating the action: "There's still a second ship—a blue ship. And the first

spared—the lasers! Oh ... oh. It destroyed my black ship. But it won't get to my blue ship. (p. 98)

Whereas literacy is stereotypically thought of as a private, solitary activity—a child sitting with a book—newer, sociocultural approaches consider narrative as a richly contextualized social practice. In play, relationships and talk are valued, and children's stories have deep personal meaning. The stories are jointly constructed, and emerge from a complex process of improvisational negotiation among peers. Stories are alive and embedded in social practices, not only decontextualized marks on a page. Dyson (1991) followed kindergartners and first graders for a year, and documented many links between their social play and the stories they wrote in their notebooks. She showed that social play may be part of the literacy-learning process.

Nicolopoulou (1997) focused on the role that narrative plays in individual and group identity. The sociocultural approach emphasizes that narrative practice links the child's developing sense of identity with the social process of jointly negotiating a constructed reality. Nicolopoulou (1996) demonstrated that children's narratives that generated in everyday, social settings are more complex and sophisticated than those demonstrated in the more constrained conditions of the research setting or laboratory. For example, some research shows that 5-year-old children cannot go beyond simple event descriptions or scripts; they cannot generate plot structures with initiating events, problems and resolutions, and formal ending devices (Hudson & Shapiro, 1991; Trabasso et al., 1992). Yet Nicolopoulou (1996) found that all of the 4- and 5-year-olds she studied told stories that contained all of these elements. What made a difference, she argued, is that these latter narratives are generated within the context of children's everyday social life, and the implication is that socially embedded activity "dramatically accelerates the development of children's narrative abilities" (p. 204).

The improvisational nature of play may also contribute to emergent writing and oral text production. Like Dyson, Nicolopoulou, Paley, and others, Daiute (1989, 1990) noted that children use improvisational play as a compositional strategy in writing. Daiute asserted that play does important work when it comes to verbal composition and thus it follows that pretend play may provide an important opportunity for children to learn generative strategies that support future written composition. Dyson (1991) likewise argued that children acquire literacy skills much more effectively if they learn to see written texts as things that are closely related to their own lives—that "the meaning embedded in written words exists because those words form worlds embedded in people's lives" (p. 115). Branscombe and Taylor (2000) made a connection between improvisation and writing, noting that many children use a generative strategy of improvising on existing texts. Variation on existing texts is common in social play, when children improvise on familiar stories from books or movies (Sawyer, 1997, 2002). Thus, even before children can read and write, improvisation during play provides an opportunity for children to interact with and operate on the texts they encounter in the wider culture (cf. Rowe, 1998, 2000).

FROM NARRATIVE PRACTICE TO COLLABORATIVE EMERGENCE

To extend the sociocultural position, we propose that play and narrative are related through *collaborative emergence*—a process found in all group improvisation, from jazz and theater to classroom and team collaboration (Sawyer, 2003a).

Because both peer play and situated narrative practices are improvisational and collaborative, the outcome cannot be controlled by any single participant. Rather, it emerges from the collective actions and contributions of each participant (Sawyer, 2003a). In collaborative improvisation, each child's contribution has to be evaluated before it is accepted by the others, and each child's turns in interaction successively build on the prior turns of the other children, resulting in the *emergence* of a narrative (Sawyer, 1997). Because both social play and co-constructed narratives are group improvisations, and the outcome emerges from the discourse of the group, we argue that the developmental benefits of these forms of peer narrative practice can only be fully understood by closely focusing on the group's conversation.

Children's sociodramatic play is improvisational. The outcome is unpredictable; there is moment-to-moment contingency from turn to turn; and the play is collaborative, with all children participating in the creation of the emergent narrative (Sawyer, 1997).

To demonstrate how the improvisation dimension of children's collaborative play contributes to narrative development, we show how a narrative emerged in a social pretend play episode between 5-year-olds in Example 1. Five years old is the peak age for social pretend play (Pellegrini, 1985) and is also the age at which children begin to frame their play narrative as distinct from everyday reality (Sachs, Goldman, & Chaille, 1984; Scarlett & Wolf, 1979). Example 1 (from Sawyer, 2002) is a transcript of a collaboratively improvised play narrative created among 5-year-olds during naturally occurring play in a preschool classroom.

Example 1

Muhammed, Corinna, and Artie are playing with jungle animals in the block area (replica play). Their talk switches between speaking as the plastic figurines (of jungle animals) and speaking out of character, as a narrator or director.

1	Corinna:	Guess what?
2		At the museum, someone is uh robbing us!
3		And they wanta take us to jail!
4	Muhammed:	That very bad.
5		How do you know a hippo, is robbing you?
6	Artie	Uh, you saw them?
7	Corinna:	Yes, I saw him last night, he was robbing my owner.
8		And I can't get him [drip of] my favorite food,
9		mashed, mashed bugs.

10	Artie:	[ ] to get out of here.
11		The [ ] took it out
12		And I can get out, BOOM.
13		I blasted open the door.
14	Corinna:	Artie, you killed, you, uh
15		got killed, alright?
16	Artie:	And, we found him, OK?
17		He wasn't dead, he just in [jail]
18	Corinna:	OK.
19	Artie:	[ ] where were you? Now they're voicing what they planned.
20	Corinna:	I'm in jail.
21	Artie:	OK!
22		Boom
23		And here's the bad guys coming in [ ]
24	Corinna:	I wanna thank you Spoken in character
25	Artie:	Let's pretend when you turned around,
26		the bad guys were [ ] in back of you, OK?

The replica play in Example 1 represents improvisation because the children do not follow a predetermined, shared script or routine. It is also collaborative because the flow of the play drama is collectively negotiated by all children through a give-and-take that creates the resulting performance. Via improvisation the play combines material drawn from a repertoire of shared cultural routines (Corsaro, 1985), such as robbery, jail, and rescue.

Clearly, the dialogue of Example 1 does not result in the emergence of a globally coherent narrative structure (Trabasso et al., 1992). Yet, even though global coherence is not present, one can identify component elements of narratives that connect across multiple turns, forming pockets of local coherence (cf. Sachs et al., 1984). At Line 2, Corinna introduces the threat of jail: "Someone is robbing us, and they wanta take us to jail." The "jail" theme stays active through Line 20, and after that, Artie introduces his "bad guy attack/fight" theme, which Corinna readily accepts.

At Line 5, in response to Corinna's proposal, "Someone is robbing us," Muhammed indirectly introduces an elaboration, that it is the hippo who is robbing: "How do you know a hippo, is robbing you?" This is a retrospective interpretation, because although Corinna did not say it was a hippo, Muhammed's utterance assumes that that was what she meant. Artie extends this question at Line 6, "You saw them?" Corinna accepts these retrospective interpretations at Line 7, voicing as an animal referencing her owner, and her favorite food, mashed bugs. At Line 10, Artie jumps ahead with the jail theme, enacting as if Corinna is already in jail; yet Corinna had only proposed "they wanta take us to jail." Artie proposes that he rescues Corinna by exploding the door to the jail. Again, Corinna accepts the modification of her proposal and extends it, suggesting that Artie was killed in the explosion (Line 14). Artie does not like the idea of his character being killed, so he responds with a modification (Lines 16–17): We found him, but he was not dead, he was in jail. Corinna agrees, and after these 17 lines of negotiation, the two begin enacting the scene they have just constructed.

At Line 19, Artie speaks in character to Corinna's play character, "Where were you?" She answers as they have planned, "I'm in jail." Artie enacts the explosion that will free Corinna's character. Then, however, Artie improvises further: The bad guys are coming in, not the good guys that would presumably rescue Corinna's character. At Line 24, Corinna has not picked up on this shift. She responds as if Artie's character is rescuing her, saying "I wanna thank you." Artie realizes that Corinna has not understood his modification of the narrative, so he repeats his new idea more explicitly, saying "Let's pretend" (Line 25).

These children use a range of interaction strategies to negotiate this group improvisation. At times they shift to explicit, out-of-character talk to propose new ideas or to modify their playmates' suggestions (e.g., Lines 23 and 25). This has been called metaplay, and as mentioned earlier, several researchers have shown that children's metaplay is related to measures of emergent literacy (Sachs et al., 1984; Trawick-Smith, 1998, 2001; Williamson & Silvern, 1991). Just as commonly, children propose or elaborate play ideas by speaking in character—an *implicit metacommunication* (Sawyer, 1997). In Lines 1 through 22, Artie and Corinna do not use the explicit metaplay that we find described in most of the research on play, yet they are negotiating nonetheless. In this negotiation the children combine a narrator's voice with their play character's voice using a *dialogic* strategy (Bakhtin, 1981; Wolf & Hicks, 1989). Lines 12 through 17 are dialogic: The children speak within the play frame and use pronouns that resolve to play frame characters ("you got killed"), and they combine this voice with a narratological voice. These children often recast information across voices: They propose a new development in the narrator voice, and then enact it with the replica character (Wolf & Hicks, 1989, p. 342). Wolf and Hicks (1989) documented recasting in a single child's narrative; in Example 1, we see recasting across speakers—Artie in Line 17, Corinna in Line 20—an important difference because it requires social negotiation and collaboration.

COLLABORATIVE EMERGENCE

How does play as an improvisation result in the emergence of a shared narrative? As analyzed earlier, Example 1 is highly embedded in the unfolding social context and thus not decontextualized. It relies on shared background knowledge among the participants. Although it contains many sophisticated elements of narrative, these are not coherently integrated in the narrative form of a children's storybook. Collaborative improvisation, in short, reflects a narrative process, whereas storybooks and texts reflect a narrative structure.

Through a sociocultural theoretical lens, relationships between improvisation and narrative become more visible, clearer, and connected through a sociocultural theoretical framework. Researchers in sociocultural psychology and situated cognition argue that knowledge and intelligence reside not only in people's heads, but are distributed across situated social practices that involve multiple participants in complex social systems. Knowing is viewed as the ability to participate appropriately in these shared cultural practices. From a sociocultural perspective, mind is considered to be "social, cultural, and embedded in the world" (Gee, 2000, p. 195).

Following this theoretical line of reasoning, we argue that the narratives that emerge from collaborative improvisation in play are collective social products. To understand this connection between improvisation and narrative requires methods that acknowledge the moment-to-moment, processual, contingent nature of improvisation, and its social and interactional nature. Structural methods of narrative analysis cannot easily do either, because they do not theorize the process whereby the narrative emerges from the dialogue—the key question from a sociocultural perspective. To theorize this process, we use Sawyer's (2003a) concept of *collaborative emergence*.

Improvised narratives are created by the collaborative efforts of the entire group. No single speaker creates the narrative; it emerges from the give and take of conversation. The narrative is constructed turn by turn; one child proposes a new development for the play, and other children respond by modifying or embellishing that proposal. Each new proposal for a development in the narrative is the creative inspiration of one child, but that proposal does not become a part of the play until it is evaluated by the other children. In the subsequent flow of dialogue, the group collaborates to determine whether to accept the proposal, how to weave that proposal into the drama that has already been established, and then how to further elaborate on it.

Narratives are collaboratively emergent from improvised dialogue for several reasons. First, they are unpredictable and contingent; their structures cannot be predicted in advance of the interaction. Second, the narrative emerges from the successive actions of all participants; it is not the conscious creation of any one person. For this reason, the interaction elements of dialogue are essential and defining features of the narratives that are generated. Third, because the narrative emerges out of an interaction process, no single child can drive its creation, and because it is a collective social product, it cannot be equated with any child's mental schema. Fourth, because improvisational discourse allows for retrospective interpretation, the emergent narrative cannot be analyzed solely in terms of a child's goal in an individual turn, because in many cases a child does not know the meaning of her own turn until the other children have responded (recall how Corinna's Turn 2 was retrospectively interpreted by Muhammed in Turn 5). In improvisational play, narrative elements emerge that cannot be understood by focusing on an individual child's mental representations and goals.

Drawing on theories of sociological emergentism (Sawyer, 2005), we argue that the emergent narrative is analytically irreducible to the actions, intentions, or mental states of participating children. Although the narrative is created by children through their collective action, it is analytically independent of their internal mental models and goals. In contrast, many cognitive psychologists assume that the emergent narrative is reducible to a participant's internal representations of it, as in Schank and Abelson's script model and in event schemata theories more generally (see Mandler, 1984; Tannen, 1979). The theory of collaborative emergence associates the narrative with an emergent and negotiated social process, rather than with any mental representation of it. Emergent narratives cannot be fully explained by analyzing the actions or mental states of the participant individuals, and then by working upward to an explanation of the emergent narrative. This sort of analysis can partially explain the collaborative emergence of narratives, but cannot adequately represent the analytic independence of the narrative, nor the conversational processes that generate them.

Collaborative emergence thus describes the connection between unstructured improvisation and the resulting narrative structure. Studying collaborative emergence requires a focus on the turn-by-turn symbolic processes that participants use to co-create the narrative. Conversation analysis can offer theory and methodology to study the emergence of narrative from improvisation; it is a common fact among scholars of conversation that individuals work together to co-construct their social reality through interaction. Conversation analysts have noted that speakers co-construct the interaction frame, and that the frame, in turn, constrains the future actions of individuals. Conversation analysts have argued that higher level structures (not only emergent narratives, but also social structures and institutions) are the product of the moment-to-moment unfolding emergence of collaborative, communicative interaction. In turn, these emergent higher level structures both constrain and enable future conversational actions (Sawyer, 2003b).

The theory of collaborative emergence suggests that the study of sociodramatic play and narrative must foundationally incorporate conversation-analytic methods that closely analyze the processual, turn-by-turn dynamics of pretend play dialogue. For example, conversation-analytic methods could be used to study metaplay and dialogic strategies in play conversation. How are such strategies combined in sequences of conversation? How does the presence or absence of these strategies affect the nature of the narratives that emerge? Answers to these questions will require a processual focus on the collaborative emergence of play conversation (e.g., Sawyer, 2002).

BENEFITS OF PEER COLLABORATION IN PRETEND PLAY

Because pretend play is both open ended and collaborative, children must continuously negotiate with each other to determine the direction of the emerging narrative and to coordinate their actions and representations. This negotiation is responsible for many of the benefits of play for literacy development. Of course, children engage in many activities that involve negotiation, but as Lillard (1998) points out, play with peers is probably the context in which children are afforded the most independence to take on such negotiations.

In the research literature on play and literacy, a significant amount of attention has been paid to the explicit negotiations or metaplay children must do to play together (Pellegrini, 1985; Rowe, 1998; Sachs et al., 1984). In metaplay, children use language to talk about language, to resolve conflicts and clarify representational ambiguities (Pellegrini & Galda, 1993). Metaplay is thought to be important to emerging literacy because it draws children's attention to features of the narrative, such as story structure, plot, and character. Reflection about the emerging narrative leads to increased facility with oral and written texts (Rowe, 1998, 2000; Williamson & Silvern, 1991). Support for this argument is provided by Williamson and Silvern (1991), who found that the directing component of metaplay (but not play itself) was related to measures of story comprehension; and by Pellegrini (1984), who found that metaplay was related to story recall and reproduction. In addition, Dickinson and Beals (1994) and Pellegrini and Galda (1991) found that metaplay among preschoolers predicted later reading performance.

Negotiating the emerging narrative is an important aspect of play not just because it draws children's attention to features of the narrative, but also because it draws attention to features of the other players. For a child to get her or his ideas into play, the child must make them clear to her or his collaborators. Whether this happens implicitly or explicitly, deciding precisely how to communicate one's ideas for play to others requires making some judgments about what others are likely to know and understand (Leslie, 1987). These same judgments are an important component of written communication as well (Clark & Brennan, 1991; Fussell & Krauss, 1989). Thus another way in which the contingent nature of play might contribute to literacy is by teaching children how to write for an audience: giving them the opportunity to develop their ideas about theory of mind and the social distribution of knowledge. Of course, as we have already established, the situation is not as simple as each child's ideas getting picked up wholesale by the group; play involves a continuous and complex process of give and take among all the players.

Playing with other children requires young people not only to make themselves clear, but to coordinate their ideas and representations with those of others. Thus the value of play for literacy development is not just in providing an audience for one's own narrative improvisation, but in placing children in interaction with other players who introduce competing ideas and representations. Some authors examine the benefits of peer interaction from a Piagetian standpoint, explaining that conceptual conflict between players leads to disequilibrium and ultimately accommodation (Pellegrini & Galda, 1993; Williamson & Silvern, 1991). However, this approach is ultimately unsatisfying, not only because Piaget himself rarely addressed accommodation to other children, but also because children often play together without the presence of conflict (Sawyer, 1997; Williamson & Silvern, 1991).

A more fruitful way to understand the benefits of play that derive from peer collaboration is found in work in sociocultural psychology that looks at the ways that peers scaffold each other's learning processes (Dauite, 1992; Forman & Cazden, 1985; Rogoff, 1990). From this standpoint, peer collaboration during play contributes to literacy learning because each child brings a unique set of cultural knowledge to the play frame, and because children are likely to direct each other's attention to aspects of the evolving narrative that differ from what each child would attend to on his or her own (Hall, 1991; Pellegrini & Galda, 1982). For example, Christie and Stone (1999) examined the ways children in a multiage class scaffolded each other's literacy behaviors during sociodramatic play, and they discovered that scaffolding during play is not unidirectional. Because literacy development occurs along several dimensions, and because each child develops uniquely, the roles of "expert" and "novice" were fluid and did not break down along the line of age.

In addition to providing an opportunity for peers to mutually support each other's literacy behaviors, the collaborative nature of play also provides a context for mutual enculturation. As Rowe (1998) explained, because children must coordinate their representations with each other, negotiation during play helps children move from idiosyncratic approaches toward more conventional sign usage and toward constructing meaning in ways shared by their interpretive community. Similarly, Kavanaugh and Engel (1998) pointed out that in the process of negotiating the play narrative, children learn about the "accepted canons of their culture" (p. 93).

CONCLUSION

The lens of improvisation allows us to view the relation between improvisational play and narrative practice in a new light. Because play is open ended and improvisational, it provides a context in which peers can interact around narrative forms and contribute to each other's developing narrative skill. They engage in sophisticated negotiation with peers, as they jointly construct a social reality, and simultaneously construct and enact social roles within that world.

The lens of improvisation focuses on one mechanism through which play contributes to literacy: collaborative emergence. In collaborative emergence, collectively created social products emerge from collectively improvised joint action. Children participate with their peers in the improvised construction of a narrative-structured play world. Collaborative emergence is the mechanism that implements the Vygotskian observation that the sophistication of social interaction always precedes the advancement of individual thought. The lens of improvisation shows the importance of another mediated stage: The narrative that emerges is a collective social product. Thus, play contributes to narrative competence through a three-stage process: First, children engage in the negotiation and collaborative activity of pretend play; second, this joint activity results in the emergence of a jointly created social product; third, children manipulate and internalize this jointly created social product. These three stages occur simultaneously and interweave with each other during situated social action, and they show how social play contributes to narrative competence and thus to literacy.

REFERENCES

Bakhtin, M. M. (1981). Discourse in the novel. In *The dialogic imagination* (pp. 259–422). Austin: University of Texas Press.

Bateson, G. (1972). A theory of play and fantasy. In G. Bateson (Ed.), *Steps to an ecology of mind* (pp. 177–193). New York: Chandler. (Original work published 1955)

Branscombe, N. A., & Taylor, J. B. (2000). "It would be as good as Snow White." Play and prosody. In K. A. Roskos & J. F. Christie (Eds.), *Play and literacy in early childhood: Research from multiple perspectives* (pp. 169–188). Mahwah, NJ: Lawrence Erlbaum Associates.

Christie, J. F. (1991). Psychological research on play: Connections with early literacy development. In J. F. Christie (Ed.), *Play and early literacy development* (pp. 27–43). Albany: State University of New York Press.

Christie, J. F., & Stone, S. J. (1999). Collaborative literacy activity in print-enriched play centers: Exploring the "zone" in same-age and multi-age groupings. *Journal of Literacy Research, 31,* 109–131.

Clark, H. H., & Brennan, S. E. (1991). Grounding in communication. In L. B. Resnick, J. M. Levine, & S. D. Teasley (Eds.), *Perspectives on socially shared cognition* (pp. 127–149). Washington, DC: American Psychological Association.

Corsaro, W. A. (1985). *Friendship and peer culture in the early years.* Norwood, NJ: Ablex.

Daiute, C. (1989). Play as thought: Thinking strategies of young writers. *Harvard Educational Review, 59,* 1–23.

Daiute, C. (1990). The role of play in writing development. *Research in the Teaching of English, 24,* 4–47.

Daiute, C. (1992). *Collaboration between children learning to write: Can novices be experts?* (Tech. Rep. No. CSW-TR-60). Washington, DC: Office of Education Research and Improvement.

Dickinson, D., & Beals, D. (1994). Not by print alone: Oral language supports for early literacy development. In D. F. Lancy (Ed.), *Children's emergent literacy: From research to practice* (pp. 29–40). Westport, CT: Praeger.

Dyson, A. H. (1991). The roots of literacy development: Play, pictures, and peers. In B. Scales, M. Almy, A. Nicolopoulou, & S. Ervin-Tripp (Eds.), *Play and the social context of development in early care and education* (pp. 98–116). New York: Teachers College Press.

Eckler, J. A., & Weininger, O. (1989). Structural parallels between pretend play and narratives. *Developmental Psychology, 25,* 736–743.

Falk, J. (1980). The conversational duet. In *Proceedings of the sixth annual meeting of the Berkeley Linguistics Society* (Vol. 6, pp. 507–514). Berkeley, CA: Berkeley Linguistics Society.

Fein, G. G. (1981). Pretend play: An integrative view. *Child Development, 52,* 1095–1118.

Fein, G. G., Ardila-Rey, A. E., & Groth, L. A. (2000). The narrative connection: Stories and literacy. In K. A. Roskos & J. F. Christie (Eds.), *Play and literacy in early child-*

hood: Research from multiple perspectives (pp. 27–43). Mahwah, NJ: Lawrence Erlbaum Associates.

Forman, E., & Cazden, C. (1985). Exploring Vygotskian perspectives in education: The cognitive value of peer interaction. In J. Wertsch (Ed.), *Culture, communication, and cognition: Vygotskian perspectives* (pp. 323–347). Cambridge, UK: Cambridge University Press.

Fussell, S. R., & Krauss, R. M. (1989). Understanding friends and strangers: The effects of audience design on message comprehension. *European Journal of Social Psychology, 19,* 509–525.

Galda, L. (1984). Narrative competence: Play, storytelling, and comprehension. In A. D. Pellegrini & T. D. Yawkey (Eds.), *The development of oral and written language in context* (pp. 105–114). Norwood, NJ: Ablex.

Gee, J. P. (2000). Discourse and sociocultural studies in reading. In M. L. Kamil, P. B. Mosenthal, P. D. Pearson, & R. Barr (Eds.), *Handbook of reading research* (Vol. 3, pp. 195–207). Mahwah, NJ: Lawrence Erlbaum Associates.

Glaubman, R., Kashi, G., & Koresh, R. (2001). Facilitating the narrative quality of sociodramatic play. In A. Goncu & E. L. Klein (Eds.), *Children in play, story, and school* (pp. 132–157). New York: Guilford.

Groth, L. A., & Darling, L. D. (2001). Playing "inside" stories. In A. Goncü & E. L. Klein (Eds.), *Children in play, story, and school* (pp. 220–237). New York: Guilford.

Hall, N. (1991). Play and the emergence of literacy. In J. F. Christie (Ed.), *Play and early literacy development* (pp. 3–26). Albany: State University of New York Press.

Heath, S. B. (1983). *Ways with words: Language, life, and work in communities and classrooms.* Cambridge, UK: Cambridge University Press.

Hudson, J. A., & Shapiro, L. R. (1991). From knowing to telling: The development of children's scripts, stories, and personal narratives. In A. McCabe & C. Peterson (Eds.), *Developing narrative structure* (pp. 89–136). Hillsdale, NJ: Lawrence Erlbaum Associates.

Kavanaugh, R. D., & Engel, S. (1998). The development of pretense and narrative in early childhood. In O. Saracho & B. Spodek (Eds.), *Multiple perspectives on play in early childhood education* (pp. 80–99). Albany: State University of New York Press.

Leslie, A. M. (1987). Pretense and representation: The origins of "theory of mind." *Psychological Review, 94,* 412–426.

Lillard, A. S. (1998). Playing with a theory of mind. In O. Saracho & B. Spodek (Eds.), *Multiple perspectives on play in early childhood education* (pp. 11–33). Albany: State University of New York Press.

Mandler, J. M. (1984). *Stories, scripts, and scenes: Aspects of schema theory.* Hillsdale, NJ: Lawrence Erlbaum Associates.

Mason, J. M., & Allen, J. (1986). A review of emergent literacy with implications for research and practice in reading. *Review of Research in Education, 13,* 3–38.

Michaels, S. (1981). "Sharing time:" Children's narrative styles and differential access to literacy. *Language in Society, 10,* 423–442.

Neuman, S. B., & Roskos, K. A. (1990). Play, print, and purpose: Enriching play environments for literacy development. *The Reading Teacher, 44,* 214–221.

Neuman, S. B., & Roskos, K. A. (1991). The influence of literacy-enriched play centers on preschoolers' conceptions of the functions of print. In J. F. Christie (Ed.),

Play and early literacy development (pp. 167–187). Albany: State University of New York Press.

Neuman, S. B., & Roskos, K. A. (1993). Access to print for children of poverty: Differential effects of adult mediation and literacy-enriched play settings on environmental and functional print tasks. *American Educational Research Journal, 30,* 95–122.

Neuman, S. B., & Roskos, K. A. (1997). Literacy knowledge in practice: Contexts of participation for young writers and readers. *Reading Research Quarterly, 32,* 10–32.

Nicolopoulou, A. (1996). Narrative development in social context. In D. I. Slobin, J. Gerhardt, J. Guo, & A. Kyratzis (Eds.), *Social interaction, social context, and language: Essays in honor of Susan Ervin-Tripp* (pp. 369–390). Mahwah, NJ: Lawrence Erlbaum Associates.

Nicolopoulou, A. (1997). Children and narratives: Toward an interpretive and sociocultural approach. In M. Bamberg (Ed.), *Narrative development: Six approaches* (pp. 179–215). Hillsdale, NJ: Lawrence Erlbaum Associates, Inc.

Paley, V. G. (1984). *Boys & girls: Superheroes in the doll corner.* Chicago: University of Chicago Press.

Paley, V. G. (1988). *Bad guys don't have birthdays.* Chicago: University of Chicago Press.

Pellegrini, A. D. (1984). Identifying causal elements in the thematic-fantasy play paradigm. *American Educational Research Journal, 21,* 691–701.

Pellegrini, A. D. (1985). The relations between symbolic play and literate behavior: A review and critique of the empirical literature. *Review of Educational Research, 55,* 107–121.

Pellegrini, A. D., & Galda, L. (1982). The effects of thematic fantasy play training on the development of children's story comprehension. *American Educational Research Journal, 19,* 443–452.

Pellegrini, A. D., & Galda, L. (1991). Longitudinal relations among preschoolers symbolic play, metalinguistic verbs, and emergent literacy. In J. F. Christie (Ed.), *Play and early literacy development* (pp. 47–67). Albany: State University of New York Press.

Pellegrini, A. D., & Galda, L. (1993). Ten years after: A reexamination of symbolic play and literacy research. *Reading Research Quarterly, 28,* 162–175.

Pellegrini, A. D., & Galda, L. (2000). Commentary—cognitive development, play, and literacy: Issues of definition and developmental function. In K. A. Roskos & J. F. Christie (Eds.), *Play and literacy in early childhood: Research from multiple perspectives* (pp. 63–73). Mahwah, NJ: Lawrence Erlbaum Associates.

Pellegrini, A. D., Galda, L., Dresden, J., & Cox, S. (1991). A longitudinal study of the predictive relations among symbolic play, linguistic verbs, and early literacy. *Research in the Teaching of English, 25,* 219–235.

Rogoff, B. (1990). *Apprenticeship in thinking.* London: Oxford University Press.

Rowe, D. W. (1998). The literate potentials of book related dramatic play. *Reading Research Quarterly, 33,* 10–35.

Rowe, D. W. (2000). Bringing books to life: The role of book-related dramatic play in young children's literacy learning. In K. A. Roskos & J. F. Christie (Eds.), *Play and literacy in early childhood: Research from multiple perspectives* (pp. 3–26). Mahwah, NJ: Lawrence Erlbaum Associates.

Sachs, J., Goldman, J., & Chaille, C. (1984). Planning in pretend play: Using language to coordinate narrative development. In A. D. Pellegrini & T. D. Yawkey (Eds.), *The development of oral and written language in social contexts* (pp. 119–128). Norwood, NJ: Ablex.

Saltz, E., Dixon, D., & Johnson, J. (1997). Training disadvantaged preschoolers on various fantasy activities. Effects on cognitive functioning and impulse control. *Child Development, 48,* 367–380.

Sawyer, R. K. (1997). *Pretend play as improvisation: Conversation in the preschool classroom.* Mahwah, NJ: Lawrence Erlbaum Associates.

Sawyer, R. K. (2002). Improvisation and narrative. *Narrative Inquiry, 12,* 321–351.

Sawyer, R. K. (2003a). *Group creativity: Music, theater, collaboration.* Mahwah, NJ: Lawrence Erlbaum Associates.

Sawyer, R. K. (2003b). *Improvised dialogues: Emergence and creativity in conversation.* Westport, CT: Greenwood.

Sawyer, R. K. (2004). Creative teaching: Collaborative discussion as disciplined improvisation. *Educational Researcher, 33*(2), 12–20.

Sawyer, R. K. (2005). *Social emergence: Societies as complex systems.* New York: Cambridge University Press.

Scarlett, W. G., & Wolf, D. (1979). When it's only make-believe: The construction of a boundary between fantasy and reality in storytelling. In E. Winner & H. Gardner (Eds.), *Fact, fiction, and fantasy in childhood* (Vol. 6, pp. 29–40). San Francisco: Jossey-Bass.

Silvern, S. B., Taylor, J., Williamson, P., Surbeck, E., & Kelley, M. (1986). Young children's story recall as a product of play, story familiarity, and adult intervention. *Merrill-Palmer Quarterly, 32,* 73–86.

Tannen, D. (1979). What's in a frame? Surface evidence for underlying expectations. In R. O. Freedle (Ed.), *New directions in discourse processing* (pp. 137–181). Norwood, NJ: Ablex.

Teale, W. H., & Sulzby, E. (1986). *Emergent literacy: Writing and reading.* Norwood, NJ: Ablex.

Trabasso, T., Stein, N. L., Rodkin, P. C., Munger, M. P., & Baughn, C. R. (1992). Knowledge of goals and plans in the on-line narration of events. *Cognitive Development, 7,* 133–170.

Trawick-Smith, J. (1998). A qualitative analysis of metaplay in the preschool years. *Early Childhood Research Quarterly, 13,* 433–452.

Trawick-Smith, J. (2001, April). *The play frame and the "fictional dream": The bidirectional relationship between metaplay and story writing.* Paper presented at the annual meeting of the American Educational Research Association, Seattle, WA.

Williamson, P. A., & Silvern, S. B. (1991). Thematic-fantasy play and story comprehension. In J. F. Christie (Ed.), *Play and early literacy development* (pp. 69–90). Albany: State University of New York Press.

Wolf, D., & Hicks, D. (1989). The voices within narratives: The development of intertextuality in young children's stories. *Discourse Processes, 12,* 329–351.

Yaden, D. B., Jr., Rowe, D. W., & MacGillivray, L. (2000). Emergent literacy: A matter (polyphony) of perspectives. In R. Barr, P. D. Pearson, & P. B. Mosenthal (Eds.), *Handbook of reading research* (Vol. 3, pp. 425–454). Mahwah, NJ: Lawrence Erlbaum Associates.

3

Bringing Books to Life: The Role of Book-Related Dramatic Play in Young Children's Literacy Learning

Deborah Wells Rowe
Vanderbilt University

At 27 months of age, my son Christopher was intensely interested in bulldozers, backhoes, and other big work machines. He and I often stopped to watch the big machines at work in our neighborhood and he owned several information books about work machines that he liked to read over and over. One day I introduced a book I remembered from my own childhood, *Mike Mulligan and His Steam Shovel* (Burton, 1939). Although the book was long, Christopher was intensely interested, listening to the story and asking questions for almost 30 minutes. The next morning, he requested that I read the book several times. In the afternoon, we went outside where Christopher played with toy trucks, rakes, shovels, and a variety of containers in his sandbox. Supervising his play from across the yard, I overheard him mutter to himself: "I don't know what its name is!" Then, with satisfaction, he loudly announced the name of Mike Mulligan's steam shovel: "Mary Ann."

Intrigued, I walked over to the sandbox. "What are you doing, Christopher?"

"I'm Mike," he corrected. "I'm digging a basement for the town of Popperville." (VT: Home)[1]

In this episode, Christopher spontaneously launched dramatic play related to a book that was his current favorite. He took on the role of the book's protagonist, Mike Mulligan, transformed a plastic rake into Mary Ann the steam shovel, and used his sandbox as the venue for physically enacting the digging he had read about. He remembered and used some of the book's language (e.g., town of Popperville) but also substituted a more familiar word, basement, for the unfamiliar term cellar that was used in the book.

---

[1]The following abbreviations are used in this chapter to indicate the data source for examples: FN = field notes; VT = videotape; Home = home-based case study; School = school-based ethnography.

Book-related dramatic play of this type was common in my home-based case study of Christopher at age 2 and also in a school-based ethnography of the literacy learning of his 2-year-old peers at Walker Preschool. Most researchers agree that a central characteristic of dramatic play is the "assimilative manipulation of symbols" (Rubin, Fein, & Vandenberg, 1983, p. 700); that is, when involved in dramatic play, children use make-believe transformations of objects and role playing to act out scripts and stories they invent (Christie, 1991). In dramatic play, children pretend as if real-world objects and people had other identities. In this chapter, I focus specifically on book-related dramatic play, which I define as involving symbolic transformations that explicitly or implicitly reflect the meanings signed in books' text or illustrations, or in the book-reading events in which children encounter books.

RESEARCH ON BOOK-RELATED PLAY

Developmental and cognitive psychologists have long been interested in understanding how patterns of dramatic play change as children grow older (e.g., Howes & Matheson, 1992; Parten, 1932) and how play may be linked to broader issues in cognitive development. Piaget (1962), for example, saw pretend play as the ultimate example of the child's assimilation of reality to the ego (Sawyer, 1997). Vygotsky (1978), on the other hand, focused on play as the arena where children learn to make abstract transformations needed in other forms of representation. Only in the last 15 years has attention turned specifically to the connection between dramatic play and reading. Most of this research has attempted to empirically establish or refute theoretical proposals concerning connections between dramatic play (or drama for older students) and reading. Educational researchers studying these questions have pursued the additional goal of establishing the effectiveness of book-related play interventions on children's reading achievement. At present there are two lines of research investigating theoretical connections between dramatic play and books—each differing in focus. A third line of research, usually conducted with older children, has investigated the impact of book-related drama on students' reading.

The first line of research, rooted in cognitive psychology, has concerned itself with the ways that play may enhance children's literacy processes. Here researchers (e.g., Galda, Pellegrini, & Cox, 1989; Pellegrini & Galda, 1991) have explored the global relationship between the basic representational abilities used in play, reading, and writing with longitudinal designs correlating measures of children's play behaviors with measures of literacy at a later time. This work has found that metaplay (Williamson & Silvern, 1991)—metacommunications about play—is more strongly related to measures of emergent literacy than are symbolic transformations (i.e., pretending a block is a car).

The second line of research, also rooted in cognitive psychology, has investigated the role of dramatic play in children's comprehension of literate content—especially the comprehension and recall of stories. In general, the premise behind these studies has been that dramatic story reenactments provide opportunities for mental reconstructions of story events and the development of story schemas, both of which are posited to increase story comprehension. Through experiments and observations of children in adult-initiated play events (e.g., Christie, 1983; Pellegrini & Galda, 1982; Saltz, Dixon, & Johnson, 1977; Silvern, Williamson, & Waters, 1983), researchers have concluded that dramatic play is related to comprehension in powerful, if complex, ways. Like the longitudinal research described earlier, these studies have identified metaplay as a more significant factor in increasing story comprehension than other aspects of play such as symbolic transformation. Williamson and Silvern (1991) hypothesized that whereas the symbolic transformations in dramatic play may remain personal, metacommunications about play may turn children's attention to story events and characters. Thus, these studies have concluded that the social nature of play is a key part of its impact on reading skills and comprehension.

The third line of research has explored the impact of various kinds of drama activities on older students' reading comprehension. Like many of the studies already cited, this research explores the impact of teacher-structured opportunities to dramatize books, rather than self-initiated play episodes launched by students for their own purposes. Although the students in these studies are generally beyond the age when one would expect to see dramatic play of the kind described in the opening of the chapter, the design of drama interventions is often based on theoretical claims similar to those advanced for book-related dramatic play interventions. Several qualitative studies have recently provided support for claims that drama encourages shifts in perspective and deep processing of book content. For example, Clyde (2003) reports that when elementary-grade children acted out the unvoiced thoughts of story characters using a "subtext strategy," they were able to take on the character's perspective and also to shift between the perspectives of different book characters. Medina (2004) reported that using drama-in-education strategies (e.g., tableau and "hot seat" activities) to respond to Latina/Latino literature helped fifth graders make sense of issues raised in the books, connect them to their lives, and eventually to examine the issues critically from the multiple perspectives represented by the characters. Wagner's (1998) review of quantitative research on the effects of drama activities also supports the contention that book-related drama can improve reading skills and comprehension. Rose, Parks, Androes, and McMahon (2000) recently added support for this claim. Comparing a book-related drama program designed to increase visual imagery around books to standard basal-reader instruction, they found that fourth graders participating in the drama intervention outperformed control students on standardized reading achievement tests. Positive effects were especially strong for measures of reading comprehension. Overall, research with both preschool and elementary-grade students presents a positive view of the effects of book-related dramatic play and drama on students' reading skills and comprehension.

Given researchers' interest in understanding the connection between dramatic play and reading, it is somewhat puzzling that there has been so little research describing the spontaneous book-related play of younger preschoolers. Only a handful of studies have extended more generally focused naturalistic descriptions of play (e.g., Haight & Miller, 1993) to specifically document the kinds of book-related play that occur in home and school contexts. Although few in number, observational studies of preschoolers' child-initiated, book-related play (Crago & Crago, 1983; Goodman, 1990; Panofsky, 1986; C. Smith, 2002; Wolf & Heath, 1992) have demonstrated that children produce this type of play in a variety of different social situations and for a wide range of social and cognitive purposes including re-creating story events and illustrations using activity and props (Crago & Crago, 1983; Goodman, 1990; C. Smith, 2002; Wolf & Heath, 1992), exploring unfamiliar words and meanings introduced in books (Crago & Crago, 1983), exploring emotionally charged problems introduced in books and the real world (Crago & Crago, 1983; Wolf & Heath, 1992), controlling social situations (Wolf & Heath, 1992), and as a means of participating in book-reading events (Panofsky, 1986; C. Smith, 2002). Classroom-based studies (Martinez, Cheyney, & Teale, 1991; Saltz et al., 1977) have demonstrated that features of the classroom context such as the amount of exposure to books and support for play as a mode of book response were related to the frequency of book-related play.

In this chapter, I extend this line of naturalistic research by describing the book-related play of one group of well-read-to 2-year-olds. Specifically, I focus on two broad research questions related to the play–reading connection: (a) What kinds of book-related play do very young children engage in at preschool and at home? and (b) What is the role of book-related dramatic play in the children's literacy learning?

METHODS FOR THE RESEARCH

Overview of the Studies

Data discussed in this chapter were collected as part of two related studies—one a 9-month naturalistic study of one group of children's literacy experiences in a preschool classroom, and the other a case study of my son's literacy learning from birth to age 4. The school-based data were recorded as I participated 2 days per week as a researcher-teacher in a preschool classroom serving 16 White, middle-class, 2- and 3-year-olds. My son, Christopher, attended this preschool class. The portion of the home-based data considered here spans a 13-month period beginning at Christopher's second birthday and continuing until the close of the school-based data collection. Data from both studies are reported here because together they provide a more comprehensive picture of literacy-related play than could be created from either data set considered by itself. The strengths of the home-based case study data are the variety of contexts in which play was observed and the intensity of observation of a single child. The school-based data provide a broader picture of literacy-related play as it occurred for a larger group of children in a school setting.

Settings for the Studies

The preschool study was conducted at Walker Preschool[2]—a "parent's day out program" designed to serve the needs of families needing part-time child care. Children attended the preschool 1 or 2 days per week, with enrollment in the 2-year-olds' classroom ranging from 12 to 15 children each day. The two classroom teachers, Ginger Wells and Michelle Raybin, worked with the children each day throughout the week. I was present in the classroom in the role of researcher-teacher 2 days per week.

During the year I collected data at the preschool, I collaborated with the classroom teachers, my research assistant Leigh Ann Copas, and the school's director, Fran Rogers, to increase the number and kinds of book-related experiences available to the young children who attended the 2-year-olds' class. We assembled text sets (Short, Harste, & Burke, 1996)—books related by theme, language patterns, author, genre, and so on—to support the teachers' thematic units. We decided to station an adult in the book center on a frequent basis for informal reading. We created a writing center for child-directed writing. We chose books related to unit themes for whole-class read-alouds and made these now-familiar books available to children for independent reading.

Much reading, talking, and playing occurred each morning at the learning centers set up around the room (i.e., blocks, manipulative toys, dramatic play, art, book center, writing table, etc.). Children moved at will from one learning center to another, playing alone, alongside peers, or with me, Ginger, or Michelle. At the book center, I was often present to read and talk informally with children about the books they selected from those displayed on the nearby shelf.

During the second semester of the study the research and teaching team made a conscious curricular decision to support book-to-play connections at the book center (Rowe, 1994). We began to help children create text and toy sets (Rowe, Fitch, & Bass, 2003) by locating book-related toys and props. We also began to explicitly talk about connections between toys and the books being read and to suggest ways that children might link future play to the books we were reading. In the book center, child-initiated forays into the world of pretend play continued to be quickly developed episodes, interspersed in the midst of book reading and informal book discussion. More developed book-related play was recorded in the dramatic play center, at the block center, and outside on the playground. Most of these instances of sociodramatic play involved adults as well as peers. Like other children their age, the 2- and 3-year-olds in this classroom often sought the participation of adults who were able to make the rich interpretations necessary to understand their pretend actions, and who were willing to follow their lead in taking roles and acting out scenes (Bergen, 1988).

---

[2]Pseudonyms have been used to identify the school and children participating in the school-based study.

Participants

All 16 children participating in the school-based study were White and from middle-class backgrounds. Parent surveys and informal contacts confirmed that these children had many experiences with books outside of school.

At the time of this study, my son, Christopher, was an only child of professional parents, and in many ways much like his peers attending Walker Preschool. At 2 years, 4 months old, he was near the middle of the age range for the class, which spanned from 1 year, 10 months to 2 years, 10 months at the start of the school year. Like his peers, Christopher had many experiences with books each day, including informal reading with me or other adults and bedtime storybook reading. However, it is possible that because of my background as an early literacy researcher he experienced a more intense emphasis on emergent reading and writing experiences than some of his peers.

When Christopher's approach to learning was compared to that of his peers at Walker Preschool, he demonstrated one of two common patterns seen in this group of children. Like 7 of his peers in the school-based study, Christopher was an *intense theme-based learner.* That is, he pursued identifiable personal learning interests (e.g., tools, work machines, dinosaurs) over long periods of time and in a variety of contexts. The remainder of his classmates pursued a more eclectic mix of interests, usually over shorter periods of time—a pattern I have labeled *sampling.* Unlike theme-based learners, samplers tended to become interested in some aspect of the classroom curriculum and explore this for a time before moving on to explore some new offering from the teachers.

Data Collection

In both research projects, data were collected using ethnographic techniques of participant observation and informal interviewing. Data were recorded using field notes, video recording, and collection of artifacts (Erickson, 1986; Guba & Lincoln, 1994; Lincoln & Guba, 1985). Methodological and theoretical notes were also recorded.

At Walker Preschool, I adopted the role of assistant teacher by reading, writing, and playing with the children. Data collected on book-related events included videotapes of informal adult–child and peer-only book reading events at the book center, video recordings of teacher-led large-group storybook reading events, field note records of play occurring outside the book center, and parent responses to a questionnaire regarding their children's reading and writing experiences and interests. Although other teachers were recorded reading informally with children at the book center, I was the most frequent adult reader on the days I was present in the classroom. Thus, my reading style and interactions had a major impact on children's expectations and experiences of events at the book center and are strongly represented in the book center data.

Data from the home-based case study of Christopher provide a comprehensive view of the ways one child linked books and play. In my role as parent, I was close enough to observe most, if not all, of his activities while we were at home together. Therefore, my field notes record literacy events throughout the day and in a broad range of settings including outdoor play, indoor play with toys, rides in the car, bath time, visits to the doctor, and so on. During the 13-month period considered here, I recorded field notes describing Christopher's reading and writing experiences an average of 4 days each week.

Data Analysis

In both studies, data analysis was ongoing during all phases of data collection using the constant comparative method. After completion of the field studies, additional analyses began with open and axial coding (Glaser & Strauss, 1967; Strauss & Corbin, 1998) of the school-based data. First, I reviewed the field notes for examples of book-to-play connections. Next, I reviewed the first 20 one-hour video tapes of classroom literacy events for book-to-play connections, and transcribed relevant portions. Using the constant comparative method, I analyzed these data to identify key characteristics of book-related play and to develop hypotheses about the role of this type of play in the children's literacy learning. In the next phase of analysis, I viewed the remaining 11 hours of videotape to challenge and refine both categories and hypotheses, with emphasis on searching for negative cases.

Next, I turned to the home-based data to refine and extend the categories of book-related play generated from the school-based data. These analyses first involved categorizing all instances of book-related play in the field notes—beginning with the categories developed from the school-based data, and refining them as needed. A final phase of data analysis involved cross-site and cross-case analysis in which book-related dramatic play was compared across the home and school-based studies, across different types of events (book reading and dramatic play), and across children to provide a broader view for the commonalities or individuality of the patterns identified.

BOOK-RELATED DRAMATIC PLAY: THE PATTERNS

Observations at school and at home revealed that children's book-to-play connections involved (a) connecting books to the world of objects by locating and holding book-related toys and props, (b) personal response to books through dramatic enactments of feelings and actions, (c) participating in book-reading events through the persona of a pretend character, (d) aesthetic reenactments of book events, (e) sorting out the author's meanings through play, (f) character studies, and (g) using book themes and characters as springboards for personal inquiries about the world.

Connecting Books With Toys and Props

One of the most noticeable ways children connected books to play was through an active, physical search for book-related toys and props. Like all patterns described in this chapter, I observed this behavior both in my own home with Christopher and with his peers at Walker Preschool.

In the studies reported here, children essentially created their own text and toy sets by physically bringing together books and related props—a pattern we began to follow as teachers by purposefully placing related sets of toys and books together in various part of the classroom. Once props were located, children sometimes moved from book reading to dramatic play, but in other instances, these toys were simply held as we read. In some cases props were realistic models of items pictured in books. For example, while reading a book about dinosaurs, Ellen rushed to the block center to gather toy dinosaurs like those pictured in the book (VT: School). Children also transformed objects with little physical resemblance to book illustrations. For example, while reading *Whatever Happened to the Dinosaurs* (Most, 1984) Adam held up a Hamburglar puppet—a fast-food chain character whose head is made of a hamburger—and announced that it was Tyrannosaurus Rex (VT: School).

Although the phenomenon of locating and holding book-related toys was common both at home and at school, the data provided few direct clues to the role of this practice in the children's literacy learning. However, there are several hypotheses that are theoretically supportable and seem worthy of further study. First, locating book-related toys may have been a part of the general learning strategy of looking for connections between background knowledge and current experiences (cf. Peirce, 1966; Piaget & Inhelder, 1969). Given the children's obvious excitement at finding and showing us toys related to the books being read, this practice may have been a physical manifestation of a more general pattern of searching for connections between books and familiar experiences. By searching out book-related toys, children connected book-reading events rooted in the adult world with play events rooted in their own experiences. Second, locating book-related toys may have provided a physical prompt for future play. Children may have located book-related toys as a means of facilitating play. Certainly, children located toys that they could, and often did, use later in exploratory or dramatic play. A third hypothesis is that holding toys may have supported comprehension by creating a more concrete link to the children's world experiences. Books required children to use verbal text and static, two-dimensional illustrations as cues for imagining a three-dimensional world full of actions and objects framed by the passage of time. I expect that toys and props, whether realistic or transformed, made book-reading events more concrete. It is possible that they lessened the cognitive load of conjuring up images from texts that were, at best, abstract and partially specified. When holding a toy dinosaur, many aspects of the text were signaled in a more concrete way, leaving more attention for other aspects of comprehension and response.

Personal Response to Books

Including props and toys was just one of the ways children made book reading a more concrete activity. When reading evoked strong emotions, role playing and physical action became a part of their response to books as well. A common pattern observed in these studies involved children in acting out their responses to a character or event. In many cases these actions were physically directed at the book's illustrations. For example, as Steve and I were reading *The Farmyard Cat* (Anello, 1987) at the book center the following exchange occurred (VT: School).

The story begins with a cat hanging on the henhouse in an attempt to catch some chickens for his dinner.

Rowe [reading]:   But ... down bent the wire, and down fell the farmyard cat. With claws stretched w-i-d-e, she landed ... on top of the farmyard dog.

Steve: Why?

Rowe: I think she was up high and fell on him. [continues reading] The farmyard dog was very angry. He began to chase the farmyard cat. "I'll get you cat!" growled the dog. "I'll get you."

[The illustration shows an obviously angry dog with bared teeth, running after the cat.]

Steve: Dop, dop, dop.

[As Steve makes these sound effects, he opens and closes the pretend alligator's mouth as if it is biting, and bangs the toy on the picture of the farmyard dog.]

This book was a favorite of Steve's, and in previous readings he had often quoted with great satisfaction the final line of the book in which the cat announces her victory over all the animals who have been chasing her. Here, once again, Steve identifies with the cat, and acts out his own angry response to the dog character.

In events such as these, children turned to the familiar medium of play to physically express their responses to book characters. These data support the hypothesis that the real-time actions and dialogue of dramatic role play provided these children with a powerful means of responding to books. Children literally jumped out of their seats in the audience and into the scene as players. Steve became a defender of his favorite character, rather than a spectator observing danger at a distance. Both at school and at home, children were constantly being reminded by adults to "use words" rather than actions to express their thoughts and emotions. These episodes suggest that play continued to provide an opportunity for combining both actions and talk as a form of response.

Participating in Book-Reading Events

Although children made use of dramatic play to catapult themselves into stories, they also used play as a medium for participating in the more distanced discussions of books that were a mainstay of adult–child book-reading events

(Rowe, 1998). Both in my home and at school, adults organized book reading events in ways that supported children's talk about books. Both children and adults commented on illustrations and story lines, asked questions, and shared personal experiences. Close analysis of interactions in these events shows that as long as talk was recognized (or could be directly defended) as related to the topic of the book, adults usually supported and encouraged it. Role play—even play obviously related to the book—was not always recognized and approved by adults during book-reading events (Rowe, 1998). In fact, despite our general commitment to supporting the connections between books and play, I and other adult readers sometimes cut short dramatic responses and role playing begun by children during book reading.

Therefore, to participate in informal book-reading events in my home and at Walker Preschool, children were learning to take a distanced, analytic stance toward books—that is, to talk about books' events and characters as objects. Although such a stance would seem to exclude role play, this was not the case. Children inserted dramatic play within the usual boundaries of adult–child book reading and discussion by playing at literacy—that is, they asked and answered questions during book discussions while pretending to be an imaginary character.

For example, Katie brought her bunny to the book center to sit in her lap and read with the group assembled there. She later took him to the writing table and produced a journal entry for herself as well as for her bunny (FN: School). In some cases, children even voiced a pretend character's responses to books. For example, while reading *Mike Mulligan and His Steam Shovel* (Burton, 1939) at home, Christopher held several plastic dinosaur toys as we read. As we came to the page where the more modern electric- and diesel-powered shovel characters tease and reject Mary Anne, the steam-powered shovel, he pointedly told me that, "The [toy] dinos don't like this part" (FN: Home). For both Sherra and Christopher, imaginary characters appeared to be the children's alter egos. Sherra's bunny produced a journal entry remarkably like her own, and Christopher's toy dinosaurs expressed his own dislike of the disparaging remarks made by the modern work machines. Here, play was adapted to fit the familiar patterns of participation in adult–child book-reading events. Children used role play as a medium for taking on adult-sanctioned roles such as asking questions or expressing personal interpretations of a book.

After looking closely at the videotapes of book-reading events, I expect that playing at literacy helped children make important connections between adult-structured book-reading events and the world of play. For these young children, dramatic play was a central means of engaging with the world. As such, it was no less central to their early encounters with books and book-reading events. At times, book reading appeared to be just a brief interlude in the midst of a larger sequence of dramatic play. Rather than making a clean break with characters and roles already developed, children bought them along from the world of play to keep them company in real-world literacy events. My hypothesis is that children used play as a medium for participating in book-reading events because it provided a connection to their familiar, playful ways of understanding and interacting with the world. Like the practice of holding toys, it may have also signaled the possibility of returning to play after book reading was finished.

Aesthetic Reenactments

In these studies, a great deal of book-related play seems to have as its purpose creating an aesthetic or lived-through experience of the book (Rosenblatt, 1978). Unlike events where play was obviously related to questions the children had expressed about the text or the world, in these events children appeared less concerned with what they would learn from the event than with the immediate enjoyment of playing out some aspect of a favorite story.

For example, on the school playground I noticed Jane looking up to the sky and letting a ball roll off her nose to the ground. When I asked what she was doing, she replied, "I'm bouncing it on my nose like the seal in the *Spot* book" (FN: School). This explanation rendered her actions entirely interpretable because we had recently read the book *Spot Goes to the Circus* (Hill, 1986), where the final pages show a seal and a dog named Spot balancing beach balls on their noses. The children appeared to have a similar purpose for playing out the scene from *The Three Little Pigs* where the wolf knocks on the door and demands that the pigs let him in. This play became a favorite on the school playground, and children often requested that we replay the scene again and again. In my child-assigned role as the wolf, I "huffed and puffed" using my most menacing voice, while clawing at the door of the playhouse. The children squealed delightedly in their roles a pigs, reveling in their power to stand up to the wolf, and relishing the fear of being threatened within the safety of play (FN: School).

Rosenblatt (1978) suggested that an aesthetic stance toward reading turns attention inward to the readers' own immediate experiences as they respond to text. In these data, children often appeared to play out scenes from books for the sheer enjoyment of experiencing the book in the multisensory medium of dramatic play. Dramatizing scenes from books brought to life, in new ways, stories that had previously been experienced primarily through text and illustrations. These observations support the hypotheses that dramatic play served as a medium for children's aesthetic responses to literature and that an aesthetic stance is an integral part of even very young children's literacy repertoire.

Sorting Out the Author's Meanings

Not all book reenactments served an aesthetic purpose, however. Children also chose to play and replay scenes they did not understand and had asked questions about during previous readings of the book. In these cases, I expect that book-related play allowed children to sort out book meanings—a task not unlike that of older students who use talk in literature discussion groups to sort out plot details and to explore personal interpretations of the author's meanings (Newbold, 1993).

Just after his second birthday, my son, Christopher, developed an intense interest in work machines that lasted for many months. He was especially taken with the book *Mike Mulligan and His Steam Shovel* (Burton, 1939) and a video version of the book introduced to him by his teacher, Ginger. Both at home and at school, his talk and play were often related to this book. A central theme of the book revolves around the demise of steam-powered work machines in the face of newer and more efficient diesel, gasoline, and electric-powered machines. Not surprisingly, the impact of changing technology was not initially an easy concept for Christopher to understand. Because he had never seen a steam-powered machine of any kind, he asked many questions about illustrations showing Mike Mulligan shoveling coal into the boiler of Mary Anne, the steam shovel. In the following episode (FN: Home), play became part of this sorting-out process.

> Christopher emerges from playing in a walk-in closet at our home.
>
> Christopher: This is Mary Anne.
>
> Mom: Um hum.
>
> [My response is noncommittal. I do not really understand what he means.
>
> He closes the closet door and runs after me.]
>
> Christopher: The *closet* is Mary Anne!!
>
> Mom: Does it have clothes in it?
>
> Christopher: No!!!!
>
> [He gets a long-handled wooden spoon from the kitchen drawer and takes me back to the closet.]
>
> Christopher: This where the coal goes.
>
> [He pretends to use the spoon to shovel coal into the door of the closet.]
>
> Mom: Oh! The closet is where the coal goes in Mary Anne!
>
> Christopher   Yeah!
> [still shoveling]:

In this episode Christopher used play to continue his exploration of steam-powered machines. By transforming the relatively small enclosed space of our closet into Mary Anne's boiler, and turning a spoon into a coal shovel, he used play to act out his understandings of steam-powered machines and as a means of checking his interpretations with me. Christopher repeated this play many times before moving on to other play scripts.

Both at home and at school, children often invented and replayed scenes related to their questions about books. All play events coded in this category preceded or followed a book discussion in which the child had voiced questions about the aspects of setting, plot, or characters that were eventually explored through play. These observations support the hypothesis that play allowed children to come to grips with book information and events by revisiting and replaying key scenes. Such play appears to require an efferent stance as described by Rosenblatt (1978). Here children were concerned with what they might take away from play, and how it could increase their understanding of the meanings of the text. I offer three hypotheses concerning the ways play supported children's comprehension. First, play allowed children to enter the world of books through the multiple avenues of language, movement, and the sensory cues provided by props, costumes, and sets. Such a multisensory experience provided new kinds of opportunities for interpreting book events and characters. Second, play often provided opportunities for children to "slow down" their interactions with books, and to revisit a problematic section at their own pace. This was particularly true because children often maintained control of their play episodes by orchestrating their play scripts with supportive adults. Third, because play involved other people, children gained access to new resources and new kinds of feedback to their ideas about books.

Character Studies

One way that children used improvisational book-related play was by taking on the role of a familiar book character. Sometimes children's play served as a character study designed to explore their inferences about aspects of the book not specified by the author. For example, during one reading of *Monster Road Builders* (Royston, 1989) at the school book center, Christopher shifted from book discussion to improvisational play to adopt the role of one of the workers pictured in the illustrations but never mentioned in the text.

> Christopher is sitting on a bulldozer riding toy as we read. He holds the receiver of a toy phone, and puts it to his ear. (VT: School)
>
> Christopher: Hey (***).
> [to imaginary character on the other end of the phone]:
>
> Christopher [to participants in the book center]: I'm calling one of the workmen.
>
> Rowe: You're calling one of the workmen?
>
> Christopher   Hello?
> [into the phone]:

In this event, Christopher launched a brief dramatic play episode in which he began to explore actions that might be taken by a workman. Using his general knowledge of workers and machines, he brought to life characters seen only in illustrations.

In another school-based episode, Melanie, Christina, Celia, and I played the Three Little Pigs outdoors in the playhouse (FN: School). The girls assigned me the role of the Big Bad Wolf and took for themselves the roles of the pigs.

> Marshall arrived and watched us playing. He began circling the playhouse, holding a sand toy in his hand.
>
> Marshall: Bricks! Bricks for sale!
>
> Christina   Give me some!
> [leaning out the window]:

Marshall:	Got any money?
Christina:	No!
Marshall:	Well, no bricks, then. I need money! [Begins circling the house again.] Bricks! Bricks for sale!

In this event, Marshall explored the story of the *Three Little Pigs* through the eyes of the brick seller. This role had been only minimally developed in the version of the story we had read in the classroom. In this version, the pigs ask a passing goose with a wheelbarrow to give them some bricks. The brick seller does not speak, but the narration states that she complies "happily." Marshall brings the brick seller to life by borrowing language patterns and intonation from our readings of *Caps for Sale* (Slobodkina, 1968). Like the peddler in *Caps for Sale*, Marshall's brick seller cannot afford to give away his wares. Selling bricks is his livelihood. In this improvisational play, Marshall gives his own unique interpretation of the role of brick seller by weaving in a theme not anticipated in the *Three Little Pigs*.

These playful character studies highlight the shifts in stance required by book-related play. Children frequently and fluidly moved from book discussions where they expressed their own perspectives on books to play episodes where they addressed the world from the perspective of a book character—an important cognitive and literary accomplishment.

Personal Inquiries

Both at home and at school, children often used book-related dramatic play as a means of personal inquiry. In contrast to events where children's play seemed aimed at understanding the meanings of books, in personal inquiry events children used books as springboards for exploring their own questions about the world. Children were no longer tightly constrained by an author's meanings. Instead book characters, language, themes, settings, and information were put to novel uses related to the children's interests and questions.

An example comes, once again, from Christopher's play related to *Mike Mulligan and His Steam Shovel* (Burton, 1939). In this book, the main character, Mike Mulligan, is shown on many pages with a smoking pipe in his mouth. During one reading of this book, Christopher asked me why Mike smoked a pipe (FN: Home). I explained that the book was written a long time ago before people knew smoking was dangerous to their health, and that many adults were smokers at the time it was written. Christopher launched book-related play by asking me to call out to him: "Hi, Mike! How are you going to get out," a direct quote of the line delivered by the townspeople looking down at Mike and his steam shovel trapped in the completed cellar. To set the scene, I suggested that Christopher use a square laundry basket as the basement. He hopped in the basket holding his toy backhoe and called for a "pipe." I provided him with a straw from the kitchen, and he promptly began puffing on it, pretending to smoke. He requested that we repeat our parts in this scene several times, each time responding by puffing strongly on his straw "pipe."

In this event, Christopher focused on two aspects of the book that were of current interest to him: the scene where the townspeople realize Mike and his steam shovel are stuck in the cellar and illustrations portraying Mike as a pipe smoker. His reenactment of the scene where the townspeople call down asking Mike how he will get out appears to be an instance of sorting out play—given his many questions about this page earlier in our reading of the book (FN: Home). The focus on the pipe is another matter, however. Here, his talk and play highlight pipe smoking—a detail in an illustration that is never mentioned in the text. Pipe smoking was important to Christopher not because it was central to the book's plot, but because it was central to his experiences in our family. As in our discussion of *Mike Mulligan,* we almost always answered his questions and comments about smoking by emphasizing that it could make people sick and that our family disapproved of the practice. Christopher used book-related play as a convenient springboard for exploring unresolved issues related to smoking. The pipe play served to explore a conflict between his family's values and his observations of smoking in books and the world at large.

Book-related play also provided opportunities for inquiries into other personal concerns such as social relationships. During one play episode (FN: Home), Christopher enlisted my help to play out a scene portrayed in the PBS television series *Marty Stouffer's Wild America,* as well as in the book by the same name (Stouffer, 1988). In the episode entitled, "The Man Who Loved Bears," a wildlife photographer named Marty Stouffer raises a tiny grizzly cub inside his wilderness cabin. The bear, Griz, is treated like a favored household pet until she grows larger, more active, and more destructive, forcing Marty to move her bed outdoors. Choosing the role of Marty for himself, he assigned me the role of the exiled Baby Griz and insisted that we play over and over a scene where Griz cries at the door to come in. With each request, he reveled in refusing—sometimes saying Griz had been "bad" or that he was "too busy."

Although his reenactment of this scene reflected a sequence of events portrayed briefly in the book and video, they took on new significance in his play. In this event, it was the inherently unequal power relationship between Marty and Griz that became the central theme of his play. As a parent it was clear to me that this event was not really about Marty Stouffer and Baby Griz. Christopher was not sorting out details of plot, but his relationship with me instead.

Play also supported children's personal inquiries by providing an arena for exploring innovative connections between their personal inquiry themes. One such event occurred as a continuation of the Marty Stouffer play just described (FN: Home).

Christopher gets on a police car riding toy and begins riding around the house in his role as Marty.

Christopher: Can Marty have a backhoe on his car?

Mom: I doubt it. Backhoes don't attach to cars.

Christopher: Yes. This is a backhoe. He uses it to dig holes for *creatures.*

Mom: Oh! like for their dens?

Christopher:	Yeah, to live in. [He rides around the room and circles back to me.]
Christopher:	Marty is a paleontologist. He digs for dinosaur bones.
Mom:	So he looks for live animals *and* fossils bones?
Christopher:	No, just dinosaur bones!

In this event, Christopher linked three personal themes that had consumed a great deal of his time and attention during the previous year: Marty Stouffer, work machines, and dinosaurs. Despite my discouraging response to his initial link between Marty Stouffer and work machines, he forged ahead to develop his play script. In so doing, he constructed a plausible, but novel, rationale for this connection. As the event continued, he constructed a second scenario in which Marty might have a backhoe—this time basing his explanation on information gained while reading about dinosaurs. Here, as in the earlier examples, play incorporated book themes and content in ways that served the child's personal purposes and inquiries.

Each of these events demonstrates that children did not always use book-related dramatic play as a means for exploring the worlds constructed by authors. Instead, book settings, characters, and events sometimes became background for broader inquiries into issues arising in the children's worlds. Because the children participating in these studies exercised considerable control over the focus of informal book-reading and dramatic play, they were able to use book-related play as an opportunity to explore questions they brought to reading from their everyday experiences.

THEORETICAL SUMMARY: PLAY AS A SUPPORTIVE ENVIRONMENT FOR LITERACY LEARNING

When the children's book-related play is examined through the lenses offered by cognitive psychology, semiotics, and transactive theories of reader response it appears that there are a number of characteristics of book-related play that may provide special motivation and opportunity for young children's literacy learning. Specifically, the self-initiated, child-directed play studied here (a) allowed children to use a familiar lens for knowing, (b) was well-matched to children's current interests and hypotheses, (c) allowed multiple entry points to books through multiple sign systems, (d) made book events more concrete, (e) provided multiple ways of connecting to books, (f) required shifts of stance to move across sign systems, (g) required shifts of stance to respond to social interaction, and (h) served as a medium for experiential response to text.

Familiar Modes of Representation

Eisner (1982) pointed out that learners become more skilled at using some forms of representation than others. As they become more adept at using particular representational forms or sign systems (Peirce, 1966; e.g., play, art, oral language), they are also more likely to choose these sign systems for learning how to express their ideas. Although every sign system, including play, has its own limitations as to what aspects of the total experience it represents, it seems important for learners to have access to those modes of representation they find most familiar. Given the importance of play in these children's interactions, I expect that book-related dramatic play allowed children to make use of familiar strategies for approaching both books and book events. This may have been particularly important as they began to explore new territory in the abstract world of books.

Well Matched to Children's Current Hypotheses

Because the play observed in these studies was largely child initiated and child directed, both the focus and pace of play were tailored to children's current hypotheses and interests. The importance of links to learners' background knowledge has been well established by cognitive psychologists (e.g., Tierney & Pearson, 1994). Further, literacy researchers (Harste, Woodward, & Burke, 1984; F. Smith, 2004) have noted that young literacy learners tend to be most interested in the aspects of literacy events that relate to their newest hypotheses. One problem with learning events that are structured by adults is the possibility that the teacher or parent's focus is not closely enough matched to the child's current understandings and interests to support the refinement and testing of the child's hypotheses. I expect that book-related play was particularly powerful for children's learning because it offered an opportunity for children to explore their own hypotheses about books and the world. Because these hypotheses were often unconventional (from an adult perspective) or highly personal, it is doubtful that I and the teachers could have designed teacher-directed play scenarios that were so well-fitted to the children's needs and interests. Children's ownership and control of play events allowed them to link book experiences to their backgrounds of experience in powerful ways.

Multiple Entry Points Through Sign Systems

From the perspectives of theorists and researchers interested in the impact of different sign systems on learning and communication (e.g., Eco, 1982; Eisner, 1982; Leland & Harste, 1994; Peirce, 1966), one of the most intriguing characteristics of book-related dramatic play is that it is inherently multimodal. That is, by nature, it often combines talk, gesture, prop selection, costuming, and set design within the same event. Following Eisner's (1982) argument about the impact of various forms of representation, dramatic play allows children the possibility of connecting to books in ways that make use of the strengths of these different systems for signaling meaning. As Eisner writes, "not everything can be said through anything" (p. 49). Each form of representation involved in dramatic play, at the same time, highlights and neglects some aspects of the total scene. For example, in play, actions may speak louder than words—or at least add different nuances of meaning—when the task is to portray a character's emotions. Dramatic play may be particularly supportive of young children's construction of new understandings because meanings are multiply coded; that is, they are simultaneously expressed through several communication systems. This allows children to use familiar sign systems to support their explorations of less familiar aspects of books.

Making Book Reading More Concrete

Because play involved multiple sign systems, these events provided a rich network of signs that could help children deal more concretely with the abstract world of books. The nature of the literate task facing young readers is well-described by Snow and Ninio's (1986) discussion of the "contracts of literacy"—understandings about the ways books represent meaning. Two of these understandings are particularly relevant to the discussion of book-related dramatic play. First, children must come to understand that "pictures are not things, but representatives of things" (p. 122). Snow and Ninio observed that children spend considerable time coming to understand that pictured items cannot be picked up, smelled, or heard. Adult readers focus on helping children learn to relate text and illustrations to objects and events in their lives. Second, children must learn that "pictures, though static, can represent events" (p. 132). In the same way that children must come to understand that two-dimensional illustrations and printed words are signs standing for socially agreed-on meanings, they must also come to understand the ways that dynamic actions, events, and sequences are represented in pictures and text.

These social conventions about the ways text and illustrations signify meanings are so basic that they are usually taken for granted by adult readers for whom two-dimensional illustrations and printed words are transparently comprehended as real-time events composed of imagined spaces, characters, and actions. Whereas adults may think of reading as a sedentary activity, children sometimes use play to redimensionalize the imagined worlds offered by books so they can feel it with their whole bodies. Play allows children to walk around in story settings. It allows them to touch, feel, and actually look at objects from the vantage points of book characters. As the young children studied here were learning to talk about the connections between books and their lives, they also acted out these connections through dramatic play—a comprehension strategy not unlike that of adults who create three-dimensional models (or more recently, computerized images) that can be turned and examined from many perspectives. Dramatic play allowed children to connect pictures and text to the concrete world of space, time, and objects.

Multiple Ways of Connecting to Books

Because dramatic play is a complex event that requires children to make a variety of book-related decisions, it also provides children with multiple entry points for engaging with books. Although play events usually involved issues of characterization, set and prop design, and plot development, children often highlighted one of these aspects for particular attention. Play exploring the perspectives offered by a particular dramatic role resulted in the pattern I have labeled character studies. Props were highlighted when children searched for book-related toys, or stopped to construct needed props. Plot development was the focus in events where children sorted out the author's meanings, or used an author's scene as an avenue for their own inquiries. All in all, dramatic play provided children with a variety of different opportunities for making connections to books.

Shifts of Stance Required by Transmediation

One of the striking characteristics of the children's connections between books and play was the necessity for taking new perspectives on books and their world knowledge. Moving from reading books to book-related play often involved *transmediation*—the expression of meanings created in one sign system through other forms of expression. For these 2-year-olds, transmediation often involved constructing meanings while transacting with text and illustrations of picture books and then expressing them through the new sign systems associated with props, costuming, set design, dialogue, and movement. Sometimes children found it necessary to use new sign systems to create dialogue and actions for characters minimally developed in books. In other cases, transmediation occurred when children moved from dramatic to constructive play to create play props.

In considering the role of transmediation in book-related dramatic play, I draw on semiotic perspectives (Eco, 1976; Siegel, 1985) that suggest that the expression of meanings in new sign systems creates anomalies that motivate a shift of stance from understanding to reflecting on and reorganizing knowledge through the lens of the new sign system. Siegel (1985) argued that transmediation differs from other instances of meaning making in that the readers' interpretation "becomes an object of thought to be conveyed in a new expression plane" (p. 21).

In this study, children frequently shifted stances between book-related dramatic play and talking about books. Data from the studies reported here support the hypothesis that dramatic play encouraged children to shift to a more reflective stance to reconsider book meanings from the perspectives offered by new sign systems. Transmediation of meanings from books to the medium of dramatic play and back again was often a transformative experience. Reading created new potentials for children's play by providing play themes, events, and characters. Play altered children's interpretations of books, often directing their attention to new aspects of the text or influencing the meanings they constructed. Children were different readers after play and different players after reading. Once children began to explore book themes through the new sign systems offered by play, new meaning potentials were available.

Shifts of Stance in Response to Social Interaction

Despite the fact that these 2-year-olds found it difficult to develop a coordinated play script with peers, book-related play was almost always a social event. Children often sought out either peers or adults as audience for their play. Adults were also sometimes drafted as co-players. Audience questions sometimes challenged children's play scripts and often encouraged them to make the basis for their play more explicit. Negotiations with co-players about roles and plot required children to shift from playing to talking about the play—a stance Williamson and Silvern (1991) called *metaplay*. Christopher's play connecting the themes of work machines, wildlife photographer Marty Stouffer, and dinosaurs is typical in that metaplay involved both discussion of the content of the play (e.g., "Can Marty have a backhoe on his car?"), and negotiation of the identity of symbolic transformations (e.g., a police car riding toy stands for a backhoe).

Researchers (e.g., Pellegrini & Galda, 1991; Williamson & Silvern, 1991) have presented evidence that it is metacommunications about play that are most strongly related to measures of emergent reading such as Sulzby's (1985) categories of emergent reading and Clay's (1972) Concepts About Print Test and measures of story comprehension such as retellings and story sequencing. Two different mechanisms—one general and one context specific—have been posited to explain the importance of metaplay. Pellegrini and Galda (1991, 1993) follow a Vygotskian approach in suggesting that play is an important arena for children to construct the general understanding that signs are arbitrarily linked to the objects they represent (e.g., *police car* is a term used to identify particular kinds of toys), and that these sign–object relationships can be severed and rearranged in new ways in play (e.g., a police car toy can be transformed into a backhoe). As Vygotsky (1978) argues, during play children are required to explain the nature of their transformations to their audience and in so doing come to understand the nature of the representational process. From this theoretical frame, it is hypothesized that it is the eventual internalization of this understanding that forms a supportive basis for children's interactions with print.

Williamson and Silvern (1991) offer a second explanation for the importance of metaplay. They suggest that while symbolic transformations in role play may be assimilative as Piaget (1962) suggested, the necessity to negotiate play with others creates disequilibrium that requires children to reflect on both the text and play transformations in ways that require accommodation to the perspectives of others. Theoretically, metaplay draws children's attention to features of the text including story structure, details of plot, and characterization. It is this increased reflection on the story that leads to increased comprehension and recall of story events and sequences, rather than role play itself. Thus, as Pellegrini and Galda's (1993) review of play and literacy learning research concludes, it is possible that dramatic play is important in young children's literacy learning because it requires negotiations with others that promote shifts of stance from playing to talking about play.

A Medium for Experiential Response

When viewed from a reader response perspective, dramatic play may be seen not only as a context for reflecting on books, but also an important part of children's reading and response processes. Through book-related dramatic play, children responded to books using interpretive strategies strikingly similar to those observed in studies of adult readers (e.g., Beach, 1991; Purves & Beach, 1972). Table 3.1 lists response strategies used by older readers (Beach, 1993) and the types of book-related dramatic play that highlighted similar response processes.

As this comparison demonstrates, the young children in these studies accomplished many of the same interpretive activities as adults through the medium of dramatic play. This is not to say that adult and child strategies were identical, but instead that children used dramatic play for purposes similar to

TABLE 3.1
Play as Experiential Response

Specific Response Processes Identified by Beach (1993, p. 52)	Patterns of Book-Related Dramatic Play

Engaging
  Becoming emotionally involved, empathizing or identifying with the text
	Personal response to books
	  Physically acting out emotional responses to book events/ characters

Constructing
  Entering into and creating alternative worlds, conceptualizing characters, events, settings
	Aesthetic reenactments
	  Replaying book events to enjoy the "lived-though" experience of the book
	Sorting out the author's meanings
	Playing out problematic scenes to understand the author's meaning
	Character studies
	  Experiencing events from the perspective a book character

Imaging
  Creating visual images
	Connecting books with toys and props
	  Locating and holding book-related toys during reading
	All book-related dramatic play events
	  Creating a multimodal image of the book

Connecting
  Relating one's autobiographical experience to the current text
	Personal inquiries
	  Exploring personal questions using book events, characters, settings

adults' use of verbal and cognitive response strategies. In this study I found that children used book-related play to make personal sense of books. Play provided an opportunity for children to explore specific aspects of their emotions, attitudes, and interests, and as such provided an opportunity for experiential readings of books. However, play was also flexible enough to allow children to move back and forth between reader-based engagements and text-based engagements (Garrison & Hynds, 1991). That is, they sometimes used book-related play to explore their own interpretations of books, and at other times they tried to sort out the details of plot and character to delve more deeply into the author's meanings. From a reader response perspective, book-related dramatic play may be valuable precisely because it allows children to make personal connections to text while bumping up against the challenges to improvisation provided by their interpretive communities (Fish, 1980).

This hypothesis about the function of role play in children's literacy learning is in contrast to findings of experimental and longitudinal research rooted in cognitive psychology. In their review of these lines of research, Pellegrini and Galda (1993) conclude that symbolic reenactments (i.e., make-believe relating to objects, roles, and situations) have only minimal effects on story comprehension and measures of emergent literacy. I would argue, however, that it is premature to conclude that role play has no part in children's comprehension and interpretation of books. Experimental research has tended to measure reading using tasks that tap efferent readings (Rosenblatt, 1978) and judge children's comprehension against the templates provided by the researcher's interpretations (e.g., story recall and sequencing tasks) or the conventions of print (e.g., concepts about print tasks). Patterns observed in this study suggest that young children may use role play, in part, to accomplish aesthetic readings that are not tapped by template-matching measures of reading comprehension (Siegel, 1985). Although factual recall and concepts about print are important aspects of reading, young children, like adults, appear to respond to books in the aesthetic mode—a type of response typically overlooked in studies of preschoolers.

SUMMARY

As the 2- and 3-year-olds in these studies became immersed in books at home and at school, they initiated a variety of types of book-to-play connections that appeared to provide a powerful mode of learning and response. However, the nature of the play–literacy connection is complex. Cognitive psychology (Pellegrini & Galda, 1993; Williamson & Silvern, 1991) supports the notion that the social nature of play has an important impact on children's story comprehension. The necessity of negotiating play scripts and roles with others requires children to talk about play and books as objects—an ability children need as they learn to read on their own. Semiotic perspectives on reading (Peirce, 1966) highlight the importance of the multiple sign systems involved in play and reading. Theoretically, the multimodal nature of play provides multiple entry points to explore book meanings (Eisner, 1982) and requires a shift of stance from comprehension to reflection as children represent book meanings in the new sign systems of play (Siegel, 1995; Suhor, 1984). Finally, reader response theories (Rosenblatt, 1978) support the contention that book-related dramatic play should be viewed as a medium for experiential response. From this perspective it appears that children often take an aesthetic stance toward books during book-related dramatic play. To understand the significance of the literacy–play connection, young readers' experiential responses must be given as much attention as factual recall of story details.

FUTURE DIRECTIONS

As this summary suggests, we are only just beginning to understand the ways that book-related dramatic play supports children's literacy learning. Although this study has generated a description of child-initiated, book-related play in one home and one preschool context, it is important that future research study more diverse groups of participants. Although research shows that early childhood play is common to most cultures around the world (Sawyer, 1997), play related to particular cultural objects such as books would be expected to vary across settings. However, if parent reports of family activities are accurate, parent–child book reading is a frequent occurrence for well over half of the preschoolers in the United States (Federal Interagency Forum on Child and Family Statistics, 2004) and the United Kingdom (National Reading Campaign, 1999). More naturalistic research is needed to document the kinds of literacy-related play generated by children from diverse backgrounds and in differing school contexts.

It should also be noted that the analyses reported in this chapter focused on children and the relation of their play to the books they were reading. In future studies it will be important to more fully analyze the cultural and interactive contexts in which this play thrives. Questions remain as to what role adults play both at home and school in providing materials, experiences, and opportunities that support book-related dramatic play. It will be important to explore the ways that family and teacher values about early childhood reading and play implicitly or explicitly shape or are shaped by children's book-related play.

When considering possible educational implications of this and related research, we can conclude that book-related dramatic play is a powerful, naturally developing resource for both efferent and aesthetic responses to books. As researchers continue to study how different features of book-related play (e.g., symbolic transformation, metaplay, adult–child interaction styles) are related to independent reading in the elementary grades, educators should be able to design more effective play environments. At the same time, it is important to continue to value the holistic, child-directed nature of the book-related play observed in this study. Even if future research identifies significant relationships between features of play events and reading behaviors (e.g., metaplay affects story comprehension), it is important to remember that these aspects of play exist only when children are offered open-ended opportunities to develop play scripts (Williamson & Silvern, 1991). Efforts to distill the active ingredients in book-related play into teacher-directed activities are likely to eliminate the complex web of motivation, sign systems, social relationships, book knowledge, and world knowledge that children bring together in play. Child-initiated dramatic play is valuable in its own right as a developmentally appropriate response to books and as a means of learning about the world. For the children at Walker Preschool, play was an irrepressible force in their exploration of the world of books. Play brought books off the page into the space and time of everyday life.

REFERENCES

Anello, C. (1987). *The farmyard cat.* New York: Scholastic.

Barnes, D., Churley, P., & Thompson, C. (1971). Group talk and literary response. *English Education, 5*(3), 63–76.

Beach, R. (1991). Research on response to literature. In R. Barr, M. Kamil, P. Mosenthal, & P. D. Pearson (Eds.), *Handbook of reading research* (Vol. 2, pp. 453–491). New York: Longman.

Beach, R. (1993). *A teacher's introduction to reader-response theories.* Urbana, IL: National Council of Teachers of English.

Bergen, D. (1988). Stages of play development. In D. Bergen (Ed.), *Play as a medium for learning and development* (pp. 49–66). Portsmouth, NH: Heinemann.

Burton, V. L. (1939). *Mike Mulligan and his steam shovel.* Boston: Houghton-Mifflin.

Christie, J. F. (1983). The effects of play tutoring on young children's cognitive performance. *Journal of Educational Research, 76,* 326–330.

Christie, J. F. (1991). Psychological research on play: Connections with early literacy development. In J. Christie (Ed.), *Play and early literacy development* (pp. 27–43). Albany: State University of New York Press.

Clay, M. (1972). *Sand: The concepts about print test.* Portsmouth, NH: Heinemann.

Clyde, J. A. (2003). Stepping inside the story world: The subtext strategy—A tool for connecting and comprehending. *The Reading Teacher, 57,* 150–160.

Crago, M., & Crago, H. (1983). *Prelude to literacy: A preschool child's encounter with picture and story.* Carbondale: Southern Illinois University Press.

Eco, U. (1976). *A theory of semiotics.* Bloomington: Indiana University Press.

Eco, U. (1982). *The role of the reader.* Bloomington: Indiana University Press.

Eisner, E. (1982). *Cognition and curriculum.* New York: Longman.

Erickson, F. (1986). Qualitative methods in research on teaching. In M. C. Wittrock (Ed.), *Handbook of research on teaching* (Vol. 3, pp. 119–161). New York: Macmillan.

Federal Interagency Forum on Child and Family Statistics. (2004). *America's children in brief: Key national indicators of well-being, 2004.* Retrieved April 13, 2005, from http://www.childstats.gov/ac2004/tables/ed1.asp.

Fish, S. (1980). *Is there a text in this class? The authority of interpretive communities.* Cambridge, MA: Harvard University Press.

Galda, L., Pellegrini, A. D., & Cox, S. (1989). Preschoolers' emergent literacy: A short term longitudinal study. *Research in the Teaching of English, 23,* 292–310.

Garrison, B., & Hynds, S. (1991). Evocation and reflection in the reading transaction: A comparison of proficient and less proficient readers. *Journal of Reading Behavior, 23,* 259–280.

Glaser, B., & Strauss, A. (1967). *The discovery of grounded theory.* Chicago: Aldine.

Goodman, J. R. (1990). *A naturalistic study of the relationship between literacy development and dramatic play in 5-year-old children.* Unpublished doctoral dissertation, Vanderbilt University, Nashville, TN.

Guba, E., & Lincoln, Y. (1994). Competing paradigms in qualitative research. In N. Denzin & Y. Lincoln (Eds.), *Handbook of qualitative research* (pp. 105–117). Thousand Oaks, CA: Sage.

Haight, W. L., & Miller, P. J. (1993). *Pretending at home: Early development in a sociocultural context.* Albany: SUNY Press.

Harste, J., Woodward, V., & Burke, C. (1984). *Language stories and literacy lessons.* Portsmouth, NH: Heinemann.

Hill, E. (1986). *Spot goes to the circus.* New York: Putnam.

Howes, C., & Matheson, C. (1992). Sequences in the development of competent play with peers: Social and social pretend play. *Developmental Psychology, 28,* 961–974.

Leland, C. H., & Harste, J. C. (1994). Multiple ways of knowing: Curriculum in a new key. *Language Arts, 71,* 337–345.

Lincoln, Y., & Guba, E. (1985). *Naturalistic inquiry.* Beverly Hills, CA: Sage.

Martinez, M., Cheyney, M., & Teale, W. (1991). Classroom literature activities and kindergarteners' dramatic story reenactments. In J. Christie (Ed.), *Play and early literacy development* (pp. 119–140). Albany: State University of New York Press.

Medina, C. L. (2004). Drama wor(l)ds: Explorations of Latina/o realistic fiction. *Language Arts, 81,* 272–282.

Most, B. (1984). *Whatever happened to the dinosaurs?* San Diego, CA: Harcourt, Brace, Jovanovich.

National Reading Campaign. (1999). *Family and education: The sixth Nestle family monitor.* Retrieved April 13, 2005, from http://www.literacytrust.org.uk/Database/Mori.html#family.

Newbold, M. (1993). Literature discussion groups aren't just for school. In K. Pierce & C. Gilles (Eds.), *Cycles of meaning* (pp. 275–290). Portsmouth, NH: Heinemann.

Panofsky, C. (1986, December). *The functions of language in parent–child book reading events.* Paper presented at the annual meeting of the National Reading Conference, Austin, TX.

Parten, M. B. (1932). Social participation among pre-school children. *Journal of Abnormal and Social Psychology, 27,* 243–269.

Peirce, C. S. (1966). *Collected papers of Charles Sanders Peirce.* Cambridge, MA: Harvard University Press.

Pellegrini, A. D., & Galda, L. (1982). The effects of thematic-fantasy play training on the development of children's story comprehension. *American Educational Research Journal, 19,* 691–701.

Pellegrini, A. D., & Galda, L. (1991). Longitudinal relations among preschoolers' symbolic play, metalinguistic verbs, and emergent literacy. In J. Christie (Ed.),

Play and early literacy development (pp. 47–67). Albany: State University of New York Press.

Pellegrini, A. D., & Galda, L. (1993). Ten years after: A reexamination of symbolic play and literacy research. *Reading Research Quarterly, 28,* 162–175.

Piaget, J. (1962). *Play, dreams, and imitations.* New York: Norton.

Piaget, J., & Inhelder, J. (1969). *The psychology of the child.* New York: Basic Books.

Purves, A., & Beach. R. (1972). *Literature and the reader: Research on response to literature, reading interests, and the teaching of literature.* Urbana, IL: National Council of Teachers of English.

Rose, D. S., Parks, M., Androes, K., & McMahon, S. D. (2000). Imagery-based learning: Improving elementary students' reading comprehension with drama techniques. *Journal of Educational Research, 94,* 55–63.

Rosenblatt, L. (1978). *The reader, the text, and the poem.* Carbondale: Southern Illinois University Press.

Rowe, D. W. (1994). Learning about literacy and the world: Two-year-olds' and teachers' enactment of a thematic inquiry curriculum. In D. Leu & C. Kinzer (Eds.), *Forty-third yearbook of the National Reading Conference* (pp. 217–229). Chicago: National Reading Conference.

Rowe, D. W. (1998). Examining teacher talk: Revealing hidden boundaries for curricular change. *Language Arts, 75,* 103–107.

Rowe, D. W., Fitch, J. D., & Bass, A. S. (2003). Toy stories as opportunities for imagination and reflection in writers' workshop. *Language Arts, 80,* 363–374.

Royston, A. (1989). *Monster road builders.* New York: Barron's.

Rubin, K. H., Fein, G. G., & Vandenberg, B. (1983). Play. In E. Hetherington (Ed.) & P. H. Mussen (Series Ed.), *Handbook of child psychology: Vol. 4. Socialization, personality, and social development* (pp. 698–774). New York: Wiley.

Saltz, E., Dixon, D., & Johnson, J. (1977). Training disadvantaged preschoolers on various fantasy activities: Effects on cognitive functioning and impulse control. *Child Development, 48,* 367–380.

Sawyer, R. K. (1997). *Pretend play as improvisation: Conversation in the preschool classroom.* Mahwah, NJ: Lawrence Erlbaum Associates.

Short, K., Harste, J., & Burke, C. (1996). *Creating classrooms for authors and inquirers* (2nd ed.). Portsmouth, NH: Heinemann.

Siegel, M. G. (1985). Reading as signification. *Dissertation Abstracts International, 45,* 2824A.

Siegel, M. G. (1995). More than words: The generative power of transmediation for learning. *Canadian Journal of Education, 20,* 455–475.

Silvern, S., Williamson, P., & Waters, B. (1983). Play as a mediator of comprehension: An alternative to play training. *Educational Research Quarterly, 7,* 16–21.

Slobodkina, E. (1968). *Caps for sale.* New York: Harper & Row.

Smith, C. R. (2002). Click on me! An example of how a toddler used technology in play. *Journal of Early Childhood Literacy, 2*(1), 5–20.

Smith, F. (2004). *Understanding reading* (6th ed.). Mahwah, NJ: Lawrence Erlbaum Associates.

Snow, C., & Ninio, A. (1986). The contracts of literacy: What children learn from learning to read books. In W. Teale & E. Sulzby (Eds.), *Emergent literacy: Writing and reading* (pp. 116–138). Norwood, NJ: Ablex.

Stouffer, M. (1988). *Marty Stouffer's wild America.* New York: Times Books.

Strauss, A., & Corbin, J. (1998). *Basics of qualitative research: Techniques and procedures for developing grounded theory* (2nd ed.). Thousand Oaks, CA: Sage.

Suhor, C. (1984). Towards a semiotic-based curriculum. *Journal of Curriculum Studies, 16,* 247–257.

Sulzby, E. (1985). Children's emergent reading of favorite storybooks: A developmental study. *Reading Research Quarterly, 20,* 458–479.

Tierney, R., & Pearson, P. D. (1994). Learning to learn from text: A framework for improving classroom practice. In R. B. Ruddell, M. R. Ruddell, & H. Singer (Eds.), *Theoretical models and processes of reading* (4th ed., pp. 496–513). Newark, DE: International Reading Association.

Vygotsky, L. (1978). *Mind in society.* Cambridge, MA: Harvard University Press.

Wagner, B. J. (1998). *Educational drama and language arts: What research shows.* Portsmouth, NH: Heinemann.

Williamson, P. A., & Silvern, S. B. (1991). Thematic-fantasy play and story comprehension. In J. Christie (Ed.), *Play and early literacy development* (pp. 69–90). Albany: State University of New York Press.

Wolf, S., & Heath, S. B. (1992). *The braid of literature: Children's worlds of reading.* Cambridge, MA: Harvard University Press.

4

COMMENTARY:
Cognition, Play, and Early Literacy

Anthony D. Pellegrini and Mark J. Van Ryzin
University of Minnesota

We are happy to have the opportunity to comment on the chapters by Rowe, Sawyer and DeZutter, and Smith. These chapters add to our knowledge of play during childhood and its relation to one dimension of performance in school, literacy. These chapters, indeed this whole book, have enormous potential to impact the fields of child development and early childhood education. The theme of the book is central to how we think about childhood and how we structure societal institutions to educate children.

Before we begin our commentary, we would first like to pay tribute to an author not included in this edition: our late colleague and friend Greta Fein. In the first edition of this book, Fein and colleagues' chapter on narrative, play, and literacy reflected her prescient view that the design features of social pretend play mapped onto the features of early literacy, thus accounting for the predictive value of play in early literacy. Fein (1979) was also very careful to note that it was the productive, not comprehension, dimension of oral language used in social pretend play that was important in this relationship. These predictions have been empirically verified in our lab (Pellegrini & Galda, 2001) and by Sawyer and DeZutter (chap. 2, this volume). More important, Greta was an avid advocate of the study of play in children's development and education. Her innovative ideas, mischievous smile, and kind, supportive demeanor will be greatly missed.

Although the study of the role of social pretend play and early reading goes back over 30 years (Pellegrini, 1980; Wolfgang, 1974), those early studies were rather global and did not identify specific processes in play that predicted early literacy. As Rowe (chap. 3, this volume) points out, in the very earliest studies, we were concerned with children's comprehension of the stories read to them and enacted (Pellegrini, 1984; Pellegrini & Galda, 1982). We set out to explore the relations between play and comprehension, not other processes such as response to stories. Since that time, however, we have used that early work to move beyond examining the role of play on comprehension, as suggested by Rowe. Instead, literacy for us and others (e.g., Heath, 1983; Olson, 1977; Snow, 1983) was defined developmentally as literate language, or the ability to produce and comprehend explicit language.

In keeping with Fein's orientation, we examine the ways in which each of these chapters defines symbolic play and early literacy and explicates predictive relations between the two. This approach is often labeled arguments by design by ethologists (Martin & Caro, 1985; Smith, chap. 1, this volume) and anthropologists (Heath, 1983). The chapters by Rowe (chap. 3, this volume) and Sawyer and DeZutter (chap. 2, this volume) carry on the work of identifying processes that predict early literacy, with Rowe's work focusing on the context of dramatic play around books and Sawyer and DeZutter on the more traditional context of social pretend play.

In our view, it is crucial to define very explicitly what is meant by play and literacy to establish links between the two constructs. As Rowe (chap. 3, this volume) points out, the specific way in which these constructs are defined will obviously impact their causal relationships. Further, and perhaps more important for readers of this volume, explicit definitions of literacy and play are crucial if educators are to use these ideas in curriculum and evaluation. School policy should spring from good ideas that have been shown to work. Good ideas usually take the form of theories that guide our attempts to understand complex phenomena. The worth of these ideas should be determined by the degree to which they explain the relation between children's play and their literacy. We would expect, for example, one set of results if pretend play is defined as anything a child does by free choice with a book or with peers rather than if it is defined according to the criteria outlined by Fein (1981). Correspondingly, defining literacy as a response to a book versus using literate language is also an important issue, especially for preschool children (Pellegrini & Galda, 1993; Snow, 1983).

PLAY IN THE MARKETPLACE OF IDEAS

Saying all this is rather high-spirited. Of course, school practice, and research, too, should be guided by what is found to be most effective. We test different hypotheses, compare different practices, expand the use of those that are found to be valid, and discard those that are not. Unfortunately, our judgments of efficacy are often tainted by what we favor, often independent of the empirical record. The study of children's play is especially vulnerable here as it is one of the "sacred cows" of child development and early childhood education. For example, child developmentalists (e.g., Hinde, 1980) assume that play serves an important role in development, despite a very spotty empirical record (Martin & Caro, 1985; Pellegrini & Smith, 1998; Smith, 1988, chap. 1, this volume). Relatedly, early childhood organizations, such as the National Association for the Education of Young Children, proclaim that young children learn best through play—again, with very little evidence in support. All of this is not to say that play is unimportant to development, but rather that valid evidence is needed before practice becomes policy.

Smith (1988, chap. 2, this volume) labeled this phenomenon the *play ethos*. Briefly, the play ethos states that play is all good for all children. More recently, Sutton-Smith (1997) made a similar point in his rhetorics of play. In the latter case, play in many fields, from anthropology to zoology, is seen as integral to development, even in cases of counterevidence. For example, experimenter or observer bias is largely responsible for the reported benefits of play in children's creativity (as reported in Dansky & Silverman, 1973, and not replicated by Smith & Whitney, 1987) and problem solving (as reported by Sylva, Brunter, & Genova, 1976, and not replicated by Simon & Smith, 1983, or Vandenberg, 1980), yet play is often cited as beneficial in these domains.

Correspondingly, the value of play has been overestimated by assuming that it accounts for a substantial part of children's development (e.g., Hinde, 1980). This argument assumes that play must serve some function because of the amount of time and energy children spend in it—something as costly as this (in terms of time and energy) would not have been naturally selected if it were not functional. In fact, there are very few time and energy budget descriptions of children's play, and those that exist suggest the opposite: Various forms of play account for less than 10% of caloric (Pellegrini, Horvat, & Huberty, 1998) and time budgets (Pellegrini & Gustafson, 2005). These estimates, consistent with those in the animal literature (Fagen, 1981; Martin & Caro, 1985), suggest that any benefits of play would be immediate, and reaped during the period of childhood, rather than deferred until adulthood. Consequently, researchers should be looking for the ways that play affects various forms of literacy during childhood per se, perhaps in the form of maximizing motivation to engage with various forms of language, rather than later in life.

Also relevant to classroom practice, the play ethos suggests that there is little need for play to be clearly defined and monitored in terms of its classroom implementation. It is often assumed that we all know what play is, and that teachers and parents intuitively understand how to implement a play curriculum. However, very different practices get labeled as play. This ambiguity may be responsible for the mixed effects of play on children's performance in school. In short, be wary of ambiguous definitions, whether they be of play or literacy.

We ask you, the reader, to consider these ideas as you read each chapter in this part and in this volume. These methodological points remain crucial in evaluating the arguments presented here. Theories and their educational manifestations should be objectively assessed if we are to keep the best interests of children and schools at the center of our enterprise.

Our brief was to discuss these chapters from a cognitive perspective. Our orientation in this task is to stress cognitive processes within a developmental context, an orientation suggesting that children are qualitatively different from adults. The implication of this approach is that play and literacy may be defined differently depending on age. Further, we do not assume that a cognitive perspective does not consider either social or emotional dimensions of play and literacy; in fact, all three affect each other dynamically. To say that all things interact and affect each other is, of course, too vague and does not advance theory or practice—the nature of the transactions must be specified. From our view (Pellegrini & Galda, 2001), the social context of play and language use (e.g., interacting with friends vs. acquaintances) affects emotional responses, which, in turn, influence children's generation of literate language. Here, too, processes must be specified and tested. It is not enough to say that children and adults process text in the same or different ways; rather, processes must be specified for each.

We first discuss different approaches to defining and measuring play and literacy and the ways this is accomplished in each chapter, including a discussion of methodological issues. Second, we discuss two different developmental views of play: play as scaffold and play as metamorphism. Although only the first view is represented in all three chapters, we argue for the importance of considering the second. As part of this discussion, we examine the developmental function of play and the ways in which play affects literacy.

DEFINITIONAL ISSUES

Defining a construct such as play is simultaneously a theoretical and methodological act. Taking theory as the starting point, we then find ways to parse occurrence or nonoccurrence of play. By parsing behavioral and linguistic streams according to definitional criteria, we are simultaneously making inferences about the meaning of those definitions as linguistic and behavioral categories.

Scholars from different orientations approach the task of definition and categorization in different ways. Some psychological researchers, for example, take a theoretical definition and then construct observable criteria corresponding to theoretically relevant dimensions. Consider Piaget's (1951/1962) theory of play, where children from infancy through late childhood engage in practice play, symbolic play, and games with rules. From these dimensions of the theory, play can be defined behaviorally, as was done by Rubin and colleagues (see Rubin, Fein, & Vandenberg, 1983, for a summary). In their work, symbolic play is defined as having one thing (e.g., a stick) represent something else (e.g., a horse).

Applying a psychological orientation to the definition of literacy, we can measure reading and writing psychometrically, or in terms of performance on tests constructed to measure literacy. In such cases, reading and writing would be defined in terms of skills, or their aggregates as measured by a test. Further, an age or grade-level criterion is often attached to psychometric definitions of literacy. So, reading for a kindergarten-age child would be defined as an exhibition of a specific set of skills. This approach to definition confuses measurement of a construct with the construct itself (Pellegrini & Galda, 1998).

Alternatively, literacy can be defined more developmentally as those skills that lead to school-based reading and writing. This has typically been done by defining literacy for preschool children as the ability to use the language and other sign systems characteristic of reading and writing. For scholars like Olson (1977), Snow (1983), Heath (1983), and ourselves (Pellegrini & Galda, 1998), literacy for young children involves the ability to talk about and reflect on oral and written language, often represented in the narrative genre.

Developmental definitions of play and literacy can also be derived from considering behaviors relationally (Martin & Bateson, 1993; Pellegrini, 2004). Here, behavior is defined and categorized in relation to who exhibits it or where it is observed. Specific to play, some biologically oriented theorists define play as anything done by a child (i.e., if a child is doing it, then it must be play). Similarly, relational definitions get applied to behaviors observed in relation to specific settings; according to relational criteria, children's behavior in the presence of toys or on the playground is considered play (Pellegrini, Horvat, & Huberty, 1998). Applying relational definitions to literacy, interacting with text would be considered a literacy event (Heath, 1983).

However, relational definitions can, in certain cases, be too global. Children can and do exhibit very different, and statistically independent, constellations of behavior in settings such as playgrounds and classroom play centers; for example, children engage in both rough-and-tumble play and aggression when they are observed on the playground but rough-and-tumble and aggression should not both be considered play, given that they do not cooccur and one does not lead to the other for most children (Pellegrini, 1988).

Another family of definitional and categorization strategies comes from sociology (Bernstein, 1971), ethology (Blurton Jones, 1972; Pellegrini, 2004; Smith, chap. 1, this volume), and ethnography (Heath, 1983). Researchers from these traditions stress the interdependence between behavior and context and inductively derive behavioral categories by applying theoretical constructs to observations of children in different contexts. Categories can be induced in terms of commonalities in physical movements (physical descriptions) or utterances and in terms of behaviors being temporally interrelated (e.g., categorization by consequence). These behavioral characteristics are considered design features. Play can be defined with this method as the constellation of behaviors such as play face, exaggerated movements or voice, and irregular sequences of behavior. Heath (1983) defined play according to the following design features: fictional character, temporal motivation, and suspension of reality. Interestingly, Heath also saw these dimensions as important components in young children's literacy events, particularly those involving narrative texts.

Similarly, Fein (1981) defined symbolic play according to the following design features: decontextualized behavior (a playful behavior is taken out of its functional context), self–other relations (pretense is directed to self, then others), substitute objects (one thing represents another), and sequential combinations (from single pretend gestures to embedded gestures). Fein, like Galda (1984) and Heath (1983), connected symbolic play and school-based literacy. Both, she argued, have design features characterizing narratives (Fein et al., 2000).

The primacy of narratives in young children's school-based literacy events may be at the heart of the symbolic play–literacy connection. Narratives are the primary genre of literacy instruction, particularly the sort of narratives represented in traditional children's books (Galda, 1984). Children who are socialized to listen and respond to these sorts of narratives are more likely to be successful at learning school-based literacy than children exposed to other genres and other sorts of narratives (Bernstein, 1972; Heath, 1983). This success is due, probably, to the similarity in the design features of the narrative speech events at home and at school, rather than to some underlying cognitive processing (Scribner & Cole, 1978). Thus, we suggest that explicit definitions of play and literacy are necessary. Further, for an educational program to be implemented effectively across multiple sites, we need to have explicit documentation of program components and should be able to document the extent to which the program is faithfully implemented, as well as the extent to which it impacts children's educational status.

Related to impact, definitions are also important in terms of gauging the developmental function of the construct. As noted briefly earlier, constructs such as literacy and play may have similar design features. This sort of argument from design (Hinde, 1980) can be used to make functional inferences about the impact of one antecedent behavior on another consequent behavior.

HOW ARE PLAY AND LITERACY DEFINED AND MEASURED HERE?

Definitions of play are numerous (Burghardt, 2005; Sutton-Smith, 1997), being proffered from fields as diverse as biology (Bateson, 2005; Byers, 1998) and literary criticism. There seems to be an essential dimension across all these fields, however: Playful behavior is considered to be without direct function or purpose. Play is considered a nonserious, or exaggerated, rendition of mature behavior and an activity in which the process of playing is more important than the end result (Pellegrini & Smith, 1998). As we discuss later, this is a curious definitional dimension for a construct for which the developmental function has been stressed.

In all three chapters in this section, following the theories of Piaget (1951/1962) and Vygotsky (1967), one form of play is considered: symbolic play. Symbolic play first appears at around 2 years of age, peaks during the preschool period, and then declines (Fein, 1981). The representational or "as if" dimension of symbolic play differentiates it from other forms of play. It is also this representational dimension that links play to aspects of literacy, such as writing, especially according to Vygostky's theory. Facility with the manipulation of symbols and signs, the argument goes, should relate to literacy, another representational activity. Social symbolic play bouts have also been described as having narrative, or story-like, qualities (Galda, 1984). Both social symbolic play and narrative have fictional, or pretend, characters who are temporally motivated, and operate in a fictional rather than real world. The extent to which the narrative features of social symbolic play match the narrative features of school literacy events should enable the former to predict the latter with reasonable accuracy. In this case, there is no underlying semiotic function, as in Piaget's theory, that is responsible for the relation between symbolic play and literacy. Instead, it is a matter of two behavioral events having similar design features (Smith, chap. 1, this volume). So the transfer from play to literacy may be the result of shared "essential elements" rather than of an underlying representational process.

The primacy of narrative structure in play and literacy is especially evident in the chapters by Rowe (chap. 3, this volume) and Sawyer and DeZutter (chap. 2, this volume). Rowe examines young children's dramatic play in relation to reading books, many of which were narratives. Like the earlier work of Cochran-Smith (1984) and Heath (1983), Rowe considers literacy in terms of the way in which children relate books to life, and life experiences to books. Rowe does not explicitly define play but does discuss it in relation to how children behave in certain sorts of responses to books or interactions with peers. Piaget's notion of play as assimilation, too, was invoked. A more precise definition would have been helpful in integrating these findings with the extant work in this field. Literacy, too, was rather loosely defined in terms of the behavior and talk that occurred around literacy props. Given her ethnographic orientation, it is unfortunate that Rowe did not derive specific categories of behavior related to play and literacy that children enacted as they progressed. It would have been especially interesting to see the degree to which the sorts of behavior she observed changed across the year, particularly in the light of the fact that these children were at the age when symbolic play is only just beginning. For example, was play around an adult different from play with peers alone? How did play differ in response to different texts? Importantly, inductively derived categories across the duration of the study would help answer an important developmental question; that is, how do children's responses to books change over time? Documentation of categorical differences in play across time would begin to answer this question. Specifically, the degree to which these categories and processes resembled those described in the adult literature, middle childhood literature, and elementary school literature is crucial to document. It is not enough to say that they are different; we must document how they are different, and how each relates to literacy development.

It also would have been interesting if Rowe had differentiated talk during play from talk about play. The ability to talk about play increases significantly across the preschool period (Garvey, 1990) and documentation of the beginnings of its ontogeny would be important. In terms of understanding play itself, we know a substantial portion of children's play with peers is spent "out of frame"; that is, most of the utterances generated by preschoolers in peer interaction around play props is spent negotiating meaning (Garvey, 1990; Sachs, Goldman, & Chaille, 1984).

This is similar to what Williamson and Silvern (1991) called metaplay. For example, children negotiate who can take what role in a situation and jointly determine what language is role appropriate. This sort of negotiation is crucial if children are to negotiate the ambiguous waters of social pretend play; if they cannot, play stops (Pellegrini, 1982). Documentation of this ability to move in and out of play is also crucial for some of the benefits of play proffered by Rowe (chap. 3, this volume). For example, there should be a relation between the children's metaplay talk and the stance shifting associated with trans-mediation and social interaction. We know that talk about play and talk about thought processes, both in and out of pretend play, is related to literacy differentially across the preschool period (Pellegrini & Galda, 1991) and into kindergarten (Pellegrini, Galda, Bartini, & Charak, 1998). For 4- and 5-year-olds, talk about talk and talk about thought processes, out of the fantasy frame, predicted literacy, whereas for younger children, metatalk in play was predictive of early literacy.

An additional concern relates to Rowe's (chap. 3, this volume) methodology and the assumptions on which it is based. For example, Rowe focuses on unidirectional book-to-play connections, where exposure to a book leads to specific types of play. We would prefer a more dynamic, reciprocal interaction where books affect the nature of play, and play in turn affects which books are selected and how a child interacts with a book. Rowe hints at how play might affect the transaction between a student and a book when she writes "when holding a toy dinosaur, many aspects of the text were signaled in a more concrete way." Unfortunately, this line of inquiry was not pursued further.

A further consideration relates to the impact of play and literacy experiences in the home, which are documented in the case of Rowe's son but not with regards to the other children in the school. Given that the home environment for these children can reasonably be expected to be rich in play and literacy experiences, it can be assumed that those experiences will undoubtedly have a major role on the evolution of play and literacy at school. Rowe provides an example of this when she documents play episodes in which her son was able to use book-related play as a platform from which to explore personal questions and make new connections between themes of interest. These types of play episodes emerge, she writes, because the children "exercised considerable control over the focus of informal book reading and dramatic play." However, we suspect these sorts of opportunities for child-controlled, one-on-one play with an adult are much more prevalent in the home than at school. Revealingly, all of Rowe's examples of this nature are from her own interactions with her son, not from the school environment.

From a practical perspective, a more reciprocal, dynamic, and ecological analysis is certainly possible given modern measurement techniques and statistical packages. If, as we suggested earlier, Rowe (chap. 3, this volume) had inductively derived categories of play and literacy behaviors across the duration of the study, she would have the basis for measuring both the impact of early types of play on subsequent literacy and the impact of early book-related behaviors on different types of play (e.g., symbolic play) that are only just emerging at this age. Further, if she had managed to conduct observations in the homes of the other children in school, she could begin to untangle the impact of home versus school play experiences on the development of literacy.

Measured across time in a longitudinal format, this sort of model would undoubtedly yield important findings that would serve as a firmer basis for educational policymaking.

That being said, we are excited to see the reference by Sawyer and DeZutter (chap. 2, this volume) to collaborative emergence, which signals the application of ideas from systems theory (e.g., Capra, 2002; Holland, 1995). Systems theory has been discovered by fields such as developmental psychology (see Magnussen & Stattin, 1998) and the result is a reciprocal, dynamic, and ecological approach to developmental theory and research. Systems theory postulates that the transactions of individuals combine to create a complex system from which emerge intricate behaviors that cannot be predicted by the individual nature of the members of the system. For example, in the game of chess, a set of simple rules regarding the movement of individual pieces gives rise to an incredibly complex game in which the outcome is impossible to predict; each move depends on the current position of each player on the board, which is an accumulation of all previous moves. Such a model is very relevant to social pretend play and literacy; as Sawyer and DeZutter put it, "narrative elements emerge that cannot be understood by focusing on the individual child's mental representations and goals."

We would like to see more direction from Sawyer and DeZutter (chap. 2, this volume) regarding how methodology must evolve to support their point of view. They state that emergent narratives are "analytically irreducible to the actions, intentions, or mental states of participating children" and suggest that conversation analysis holds some promise for analyzing the dynamic, moment-to-moment evolution of these narratives. Although we are not certain that conversation analysis is the key, we are willing to see how the field reacts to this suggestion and how conversation analysis as a technique evolves in response to the demands of collaborative emergence. From a systems theory perspective, we would expect that such analysis would include a consideration of the children's background knowledge and experience, as well as the social context for the emergent narratives.

Given this, it is somewhat surprising that the example provided by Sawyer and DeZutter (chap. 2, this volume) is a simple dialogue, bereft of any references to the setting, the children's characteristics, their behaviors during the dialogue, or any discussion of how conversational analysis techniques would add value. A more complete recounting of this dialogue could not only serve as a working model of their new ideas but could also bring us closer to understanding exactly how, in their view, collaborative emergence relates to literacy. We would also like to see a tighter definition of emergence such that it can be clearly identified during the give-and-take of everyday peer interactions. This would also give us a foothold on the issue of how the characteristics of the children involved (e.g., dominance status) may influence the dynamic path of the narrative and, in turn, affect literacy development. Without this, we find ourselves intrigued by the theory of collaborative emergence, but at the same time we find it difficult to apply the theory constructively to the study of play and literacy and we see no immediate benefit for those interested in educational policy.

It is refreshing, then, to see a reference early in the chapter by Smith (chap. 1, this volume) to how play and literacy research can inform educational policymaking, as the ultimate goal of any research effort in this field is the improvement of the educational experience for young children. Unfortunately, this discussion is not pursued in Smith's chapter, which is devoted to a discussion of methodological issues in play research. For example, Smith argues that much of play research is correlational and argues that correlations do not prove causation; they may, in fact, involve a third factor that is actually responsible for the observed covariance between two measures. Smith presents longitudinal data collection and cross-lagged correlations as one solution to be used in those situations where experimental studies are not feasible. We agree with this position, but would add that more modern techniques such as structural equation modeling (SEM; Maruyama, 1998) and hierarchical linear modeling (HLM; Raudenbush & Bryk, 2002) may be more appropriate than simple correlations. SEM analysis not only generates model fit statistics that can be compared across models, but seamlessly handles missing data issues that often arise in longitudinal studies and that can negatively impact a correlational analysis. HLM can also handle missing data issues and, in addition, enables the researcher to model the hierarchical nature of school-based data (i.e., students nested within classrooms, or classrooms within schools). Through this hierarchical modeling, the researcher can eliminate the bias that is introduced through the use of single-level analysis techniques (e.g., correlation) on multilevel data.

Various methodological issues are also raised by Smith (chap. 1, this volume) with regard to experimental studies, highlighting the intervention studies inspired by Smilansky's (1968) argument in favor of sociodramatic play. Smith argues that these studies suffered from multiple methodological problems, such as experimental bias and inappropriate control groups. Given that many of the studies utilized multiple classes in the same school, we believe that contamination between experimental and control classrooms, as well as the novelty or Hawthorne effect of being part of the treatment group, may be an even greater issue. Future intervention research should certainly take these issues into account.

To summarize, all chapters are concerned with play and how play may impact literacy. In each case, however, play is, in fact, defined very differently. In one case, play is defined as transformations based on book-related themes as well as talk about those themes. In this definition, enactments are kept distinct from talk about play, story productions, reading, and word games. In another case, pretend and sociodramatic play are emphasized. Different mechanisms are also given to explain the benefits of play on literacy, including scaffolding, narrative, and theory of mind. Given this diversity, it is very difficult to understand what is meant by play without reading the chapters very closely; even then it is difficult to determine in some cases. Consequently, it is very difficult to draw global conclusions across the chapters about the impact of play on children's literacy. This ambiguity is especially problematic in terms of recommending educational policy. How could we recommend "based on the research" that children learn best through play when there is very little commonality in different play definitions? Unfortunately, we can do no better than to agree with Smith (chap. 1, this volume) when he writes that play undoubtedly has an important role in literacy, but we can find no evidence to show that it plays an essential role.

DEVELOPMENTAL AND FUNCTIONAL ISSUES

As we discussed earlier, one way to define play is to simply categorize all that children do as play. Such an orientation is a direct result of the recognition that children are qualitatively different from adults. This difference is very often expressed as children's behavior being considered a nonserious and imperfect variant of adult behavior, a view that is reflected in the play theories of Piaget (1951/1962, 1983) and Vygotsky (1967), and Groos (1898, 1901) before them. In such cases, the developmental function of play is considered in terms of what it contributes to later development, not in terms of its intrinsic value during childhood. The developmental metaphor for this view of play is play as scaffolding (Bateson, 1981, 2005). In this view, play occurs during childhood to aid in skill assembly and is disassembled when the skill is mastered. Accordingly, benefits of play are not immediate, but deferred until after childhood. Indeed, the idea of deferred benefits of play, rather than immediate benefits, is one of the only ways to solve the logical conundrum of contrasting views of play. Play can be defined as having no apparent purpose for children and, simultaneously serving an important developmental function, only if benefits are deferred until after childhood. Interestingly, many studies of children's play follow Piagetian and Vygotskian theories, which posit deferred benefits for play (Bjorklund & Green, 1992), yet at the same time they search for immediate benefits. As we (e.g., Pellegrini & Smith, 1998) and others (Byers & Walker, 1995; Martin & Caro, 1985) have shown, the evidence for long-term benefits of play is very weak.

An alternative view of play is to not consider it an inferior or imperfect version of adult behavior but to consider it beneficial and specific to the niche of childhood. In Bateson's (2006) terms, this is considered the metamorphic view of play. Evidence in support of this view of play comes from studies documenting the occurrence of play during periods of childhood when developmental trajectories can be modified (Byers & Walker, 1995; Pellegrini & Smith, 1998). To determine immediate function, scholars have, as a first step, examined the frequency of certain forms of play during early childhood and examined its co-occurrence with other rapidly developing systems, such as locomotion during early infancy (Thelen, 1979). Specific to social symbolic play, its natural frequency of occurrence relates to social understanding (e.g., Dunn, 1988; Smith, chap. 1, this volume). Developmental function, or benefits associated with play, can be measured in a number of different ways (see Pellegrini & Smith, 1998), such as through experimental enrichment (Fein, Ardila-Rey, & Groth, 2000) and deprivation paradigms (Pellegrini,

Horvat, et al., 1998; Smith & Hagan, 1980), longitudinal correlational studies, and design features arguments (Rowe, chap. 3, this volume).

As noted, the three chapters in this section use very different means by which to make inferences about play and literacy. For example, Sawyer and DeZutter (chap. 2, this volume) emphasize the benefits of metaplay from several perspectives. This explicit negotiation that children undertake during a collaborative play session, they argue, often leads children to pay closer attention to narrative structure and theme, which has benefits for literacy measures such as comprehension and recall. Although we agree with the emphasis on metaplay, we believe that it involves reflection on language and thought, which is necessary for constructing decontextualized meaning.

Sawyer and DeZutter also explore the relationship between improvisation and narrative, and suggest that sociocultural psychology and situation cognition can provide some guidance. Although we believe that the link between improvisation and play is important, we find their explanation to be somewhat vague and would like to see this line of thought expanded. For example, what are some specific tenets of the theory that would lead to hypotheses, and how could these hypotheses be tested? We would also like to see a consideration of related issues, such as how emergent narratives may impact and be impacted by aspects of symbolic play, which in turn could impact literacy. Research has shown that, for preschoolers, symbolic play and some aspects of metalinguistic awareness are positively and significantly correlated (Pellegrini & Galda, 1991). More directly, play with language, often occurring in symbolic play bouts, is directly related to phonological awareness, which in turn predicts literacy.

Rowe's (chap. 3, this volume) study of 2-year-olds' book-related symbolic play is particularly interesting because the children under study were at the age when symbolic play is only just beginning. Rowe examined the important interchange between stories, talk about books, and pretend talk. Following up on the earlier work of Cochran-Smith (1984), she notes that this interchange is dynamic, in that changes in one aspect affect changes in the others. Such contrastive interchanges between sign systems, consistent with Piaget's (1983) equilibration theory, broadens children's conceptual categories.

Although we agree at one level with this analysis, we also question the place of play in the greater scheme of contrastive experiences. For children, especially 2-year-olds, not all cross-media or social experiences are capable of maximizing conceptual regrouping. Our developmental orientation posits that play, specifically, helps young children negotiate the conceptual disequilibration specific to childhood. In a sense, play is adaptive for childhood, whereas other strategies and media may be adaptive for adulthood but not for childhood.

Finally, our bias, following McCall (1977), is that longitudinal designs are the lifeblood of developmental studies. Smith does the field a service by arguing for cross-lagged longitudinal research, and we would add, as earlier, that modern techniques, such as SEM and HLM, could be enormously helpful. We hope that researchers in the field, including Rowe and Sawyer and DeZutter (and indeed Smith himself), take advantage of the opportunities that this technology provides to further explore the relationship between play and literacy.

CONCLUSION

These chapters are a testament to the continued interest in the connections between play and early literacy as well as a testament to both the continuity and the change in the ways in which these phenomena are studied. The continuity lies in the theoretical guidance provided by Piaget's theory, as evidenced by Wolfgang's (1974) early study, later complemented by Vygotsky's theory. As noted elsewhere (Pellegrini & Galda, 1993), the theories have quite a bit of overlap as well as some major points of disagreement. Theoretical consistency also relates to the way in which we view play as beneficial for children. Is it immediately beneficial, as the theories would suggest, or are the benefits delayed, as many studies conclude?

Aside from theoretical consistency, studies of children's play can benefit from clarity of definition and rigor of observational methods. What counts as play and how it is observed and categorized varies tremendously across studies, and the temptation to fall victim to the "play ethos" (Smith, 1988, chap. 1, this volume) by assuming that all play is good for young children have negative implications for educational policymaking. There are many types of play, varied benefits that derive from play, and developmental influences on both type and benefits. There are also other experiences through which children learn and develop. Play is likely to be important in children's development, but there are other routes to competence—play is only one of many.

REFERENCES

Bateson, P. P. G. (1981). Discontinuities in development and changes in the organization of play in cats.In K. Immelmann, G. Barlow, L. Petrinovich, & M. Main (Eds.), *Behavioral development* (pp. 281–295). New York: Cambridge University Press.

Bateson, P. P. G. (2005). Play and its role in the development of great apes and humans. In A. D. Pellegrini & P. K. Smith (Eds.), *The nature of play: Great apes and humans* (pp. 13–26). New York: Guilford.

Bernstein, B. (1971). *Class, codes, and control* (Vol. 1). London: Routledge & Kegan Paul.

Bjorklund, D. F., & Green, B. L. (1992). The adaptive nature of cognitive immaturity. *American Psychologist, 47,* 46–54.

Blurton Jones, N. (1972). Categories of child–child interaction. In N. Blurton Jones (Ed.), *Ethological studies of child behaviour* (pp. 97–129). London: Cambridge University Press.

Burghardt, G. M. (2005). *The genesis of animal play: Testing the limits.* Cambridge, MA: MIT Press.

Byers, J. A. (1998). Biological effects of locomotor play: Getting into shape or something more specific? In M. Bekoff & J. A. Byers (Eds.), *Animal play: Evolutionary, comparative, and ecological perspectives* (pp. 205–220). Cambridge, UK: Cambridge University Press.

Byers, J. A., & Walker, C. (1995). Refining the motor training hypothesis for the evolution of play. *American Naturalist, 146,* 25–40.

Capra, F. (2002). *The hidden connections: A science for sustainable living.* New York: Anchor.

Cochran-Smith, M. (1984). *The making of a reader.* Norwood, NJ: Ablex.

Dansky, J., & Silverman, I. W. (1973). Effects of play on associative fluency in preschool-age children. *Developmental Psychology, 9,* 38–43.

Dunn, J. (1988). *The beginnings of social understanding.* Cambridge, MA: Harvard University Press.

Fagen, R. (1981). *Animal play behavior.* New York: Oxford University Press.

Fein, G. G. (1979). Echoes from the nursery: Piaget, Vygotsky and the relationship between language and play. In E. Winner & H. Gardner (Eds.), *Fact, fiction, and fantasy in childhood* (pp. 1–17). San Francisco: Jossey-Bass.

Fein, G. G. (1981). Pretend play in childhood: An integrative review. *Child Development, 52,* 1095–1118.

Fein, G. G., Ardila-Rey, & Groth, L. A. (2000). The narrative connection: Stories and literacy. In K. A. Roskos & J. F. Christie (Eds.), *Play and literacy in early childhood* (pp. 27–44). Mahwah, NJ: Lawrence Erlbaum Associates.

Galda, L. (1984). Narrative competence: Play, storytelling and comprehension. In A. Pellegrini & T. Yawkey (Eds.), *The development of oral and written language in social context* (pp. 105–119). Norwood, NJ: Ablex.

Garvey, C. (1990). *Play* (2nd ed.). Cambridge, MA: Harvard University Press.

Groos, K. (1898). *The play of animals.* New York: Appleton.

Groos, K. (1901). *The play of man.* London: Heinemann.

Heath, S. (1983). *Ways with words.* New York: Cambridge University Press.

Hinde, R. A. (1980). *Ethology.* London: Fontana.

Holland, J. H. (1995). *Hidden order.* Reading, MA: Addison-Wesley.

Magnusson, D., & Stattin, H. (1998). Person–context interaction theories. In W. Damon (Series Ed.) & R. Lerner (Vol. Ed.), *Handbook of child psychology: Vol. 1. Theoretical models of human development* (pp. 685–760). New York: Wiley.

Martin, P., & Bateson, P. P. G. (1993). *Measuring behaviour.* Cambridge, UK: Cambridge University Press.

Martin, P., & Caro, T. (1985). On the function of play and its role in behavioral development. In J. Rosenblatt, C. Beer, M.-C. Bushnel, & P. Slater (Eds.), *Advances in the study of behavior* (Vol. 15, pp. 59–103). New York: Academic.

Maruyama, G. M. (1998). *Basics of structural equation modeling.* Thousand Oaks, CA: Sage.

McCall, R. B. (1977). Challenges to a science of developmental psychology. *Child Development, 48,* 333–344.

Olson, D. R. (1977). From utterance to text: The bias of language in speech and writing. *Harvard Educational Review, 47,* 257–281.

Pellegrini, A. (1980). The relationship between kindergartners play and achievement in pre-reading language, and writing. *Psychology in the Schools, 17,* 530–555.

Pellegrini, A. (1982). Explorations in preschoolers' construction of cohesive test in two play contexts. *Discourse Processes, 5,* 101–108.

Pellegrini, A. (1984). Identifying causal elements in the thematic-fantasy play paradigm. *American Educational Research Journal, 21,* 691–703.

Pellegrini, A. D. (1988). Elementary school children's rough-and-tumble play and social competence. *Developmental Psychology, 24,* 802–806.

Pellegrini, A. D. (2004). *Observing children in the natural worlds: A methodological primer* (2nd ed.). Mahwah, NJ: Lawrence Erlbaum Associates.

Pellegrini, A. D., & Galda, L. (1982). The effects of thematic fantasy play training on the development of children's story comprehension. *American Educational Research Journal, 19,* 443–452.

Pellegrini, A. D., & Galda, L. (1991). Longitudinal relations among preschoolers' symbolic play, metalinguistic verbs, and emergent literacy. In J. Christie (Ed.), *Play and early literacy development* (pp. 47–68). Albany: State University of New York Press.

Pellegrini, A., & Galda, L. (1993). Ten years after: A reexamination of symbolic play and literacy research. *Reading Research Quarterly, 28,* 163–175.

Pellegrini, A., & Galda, L. (1998). *The development of school-based literacy: A social ecological approach.* London: Routledge.

Pellegrini, A. D., & Galda, L. (2001). I'm so glad, I'm glad, I'm glad: The role of emotions and close relationships in children's play and narrative language. In A. Göncü & E. Klein (Eds.), *Young children in play, story, and school: Essays in honor of Greta Fein* (pp. 204–219). New York: Guilford.

Pellegrini, A. D., Galda, L., Bartini, M., & Charak, D. (1998). Oral language and literacy learning in context: The role of social relationships. *Merrill-Palmer Quarterly, 44,* 38–54.

Pellegrini, A. D., & Gustafson, K. (2005). Boys' and girls' uses of objects for exploration, play, and tools in early childhood. In A. D. Pellegrini & P. K. Smith (Eds.), *The nature of play: Great apes and humans* (pp. 113–138). New York: Guilford.

Pellegrini, A. D., Horvat, M., & Huberty, P. D. (1998). The relative cost of children's physical activity play. *Animal Behaviour, 55,* 1053–1061.

Pellegrini, A. D., & Smith, P. K. (1998). Physical activity play. *Child Development, 69,* 577–598.

Piaget, J. (1962). *Play, dreams, and imitation in childhood* (C. Gattengno & F. M. Hodgson, Trans.). New York: Norton. (Original work published 1951.)

Piaget, J. (1983). Piaget's theory. In W. Kessen (Ed.), *Handbook of child psychology: History, theory, and methods* (pp. 103–128). New York: Wiley.

Raudenbush, S. W., & Bryk, A. S. (2002). *Hierarchical linear models: Applications and data analysis methods* (2nd ed.). Thousand Oaks, CA: Sage.

Rubin, K. H., Fein, G., & Vandenberg, B. (1983). Play. In E. M. Hetherington (Ed.), *Handbook of child psychology: Vol. IV. Socialization, personality and social development* (pp. 693–774). New York: Wiley.

Sachs, J., Goldman, J., & Chaille, L. (1984). Planning in pretend play. In A. Pellegrini & T. Yawkey (Eds.), *The development of oral and written language in social context* (pp. 119–128). Norwood, NJ: Ablex.

Scribner, S., & Cole, M. (1978). Literacy without schooling. *Harvard Educational Review, 48,* 448–461.

Simon, T., & Smith, P. K. (1983). The study of play and problem solving in preschool children. *British Journal of Developmental Psychology, 1,* 289–297.

Smilansky, S. (1968). *The effects of sociodramatic play on disadvantaged preschool children.* New York: Wiley.

Smith, P. K. (1988). Children's play and its role in early development: A re-evaluation of the "play ethos." In A. D. Pellegrini (Ed.), *Psychological bases for early education* (pp. 207–226). Chichester, UK: Wiley.

Smith, P. K., & Hagan, T. (1980). Effects of deprivation on exercise play in nursery school children. *Animal Behaviour, 28,* 922–928.

Smith, P. K., & Whitney, S. (1987). Play and associative fluency: Experimenter effects may be responsible for previous positive findings. *Developmental Psychology, 23,* 49–53.

Snow, C. (1983). Literacy and language: Relationships during the preschool years. *Harvard Educational Review, 53,* 165–189.

Sutton-Smith, B. (1997). *The ambiguity of play.* Cambridge, MA: Harvard University Press.

Sylva, K., Bruner, J., & Genova, P. (1976). The role of play in the problem-solving of children 3–5 years old. In J. Bruner, A. Jolly, & K. Sylva (Eds.), *Play: Its role in development and evolution* (pp. 244–261). New York: Basic Books.

Thelen, E. (1979). Rhythmical sterotypies in normal human infants. *Animal Behaviour, 27,* 699–715.

Vandenberg, B. (1980). Play, problem solving, and creativity. In K. Rubin (Ed.), *Children's play* (pp. 49–68). San Francisco: Jossey-Bass.

Vygotsky, L. (1967). Play and its role in the mental development of the child. *Soviet Psychology, 12,* 62–76.

Williamson, P., & Silvern, S. (1991). Thematic fantasy play and story comprehension. In J. Christie (Ed.), *Play and early literacy development* (pp. 69–90). Albany: State University of New York Press.

Wolfgang, C. (1974). An exploration of the relationship between the cognitive area of reading and selected developmental aspects of children's play. *Psychology in the Schools, 11,* 338–343.

THE PLAY–LITERACY
INSTRUCTIONAL ENVIRONMENT

5

Play in the Context
of the New Preschool Basics

Kathleen A. Roskos
John Carroll University

James F. Christie
Arizona State University

Play has long been at center of early childhood education, where it has been viewed as an effective means for promoting all aspects of child development. Preschool programs have routinely allocated large blocks of time to free-choice center time during which children could choose to engage in a variety of play-related activities. Recently, major policy shifts in preschool education and a new science-based perspective on early learning are starting to erode play's curricular status, raising the possibility that play-based activities will be pushed aside in favor of more direct forms of instruction that address the new pre-K basics of language, early literacy, and numeracy skills (Christie & Roskos, 2006; Zigler & Bishop-Josef, 2004). Many early childhood educators are concerned that the current skills-based movement will go too far, resulting in children receiving age-inappropriate forms of instruction that may actually undermine their learning of the basics (Neuman & Roskos, 2005).

We begin this chapter by looking back at why play has been regarded as an essential component of preschool programs, examining theory and research on play's role in development and several widely implemented early childhood curriculum models. Next, we discuss the rise of the new preschool basics—language, literacy, and math—and their impact on the early childhood curriculum and on play's role in general learning. Special emphasis is given to the new "science-based" perspective on early literacy and its curricular demands, which threaten to squeeze play out of many preschool programs. Finally, we look to the future and discuss the concept of networking play and academics, an approach that promises to enrich children's classroom play experiences and promote learning of the basics. We also recommend expanding the scope of the new basics to include self-regulation, an important prerequisite to academic success that has strong ties to play activity.

LOOKING BACK: PLAY AT THE CENTER OF THE CURRICULUM

Play's central role in early education can be traced back to the beginnings of formal preschools in 16th- and 17th-century Europe and the work of Rousseau, Pestalozzi, and Froebel (Johnson, Christie, & Wardle, 2005). These early play proponents argued that play-related activities provided educational advantages over the strict methods of rote instruction that were used to teach young children. In the United States, play was a bit late in arriving in early education programs because of the pervasive influence of the Puritan and Protestant work ethic. Play finally established a firm foothold in U.S. preschool programs during the 1920s and 1930s with the rise of the child study movement, progressive education, and Dewey's experimentalist philosophy of education (Glickman, 1984; Varga, 1991). Play has stayed at the center of U.S. early childhood from that time forward.

Currently, play has an important role in most of the major "brand-name" early childhood education programs, such as Montessori, Reggio Emilia, High Scope, and the Creative Curriculum, although the nature of the play activities varies considerably from program to program. Montessori programs feature independent activity with semistructured play materials that teach specific concepts, whereas Reggio schools emphasize creative expression with unstructured art materials and group dramatic play. The defining feature of High Scope curriculum is the "plan, do, and recall" activity period in which children state in advance what they intend do, then engage in play and other activities, and finally reflect on their play experiences with guidance from the teacher. The Creative Curriculum (Dodge, Colker, & Heroman, 2000) organizes learning activities around interest areas or learning centers, many of which involve play (e.g., blocks, house corner, table toys, sand and water). The role of the teacher is to set up rich interest areas and then scaffold children's learning as they interact with these environments. For more information about play's role in curriculum models, see Roopnarine and Johnson (2000).

Play's central role in these curriculum models is based on two underlying tenets: that early childhood education should focus on the whole child and use age-appropriate teaching strategies. These beliefs have been translated into broad policy initiatives, such as (a) the mandate that Head Start programs focus on promoting social and emotional development, as well as cognitive processes and skills (Zigler & Muenchow, 1992); and (b) the National Association for the Education of Young Children's advocacy of "developmentally appropriate practice" (Bredekamp & Copple, 1997) in a nationwide system of early childhood program certification. In the sections that follow, we examine the theory and research that support each of these basic assumptions about play.

Play and the Development of the "Whole Child"

The contention that play contributes to all aspects of child development has broad research and theoretical support. Connections between play and physical development are the most obvious. Research has shown that "the vigorous physical component of exercise play has immediate beneficial consequences" for children's motor development (Pellegrini & Smith, 1998, pp. 591–592). Given the recent increase in childhood obesity and its connection with Type II diabetes (Gabbard, 2000; Sutterby & Frost, 2002), the physical benefits of play are more important than ever.

Sociodramatic play occurs when groups of children adopt roles and act out make-believe stories and situations (Johnson et al., 2005). This complex type of play places heavy linguistics and social demands on children. Children must make intentional use of lexical and syntactical features of language to (a) signify the person, object, and situational transformations that occur in pretense play; and (b) identify and elaborate on play themes as they unfold during the play episode. Sociodramatic play also raises the bar for social skills. Children need to collaborate, take turns, share props, and inhibit aggression to successfully engage in group dramatizations. Thus, it is not surprising that research has documented firm connections between sociodramatic play and oral language development (e.g., Dickinson & Tabors, 2001) and social competence (Creasey, Jarvis, & Berk, 1998).

Research has also established links between play and many areas of cognition, including conceptual development, representational thinking, problem solving, divergent thinking, and the development of theory of mind, the awareness that other people's knowledge and beliefs may be different than one's own (Johnson et al., 2005; Zigler & Muenchow, 1992). In general, evidence indicates that play can make important contributions to these aspects of cognitive development but is not absolutely necessary for their development (Smith, 2005).

Most of the work on play's role in emotional adjustment has been clinical rather than experimental, so research evidence on play's contribution to this area of development is rather thin. However, there is strong theoretical support that the fantasy component of play promotes emotional resilience and coping in young children. Singer and Singer (1990) developed a cognitive-affective framework in which children who are more imaginative in their play are more open to their affect system and are thus able to develop a more elaborate and richer storehouse of affect-laden symbols and memories. This, in turn, enables children to draw on a wider range of mental associations or connotations to solve problems and cope with stress (Russ, 1998).

Perhaps the strongest theoretical support for the notion that play promotes development of the whole child comes from Vygotsky. His student Elkonin's theory of child development maintained that there are leading activities that make unique contributions to specific periods of child development (Bodrova & Leong, 2000). According to Elkonin, sociodramatic play is the leading activity during the preschool years. This aligns with Vygotsky's (1966) contention that play "contains all the developmental tendencies in a condensed form" (p. 16; physical, cognitive, emotional) and thus creates a zone of proximal development that pulls the child forward. For this reason, play activity is essential in the preschool years because it leads development, giving rise to symbolic thought (thought separate from action or object), self-awareness, and self-regulation (the set of abilities that enables children to control their behavior, engage in positive interactions with others, and become independent learners).

Play as Age-Appropriate Pedagogy

Play is a pattern of activity with salient features, such as positive affect, nonliterality, means-over-ends orientation, flexibility, and autonomy (King, 1979; Rubin, Fein, & Vandenberg, 1983; Smith & Vollstedt, 1985). Play proponents believe that these characteristics make play an ideal context for teaching young children. The basic argument is that play can help children achieve specific educational goals through a vehicle that is, from the child's perspective, inherently engaging, self-motivating, and highly meaningful (Johnson et al., 2005).

A substantial body of research has shown that literacy-enriched play settings provide effective opportunities for learning and teaching early reading and writing skills. This ecologically focused intervention involves supplying sociodramatic play settings with theme-related literacy tools and materials. For example, the kitchen area in a home center could be supplied with cookbooks, food coupons, a telephone book, pencils, and notepads. A doctor play setting might include pens, prescription pads, patient charts, an appointment book, wall signs ("Payment due at time of service"), and magazines for waiting patients to read.

Studies conducted in preschool and kindergarten classrooms have shown that literacy-enriched play settings result in large increases in emergent reading and writing activity during play (Morrow & Rand, 1991; Neuman & Roskos, 1992). Evidence is also accumulating that children learn about the functional uses of print (Vukelich, 1991) and acquire environmental print recognition (Neuman & Roskos, 1992; Vukelich, 1994) and comprehension skills (Neuman & Roskos, 1997). In addition, literacy-enriched play centers have also been found to enhance the duration and complexity of children's play episodes (Neuman & Roskos, 1992).

Linking play and academics has not been limited to literacy. Van Hoorn, Scales, Nourot, and Alward (1999) present a rich description of how a kindergarten teacher equipped a store play center with a variety of numeracy props, including balance scales, a stamp and ink pad set with rotating numbers, calculators, adding machines, and small objects such as Unifix cubes to count and sell. The teacher's goal was to help children learn how to count and recognize numerals from 1 to 20, important objectives in her school district's mathematics curriculum. The children gained additional mathematical knowledge by making money for use in the store and by using coupons to save money when buying items at the store. Play centers can also be enriched to promote learning other curriculum areas such as science and social studies. For example, Roskos (1994) detailed how two kindergarten teachers developed play settings that were closely connected with science content. For example, during a 6-week unit on winter, the teachers provisioned the Math and Science Lab play center with various types of thermometers, note pads and pencils for recording data, materials for an "experiment" measuring the temperature of water under different circumstances, lab coats for dress-up, and printed matter related to the topic. Roskos concluded that "the combination of setting cues (e.g., the 145>lab'), objects (i.e., the experiment, paper and writing tools), and opportunities for peer interaction around a common purpose appeared to create sufficient conditions for enjoyment that urged children to persist in the content-focused task as a form of play activity" (p. 10).

We have evidence, albeit indirect, that the elements of play may benefit learning in general that is needed for academic success. Play may generate a mental engagement spill-over effect that boosts the chances of learning new information; that is, forming mental constructions and remembering words. This heightened engagement is especially important for young children because their self-regulation is still in the formative stages and their attention span to more traditional, adult-centered forms of instruction is quite limited.

THE CURRENT SITUATION: SCIENCE, STANDARDS, AND THE NEW BASICS

Play has maintained its centrality in early childhood education for quite a long time. It is no accident that, during this same time period, modern societies increasingly came to view children not as miniature adults, but as developing persons in their own right. Play served to bracket childhood as distinct from adulthood, giving children space and time to learn on their own terms. Play, as 20th-century early educators observed, was the "business of children."

In a 21st-century world, however, play as the business of children faces serious competition. Megatrends are restructuring education in the face of global economies, based on the creation and distribution of information (Carneiro & Heckman, 2003). These trends are resulting in sweeping reconceptualizations about what it means to know, think, learn, and play in an information age. Three megatrends in particular are shaping and changing play's role in helping young children learn about print as a communication tool. We briefly describe these next.

Megatrend 1: A Science of Early Childhood Development

Toward the end of the 20th century, neurobiological, behavioral, and social science research converged to strengthen the hypothesis that early experiences have powerful effects on human development over the life span. The old saying, "As the twig is bent, so grows the tree," speaks true, swiftly summing up decades of research that show that the quality of early life experiences shapes human capacities for future learning and achievement. Synthesized in a landmark report titled *From Neurons to Neighborhoods: The Science of Early Childhood Development* (Shonkoff & Phillips, 2000), the research evidence establishes four scientific principles of early childhood development (see Table 5.1) and builds a strong case that education needs to start earlier so that young children arrive at school eager and ready to learn. Challenging the deeply held 20th-century idea that infants, toddlers, and preschoolers are "too young" to learn, this new evidence calls for enlightened action in early childhood policies and early learning programs.

Two initiatives, grounded in the new science of early childhood, bear watching for paradigm shifts in young children's early learning experiences. One is Universal Pre-K (UPK), a state-funded program, currently gaining momentum across the United States (see CED, 2002). UPK is designed to provide all preschool-aged children with an opportunity to participate in supportive, high-quality, literacy-rich educational environments prior to entering kindergarten. Georgia, a state leader in this model, serves 70% of its 4-year-olds through UPK programs, and many other states are following suit. Each state sets its own program requirements, but in general these call for quality teaching staff, developmentally appropriate curriculum, ongoing professional development, and meeting the needs of working families.

Another initiative is Early Reading First (ERF), a competitive grant program federally funded through the No Child Left Behind Act (2001). It is designed to prepare preschoolers, especially those at risk due to poverty, disabilities, and limited English proficiency, to enter kindergarten with the necessary cognitive, language, and early literacy skills for success in school. ERF has five purposes: (a) to enhance preschoolers' language, cognitive, and early reading development by using scientifically based teaching strategies and professional development; (b) to create high-quality language and print-rich envi-

TABLE 5.1
Scientific Principles of Early Childhood Development

Principle 1	Each of us is the product of an ongoing interaction between the influence of our personal life experiences and the contribution of our unique genetic endowment, within the culture in which we live.
Principle 2	Human relationships are the "active ingredients" of environmental impact on young children.
Principle 3	The development of intelligence, language, emotions, and social skills is highly inter-related.
Principle 4	Early childhood interventions can shift the odds toward more favorable outcomes, but programs that work are rarely simple, inexpensive, or easy to implement.

Adapted from Shonkoff, J.P. (2004). *Science, policy, and the developing child: closing the gap between what we know and what we do.* Chicago, ILL: Ounce of Prevention Fund.

ronments so children learn fundamental language and literacy skills; (c) to implement research-based language and literacy activities into practice for development of oral language, phonological awareness, print awareness, and alphabet knowledge; (d) to assess and monitor children's progress; and (e) to integrate early reading curriculum based on scientifically based reading research into preschool programs. More specific than UPK requirements, ERF specifies the structure and curricular content of an early literacy program with a strong emphasis on a scientific approach to early literacy pedagogy.

Underlying both initiatives is the premise that skill begets skill in a dynamic process: Skills gained early in life help children gain additional skills in the next stage of development (Carneiro & Heckman, 2003). As a corollary, skills missed early in life are hard to compensate for later on, as dramatically shown in the early language studies of Hart and Risley (1995, 1999). They report a 30-million word gap by age 3 that accrues as a result of families' language and use across different income groups. In sum, early advantages accumulate, as do early disadvantages. Focusing on learning and skill development at an early age, therefore, can be particularly valuable, contributing to children's educational attainment as well as social and behavioral development. How play fits into this skills beget skills view, however, is uncertain. The shrinking amount of time allowed for child play in preschool programs is not a good sign. Attributes of fun (as opposed to learning) commonly associated with play by parents, grandparents, caregivers, and the general public do not help build support for play in this new skills-focused environment.

Megatrend 2: Early Learning Standards and Standards-Based Education

The K–12 standards movement, originating in the 1980s, swept with the force of a tidal wave into the early education field at the start of the 21st century. The Bush administration federal policy (*Good Start, Grow Smart*, 2002) vigorously endorsed early learning standards as integral to a comprehensive system of education and care for young children. Professional organizations, such as the National Association for the Education of Young Children, have somewhat reluctantly followed along. Early learning content standards in the major domains of development (what young children should know and be able to do) have rapidly become part of the states' educational architecture in developing systems of service delivery for young children. Today, for example, 45 states have approved early learning standards for preschoolers (www.mcrel.org; www.nieer.org). As a structural element of education reform, early learning standards frame the content of curriculum, the goals of professional development, and the focus of assessment aimed at improving children's school readiness. They are increasingly seen as a powerful lever for improving preschool instruction.

Standards, by definition, are about outcomes that describe what children should know and be able to do, and that share a consensus of acceptance. Although standard setting is a sensitive endeavor in early childhood education, given the plasticity in early learning and the variability of experience, it none-theless serves the important purpose of making expectations transparent, thus opening the door to building an early education system that supports school readiness for all children.

Play and standards, however, have a strained relationship for a couple of reasons. For one, the cognitive focus of standard setting has riveted attention to the content areas of early literacy and mathematics, giving short shrift to the vital socioemotional competencies in play's province. The essential skills of self-regulation that play so beautifully builds, for example, have not been part of the standards-making conversation (Bodrova & Leong, 2005). Another reason is that play's inherent complexity makes it very difficult to measure objectively. Play is dense with multilayered interactions that reflect at best large patterns of change; that is, from sensorimotor play to symbolic play to games (Piaget, 1962; Smilansky, 1968) or from self-pretend to simple pretend about familiar situations to highly complex bouts of sociodramatic play with others (Weitzman & Greenberg, 2002). So it is quite difficult (and intellectually challenging) to tease out how play is progressing and what learning benefits are for the young child. Standards indicators that describe play, therefore, do not yield easily to one of the foundational principles of the standards movements, that a standard must be measurable. As a result, play has not been a focal topic in the standards-making process despite its centrality in human development as a learning mechanism. How to make the connections among play, early learning, and early literacy clear in standards frameworks and language remains a hard problem, and one that continues to reduce play's role in a standards-driven world (Christie & Roskos, 2006; Johnson et al., 2005, pp. 151–153).

Megatrend 3: Early Literacy as a Critical Period of Literacy Development

Publication of *Learning to Read and Write: Developmentally Appropriate Practices for Young Children*, a joint statement of the International Reading Association and the National Association for the Education of Young Children (IRA/NAEYC, 1998), is a milestone in the evolution of early literacy as a recognized domain of development from birth to 5 years of age. Rooted in early childhood (ages 0–8) as well as early literacy research, the statement legitimated early literacy as a developmental domain of early childhood. The position rests on a dynamic, bioecological view of human growth and learning (Bronfenbrenner, 1995; Thelen & Smith, 1995). Children learn and grow through proximal processes that vary as a function of who they are (biopsychological characteristics), where they are (near–far environments) and what is expected (nature of learning outcomes). There ensues, therefore, a continual interplay between development and learning. Instruction both follows and leads this interplay (Hawkins, 1996). Not fully grasped at the time perhaps, the position statement's claim in effect extended literacy education into the preschool years, thus expanding the learn-to-read period from age 3 to Grade 3.

Around the same time that the IRA/NAEYC position was published, the National Research Council published a synthesis of early reading research entitled *Preventing Reading Difficulties in Young Children* (Snow, Burns, & Griffin, 1998). The research report identified early risk factors, such as vocabulary deficits, that significantly increased chances for children's reading failure, a condition already linked to broader social and economic problems (e.g., crime, poverty, joblessness). The significance of the early years, not only in learning to read and write, but also for learning in general, was well-documented in two subsequent reports of the National Research Council: *From Neurons to Neighborhoods* (Shonkoff & Phillips, 2000), which synthesized scientific knowledge about the nature of early development and the role of early experiences, and *Eager to Learn* (Bowman, Donovan, & Burns, 2000), which reviewed and synthesized the knowledge base on early childhood pedagogy.

Firmly footed in the professional literature—as a developmental domain of early childhood, as a significant period of literacy development over the life span, and as a category of learning—early literacy became the cornerstone of school readiness, increasingly seen as a major outcome of early education and care (American Federation of Teachers, 2002). A corpus of research-based evidence (e.g., Neuman & Dickinson, 2006; Snow et al., 1998; Whitehurst & Lonigan, 2001) points to core early literacy knowledge and skills predictive of or highly correlated with future reading achievement, namely oral language, phonological awareness, alphabet letter knowledge, and print awareness. Background knowledge, print motivation, and self-regulation are also described as playing key roles in the early stages of reading acquisition (Bodrova & Leong, 1996; Neuman, 2001). Describing in essence the early literacy content that young children should be learning before school, the synthesizing trio of reports brought a new level of detail to the early years as the beginnings of literacy. Joined by demands for early math and increased language experiences (vocabulary in particular), it was inevitable that the new pre-K basics of literacy, math, and language would replace play as the centerpiece of the early childhood curriculum. This is exactly what happened as early childhood curriculum entered a new century, and left play behind in the old.

LOOKING AHEAD: UNITING PLAY AND THE PRE-K BASICS

The megatrends of the 21st century are pushing on play and forcing a reconceptualization of its role in the early childhood curriculum. Once central, it now must compete with the new early basics essential to the young child's future in an information society. Caught in a time of transition, play, as a medium for learning, must itself adapt to the emerging future of early education, which is one of science, standards, and new pedagogies. But how? What should play's role be? What does it look like in a brave new world of early literacy education?

Complementing the New Basics

Play in preschool, we would argue, must expand its educational role to complement and enhance the new pre-K basics. *Educational play* refers to play activities that are linked to educational goals, objectives, and outcomes (Johnson et al., 2005). By definition, educational play implies some degree of planning or structure by teachers. This structure can be minimal as in the case where a teacher arranges the physical environment to encourage certain types of play. For example, teachers may add theme-related literacy props to a play setting. Or it can be more substantial as in the case of direct teacher involvement in play. For example, Roskos and Neuman (1993) found that preschool teachers frequently intervened as a co-player or coach to encourage children to incorporate literacy into their play activities.

In the past, classroom play has tended to be a stand-alone activity. We believe that a considerable amount, but not all, play must be networked with instructional goals of the new basics. Play, in and of itself, is a network of interactions characterized by elements of nonliterality, intrinsic motivation, self-initiation, and means over ends. However, this highly motivating network must be joined with other activity settings in the preschool classroom in clear and consistent ways to support the learning progression of difficult ideas, such as the alphabetic principle (i.e., that the sounds of oral language are represented by letters). In large and small groups children can be taught how speech maps to print, but it is in play that they can put such concepts to practical use (from the child's point of view), and thus practice the transfer of new ideas to real situations.

Old, hierarchical curriculum structures that privilege one learning domain over another falter in the face of new early learning demands, in large part because a hierarchical approach lacks the multidirectional and overlapping linkages young children need to master the new basics. What must evolve is a network style of curriculum management where high-power learning domains (e.g., early literacy and math) criss-cross and instructional communication flows across settings. Play's networking role means:

- Some play settings are directly linked to standards-based content.
- Some play settings and play objects are deliberate extensions of key concepts and skills taught during circle time and small-group activities (e.g., play props are related to the stories that the teachers read to children).
- Teachers actively support and guide play toward instructional goals (e.g., learning new vocabulary words).

Faced with new challenges for more complex early learning, the early childhood curriculum can neither afford to privilege play nor to exclude it, because the demand for the exchange of education-oriented ideas and skills is so high. It will take all the activity settings in the early childhood classroom working together to provide sufficient opportunity for learning the basic skills necessary to be well-prepared for school entry.

The Arizona Centers for Excellence in Early Education (ACE[3]) is a good example of the nexus of the science-based instruction and early childhood standards movements (Zepeda, Christie, Blanchard, Burstein, & Bryan 2003). ACE[3] was an ERF project that served children in 24 Head Start and state-funded preschool classrooms in San Luis and Somerton, Arizona. A vast majority of these children were native Spanish speakers who were learning English as a second language. Like all ERF projects, the primary goal of ACE[3] project was to promote preschoolers' readiness for kindergarten by teaching them science-based early reading skills—oral language, phonological awareness, alphabet knowledge, and concepts of print. Because of the population being served, oral language received top instructional priority.

The ACE[3] project used a commercially published curriculum, *Doors to Discovery* (Wright Group/McGraw-Hill, 2002), which is organized into 1-month "explorations" or units that focus on topics that appeal to young children, such as transportation, nature, food, and school. The Doors curriculum consists of three interrelated components:

- *Large group time.* Theme-related song and rhyme posters were used as a warm-up and to teach phonological awareness (e.g., rhyme recognition). This was followed by shared reading of big books in which the teacher encouraged children to read along and engage in book-related talk. Instruction on concepts of print, phonological awareness, and alphabet knowledge was incorporated into these shared reading sessions.
- *Discovery centers.* During a 60-minute period, children engaged in self-selected activities in a variety of learning centers, including dramatic play, art, blocks, writing, mathematics, and science. Many of these activities were linked to the unit theme and to the stories that are read during shared reading. For example, during the unit on transportation, the dramatic play center was turned into a gas station. Props included a gas station sign (e.g., "Chevron") and a cardboard gas pump with a label ("gas") and numerals to represent the gallons and cost of gas that was pumped.
- *Small group time.* This instruction was embedded in the 60-minute center time. The teacher met with groups of four to six students at a table, and the assistant teacher worked with children at the centers. Two types of small group instruction occurred:
  1. *Interactive book lesson.* During the second 10-minute segment of discovery center time, the teacher met with small groups of students and conducted a vocabulary lesson using a wordless big book that contains a number of illustrations that were related to the unit theme. For example, *Our Big Book of Driving,* which was used in the unit on transportation, contains pictures of different types of vehicles (bus, ambulance, motorcycle), parts of a car (door, tire, speedometer), and a scene of a busy intersection. Children were encouraged to discuss the pictures, initially in Spanish and then in English.
  2. *Big scrapbook lesson.* Once a week, during the third 10-minute segment of discovery center time, the teacher also conducted a shared

writing lesson with a small group of children using a blank big book. In a variation of the language experience approach, the teacher wrote down children's oral language while they watched. The subject of the children's dictation was often photographs of children's play activities or samples of the children's artwork. For example, children would draw pictures of the type of vehicle that their parents drive. Each child would then dictate a sentence ("My mom drives a _____"), which the teacher wrote below his or her picture. Completed scrapbooks were placed in the classroom library center for children to read during the center time.

This curricular integration in the ACE[3] presented opportunities for children to encounter and use vocabulary and skills on multiple occasions, increasing the chance that newly learned content would be learned and retained. The following vignette, which occurred during a unit on building and construction, illustrates how play was networked with the instructional components of the curriculum:

During large group circle time, the teacher began with a rhyme poster that was about building a tree house. The teacher paused to point out the words that rhymed in the story, and then encouraged the children to come up with other words that ended with the same rhyming sound. She also focused on several tool-related vocabulary terms: *hammer* and *nail* (*tiny little nails*). Next, the teacher did a shared reading lesson with a big book about building a doghouse. Before reading the book with the children, she did a "picture walk," engaging the children in a discussion about objects in the photos in this informational book. The teacher focused children's attention on several tool vocabulary terms: *hammer, nail, saw, measuring tape,* and *safety goggles* in the illustrations. Then the teacher read the book and encouraged the children to read along. Some were able to do so because of the simple text and picture clues. The teacher paused after the first several pages and asked the children, "What kind of tools will they need to build their dog house?" Children responded with *hammer, saw, tape measure,* and *tiny little nails* (carried over from the rhyme poster).

During center time, several children chose to play in a dramatic play center that was set up as a house construction site. There was a "house" made out of large cardboard boxes. In addition, there were toy tools (hammers, saw, measuring tape, level), safety goggles, hard hats, some golf tees that were used as make-believe nails, and several signs (Hard Hat Area, Danger, Construction Site). Two girls and a boy spent 30 minutes in the center, using the toy tools to measure, plan, and build the house. During this play, they used the target vocabulary repeatedly and also explored the uses of the tools. For example, when the boy attempted to use the toy saw without first putting on his safety goggles, one of the girls reminded him to put the goggles on (which he did, very reluctantly). The dramatic play center was used a means to provide children with an opportunity to practice and consolidate the vocabulary and concepts that were being taught in the instructional part of the curriculum.

This type of educationally networked play was not the only opportunity for play. Children could also engage in free play with blocks, table toys, wheeled vehicles, and other materials. They also had a lengthy outdoor play period. However, a significant part of the play "menu" was linked with the concepts and skills being taught in the *Doors* curriculum. We believe that this type of networking is necessary to allow play to continue to thrive in the era of the new basics.

Extending the New Basics

Play, we also strongly argue, must assume a vigorous leadership role in extending the new pre-K basics to include self-regulation, along with the reflective abilities it fosters. All we know about school readiness from research and years of practice confirms that self-regulatory competence is absolutely critical for the academic and social challenges of the school years (Blair, 2002). The root of self-regulation is the ability to inhibit impulsive behavior, emerging at the end of the first year of life, and from then on progressively requiring the child to actively suppress or initiate behaviors inconsistent with reactive tendencies. The desire to hit another, for example, must be restrained despite provocation. Language serves as a powerful self-regulatory tool for initiating behaviors (e.g., "We can share the cookies") and also inhibiting impulses of the self when faced with the norms, conventions, and rules of the social environment (e.g., "Use your words, not your fists").

According to Vygotsky's sociocultural theory, children learn to consciously regulate their behavior and exercise self-restraint in collaborative sociodramatic play (CSD), because it demands language use, adherence to rules, and the coordination of goals and behavior with others. Vygotsky (1934/1978) argued that young children achieve their "greatest self-control" (p. 99) in play, viewing it as the leading developmental activity of the preschool years. Research supports the Vygotskian supposition that CSD is influential in the development of self-regulation (Elias & Berk, 2002; Krafft & Berk, 1998), and especially beneficial for highly impulsive youngsters (Elias & Berk, 2002). There is also some neurobiological evidence that rough-and-tumble play, in affording emotional reactivity, may support the cognitive self-regulation (Blair, 2002; Panksepp, 1998) necessary for beginning reading; that is, learning to pay attention on purpose.

Relatedly, CSD fosters young children's reflective skills; that is, the ability to think about one's own thought and action. These essential skills, first practiced in play, are the foundations of metacognition—predicting, explaining to oneself, noting mistakes, planning ahead, and allocating effort. Strong metacognitive skills help learners take control of their own learning and spur motivation to persevere when learning is difficult (Bransford, Brown, & Cocking, 2000).

In early childhood, play gives rise to reflection (and therein metacognitive skills) because it makes demands on children's emerging planning skills.

Early games like peek-a-boo, search and find, and hide and seek nurture abilities to retrieve information from memory, the taproot of planning. In more advanced forms of social play (e.g., CSD), playing well with others requires deciding what will happen (e.g., "I'll feed the baby and then it will get sick, okay?"), deliberate remembering (e.g., "Always put the baby's bottle in the fridge, so we can find it"), problem solving (e.g., "Three kids is too many, so you can play over there"), and evaluating play activity (e.g., "Teacher ... she's not doing what moms do"). Play, therefore, creates a compelling situation for young children to use and practice general cognitive processes, such as planning ahead, monitoring progress, evaluating success, correcting errors, and so forth, that are essential for early school success. Theoretically (Bronfenbrenner & Ceci, 1994; Deloache & Brown, 1984; Thelen & Smith, 1995), the planning skills that play demands may support a developing neural grid, so to speak, for more complex, general cognitive skills, also essential in learning to read.

Some early literacy research shows evidence of these emerging planning skills. Rowe (1998), for example, describes preschoolers' use of metacognitive knowledge (e.g., knowledge of oneself as a writer) and structures (e.g., "how to" write strategies) in their writing play. Pellegrini, Galda, Dresden, and Cox (1991) show how symbolic play necessitates the use of metalanguage (endophora, elaborated nominal groups, linguistic verbs, temporal conjunctions) in 3- and 4-year-old children, and its relationship to emergent reading and writing. Their analysis of linguistic verbs (read, say, write, tell) used in make-believe play is especially relevant to this discussion, as these verbs indicate children's reflection on linguistic processes. Age differences as to proportional use of linguistic verbs aside, the important observation is that symbolic play provided a context for young children to lexicalize meaning and practice metalinguistic awareness. It afforded, in short, the use of oral language skills (speech) necessary for later decoding and encoding of print (written language). As Perfetti (1987) pointed out (following Tversky's [1977] theory of similarity), "for children learning to read, print is more similar to speech, than speech is to print" (p. 357). In other words, the learning progression is from speech as the source of meaning to print, and complex play (as the research seems to indicate) may scaffold the use of speech toward this more abstract purpose in its demand for metalanguage.

CONCLUSIONS

With the advent of new pre-K basics, play faces an uncertain future. Like the toys of yesteryear, play (some observe) may be well on its way to being shelved in the preschool curriculum, just like it was in kindergarten not all that long ago and Grade 1 before that. This is a dangerous direction to go for all the reasons we have discussed in this chapter, and we urge strong resistance to it. We must redirect the question from whether there should be play to how play contributes to the learning child who is well-prepared for school and for life. Time for play in the early childhood curriculum cannot be our leading question. No, this is not the best question. Rather, we should ask (loudly): How is play helping young children learn? How is it integrated into supportive environments for early learning? How is play maximized to ensure the integration of multiple abilities and skills so necessary for learning? Questions like these pull play into curriculum development and implementation, requiring a more deliberate and strategic approach to play's role and calling for a new, differentiated approach to play in the preschool setting. Questions like these situate play in 21st-century early education.

REFERENCES

American Federation of Teachers. (2002). *At the starting line: Early childhood education programs in the 50 states.* Washington, DC: Author.

Blair, C. (2002). School readiness. *American Psychologist, 57,* 111–127.

Bodrova, E., & Leong, D. (1996). *Tools of the mind: The Vygotskian approach to early childhood education.* Columbus, OH: Merrill.

Bodrova, E., & Leong, D. (2000). Imaginative, child-directed play: Leading the way in development and learning. *Dimensions of Early Childhood, 28,* 25–30.

Bodrova E., & Leong, D. J. (2005). High quality preschool programs: What would Vygotsky say? *Early Education & Development, 16,* 435–444.

Bowman, B., Donovan, M. S., & Burns, M. S. (Eds.). (2000). *Eager to learn: Educating our preschoolers.* Washington, DC: National Academy Press.

Bransford, J., Brown, A., & Cocking, R. (2000). *How people learn: Brain, mind, experience and school.* Washington, DC: National Academy Press.

Bredekamp, S., & Copple, C. (1997). *Developmentally appropriate practice in early childhood programs* (Rev. ed.). Washington, DC: National Association for the Education of Young Children.

Bronfenbrenner, U. (1995). Developmental ecology through space and time: A future perspective. In P. Moen., G. Elder, & K. Lúscher (Eds.), *Examining lives in context* (pp. 619–647). Washington, DC: American Psychological Association.

Bronfenbrenner, U., & Ceci, S. J. (1994). Nature–nurture reconceptualized in developmental perspective: A bioecological model. *Psychological Review, 101,* 568–586.

Carneiro, P., & Heckman, J. J. (2003). Human capital policy. In J. J. Heckman & A. Krueger (Eds.), *Inequality in America: What role for human capital polices?* (pp. 77–240). Cambridge, MA: MIT Press.

Christie, J., & Roskos, K. (2006). Standards, science, and the role of play in early literacy education. In D. Singer, R. Golinkoff, & K. Hirsh-Pasek (Eds.), *Play = learning.* Oxford, UK: Oxford University Press.

Committee for Economic Development. (2002). *A new framework for assessing the benefits of early education.* Pew Charitable Foundations.

Creasey, G. L., Jarvis, P. A., & Berk, L. (1998). Play and social competence. In O. Saracho & B. Spodek (Eds.), *Multiple perspectives on play in early childhood education* (pp. 116–143). Albany: State University of New York Press.

Deloache, J., & Brown, A. (1984). Where do I go next? Intelligent searching by very young children. *Developmental Psychology, 20,* 37–44.

Dickinson, D., & Tabors, P. (2001). *Beginning literacy with language: Young children learning at home and school.* Baltimore: Brookes.

Dodge, D., Colker, L., & Heroman, C. (2000). *Creative curriculum for early childhood: Connecting content, teaching and learning.* Washington, DC: Teaching Strategies.

Elias, C., & Berk, L. (2002). Self-regulation in young children: Is there a role for sociodramatic play? *Early Childhood Research Quarterly, 17,* 216–238.

Gabbard, C. (2000). Physical education: Should it be part of the core curriculum? *Principal, 79*(3), 29–31.

Glickman, C. (1984). Play in public school settings: A philosophical question. In T. Yawkey & A. Pellegrini (Eds.), *Child's play: Developmental and applied* (pp. 255–271). Hillsdale, NJ: Lawrence Erlbaum Associates.

Good Start, Grow Smart. (2002, April). Washington, DC: U.S. Department of Education.

Hart, B., & Risley, T. (1995). *Meaningful differences in the everyday experience of young American children.* Baltimore: Brookes.

Hart, B., & Risley, T. (1999). *The social world of children learning to talk.* Baltimore: Brookes.

Hawkins, D. (1996). Learning the unteachable. In L. S. Shulman & E. R. Keislar (Eds.), *Learning by discovery: A critical appraisal* (pp. 3–12). Chicago: Rand McNally.

International Reading Association and the National Association for the Education of Young Children. (1998). Learning to read and write: Developmentally appropriate practices for young children. *Young Children, 53*(4), 30–46.

Johnson, J., Christie, J., & Wardle, F. (2005). *Play, development, and early education.* New York: Allyn & Bacon.

King, N. (1979). Play: The kindergartners' perspective. *Elementary School Journal, 80,* 81–87.

Krafft, K., & Berk, L. (1998). Private speech in two preschools: Significance of open-ended activities and make-believe play for verbal self-regulation. *Early Childhood Research Quarterly, 13,* 637–658.

Morrow, L., & Rand, M. (1991). Preparing the classroom environment to promote literacy during play. In J. Christie (Ed.), *Play and early literacy development* (pp. 141–165). Albany: State University of New York Press.

Neuman, S. (2001). The role of knowledge in early literacy. *Reading Research Quarterly, 36,* 468–475.

Neuman, S., & Dickinson, D. (Eds.). (2006). *The handbook of early literacy research* (2nd ed.). New York: Guilford.

Neuman, S., & Roskos, K. (1992). Literacy objects as cultural tools: Effects on children's literacy behaviors during play. *Reading Research Quarterly, 27,* 203–223.

Neuman, S., & Roskos, K. (1997). Literacy knowledge in practice: Contexts of participation for young writers and readers. *Reading Research Quarterly, 32,* 10–32.

Neuman, S., & Roskos, K. (2005). The state of the state prekindergarten standards. *Early Childhood Research Quarterly, 20,* 125–145.

NCLB Act. (2001). No child left behind: Revitalization of the Elementary and Secondary Education Act. http://www.ed.tv/offices/OESE

Panksepp, J. (1998). Attention deficit hyperactivity disorders, psychostimulants, and intolerance of childhood playfulness: A tragedy in the making? *Current Directions in Psychological Science, 7*(3), 91–98.

Pellegrini, A., & Smith, P. (1998). Physical activity play: The nature and function of a neglected aspect of play. *Child Development, 69,* 577–598.

Pellegrini, A., Galda, L., Dresden, J., & Cox, S. (1991). A longitudinal study of the predictive relations among symbolic play, linguistic verbs, and early literacy. *Research in the Teaching of English, 25,* 215–235.

Perfetti, C. (1987). Language, speech and print: Some asymmetries in the acquisition of literacy. In R. Horowitz & S. J. Samuels (Eds.), *Comprehending oral and written language* (pp. 295–325). San Diego, CA: Academic.

Piaget, J. (1962). *Play, dreams and imitation in childhood.* New York: Norton.

Roopnarine, J., & Johnson, J. (2000). *Approaches to early childhood education* (3rd ed.). Upper Saddle River, NJ: Merrill/Prentice-Hall.

Roskos, K. (1994, April). *Connecting academic work and play at school: Preliminary observations of young children's content-oriented interaction and talk under conditions of play in kindergarten.* Paper presented at the meeting of the American Educational Research Association, New Orleans, LA.

Roskos, K., & Neuman, S. (1993). Descriptive observations of adults' facilitation of literacy in play. *Early Childhood Research Quarterly, 8,* 77–97.

Rowe, D. (1998). The literate potentials of book-related dramatic play. *Reading Research Quarterly, 33,* 10–35.

Rubin, K., Fein, G., & Vandenberg, B. (1983). Play. In E. Hetherington (Ed.), & P. Mussen (Series Ed.), *Handbook of child psychology: Vol. 4. Socialization, personality, and social development* (pp. 693–774). New York: Wiley.

Russ, S. (1998). Play, creativity, and adaptive functioning: Implications for play interventions. *Journal of Clinical Child Psychology, 27,* 469–480.

Shonkoff, J., & Phillips, D. (Eds.). (2000). *From neurons to neighborhoods.* Washington, DC: National Academy Press.

Singer, D., & Singer, J. (1990). *The house of make-believe: Children's play and developing imagination.* Cambridge, MA: Harvard University Press.

Smilansky, S. (1968). *The effects of sociodramatic play on disadvantaged preschool children.* New York: Wiley.

Smith, P. (2005). Social and pretend play in children. In A. D. Pellegrini & P. K. Smith (Eds.), *The nature of play: Great apes and humans* (pp. 173–209). New York: Guilford.

Smith, P. K., & Vollstedt, R. (1985). On defining play: An empirical study of the relationship between play and various play criteria. *Child Development, 56,* 1042–1050.

Snow, C., Burns, M. S., & Griffin, P. (1998). *Preventing reading difficulties in young children.* Washington, DC: National Academy Press.

Sutterby, J., & Frost, J. (2002). Making playgrounds fit for children and children fit for playgrounds. *Young Children, 57*(3), 36–41.

Thelen, E., & Smith, L. B. (1995). *A dynamic systems approach to the development of cognition and action.* Cambridge, MA: MIT Press.

Tversky, A. (1977). Features of similarity. *Psychological Review, 84,* 327–352.

Van Hoorn, J., Scales, B., Nourot, P., & Alward, K. (1999). *Play at the center of the curriculum* (2nd ed.). Upper Saddle River, NJ: Merrill.

Varga, D. (1991). The historical origins of children's play as a developmental task. *Play and Culture, 4,* 322–333.

Vukelich, C. (1991, December). *Learning about the functions of writing: The effects of three play interventions on children's development and knowledge about writing.* Paper presented at the meeting of the National Reading Conference, Palm Springs, CA.

Vukelich, C. (1994). Effects of play interventions on young children's reading of environmental print. *Early Childhood Research Quarterly, 9,* 153–170.

Vygotsky, L. (1966). Play and its role in the mental development of the child. *Soviet Psychology, 12*(6), 62–76.

Vygotsky, L. (1978). *Mind in society: The development of higher mental processes.* Cambridge, MA: Harvard University Press. (Original work published 1934)

Weitzman, E., & Greenberg, J. (2002). *Learning language and loving it* (2nd ed.). Toronto: The Hanen Centre.

Whitehurst, G., & Lonigan, C. (2001). Emergent literacy: Development from pre-readers to readers. In S. Neuman & D. Dickinson (Eds.), *Handbook of early literacy research* (pp. 11–29). New York: Guilford.

Wright Group/McGraw-Hill. (2002). *Doors to discovery.* Bothell, WA: Author.

Zepeda, O., Christie, J., Blanchard, J., Burstein, K., & Bryan, T. (2003). *Arizona Centers of Excellence in Early Education.* Washington, DC: U.S. Department of Education.

Zigler, E., & Bishop-Josef, S. (2004). Play under siege: A historical overview. In E. Zigler, D. Singer, & S. Bishop-Josef (Eds.), *Children's play: The roots of reading* (pp. 1–14). Washington, DC: Zero to Three Press.

Zigler, E., & Muenchow, S. (1992). *Head Start: The inside story of America's most successful educational experiment.* New York: HarperCollins.

6

Supporting Literacy and Play in Early Childhood Programs: Promising Practices and Continuing Challenges

Loraine Dunn and Sara Ann Beach
University of Oklahoma

Over the past decade research has begun to provide a window into preschool literacy environments and the literacy learning of children in those settings. The National Early Literacy Panel (Shanahan et al., 2004) has reviewed research to determine strong predictors from the preschool years of later success in learning to read and to identify instructional strategies that best support the development of these evidence-based precursors. Other recent reviews of the research in early literacy (cf. Dickinson & Neuman, 2006; Hall, Larson, & Marsh, 2003; Neuman & Dickinson, 2001; Snow, Burns, & Griffin, 1998) have advocated many preschool classroom strategies including a richly stocked library area, interactive story reading, and the inclusion of a plethora of common literacy artifacts and environmental print. Specifically, food containers, telephone books, stationary, pencils, and labels in dramatic play centers encourage children to experiment with literacy through play. Enriching play centers with literacy artifacts has been shown to provide opportunities for children to practice literary behaviors, particularly the uses of literacy in everyday life. In addition, teachers who enter the play setting and are responsive to the ongoing play in a literacy-enriched play center can positively enhance children's literacy learning (Morrow & Schickedanz, 2006).

In addition to enriching dramatic play centers with literacy artifacts, teachers are encouraged to provide multiple readings of big and small books, talk about stories, and demonstrate concepts about print (i.e., one reads from left to right and reads the print, not the pictures), thus making explicit what is invisible about reading and encouraging children to construct meaning with print. Writing should play a significant role in classroom life as adults model writing behaviors and provide writing materials for children in multiple settings, allowing them to experiment with writing as a communicative tool. Key to these classroom practices is the availability of appropriate literacy resources, interactions between peers and between children and adults, and the mediation of adults to scaffold learning (Dickinson & Tabors, 2001; Makin, 2003). These classroom practices have been found to significantly impact children's knowledge about the functions and uses of literacy (Roskos & Neuman, 2001), their vocabulary and knowledge of story (Dickinson & Tabors, 2001), and their phonemic awareness and knowledge of the written language system (Richgels, 1995).

In addition to the empirical work supporting these practices, current theoretical views of development imply linkages between literacy knowledge and the environments children experience. According to Bronfenbrenner and Morris (1998), the proximal processes, or everyday experiences, of children interact synergistically with the environment and children's own characteristics to produce developmental outcomes. Applying these notions to children's literacy development, Roskos (1997; Roskos & Neuman, 2001) posited that children's literacy experiences in everyday life (proximal processes) interact with the environment (the context of development that varies in its support for literacy) and together influence children's sense of being literate. In other words, the nature of children's participation in the literacy community determines their sense of being literate. If they have little participation in literacy events, then their sense of literacy might include a notion that only adults and older children can interact with print. Alternatively, if children are able to participate in literacy activities, they may begin to understand the functions that literacy has in everyday life for both children and adults. They begin to create identities in practice (Wenger, 1998). Constructing identities in practice is the fundamental work of learners in any context. According to Wenger, who you are as a member of a community shapes what you know and how you participate in that community.

Thus, there are strong indications from both theory and research regarding the power of the environment and the role of the teacher in children's literacy development. The practices described earlier represent current knowledge of environmental features known to enhance children's emerging literacy. But what is the state of the typical early childhood environment and how do typical environments support children's literacy development? Our studies indicate that community-based environments for preschool-age children have far to go before they can be considered optimal in this regard. We report on two sets of germane studies focusing on the types of educational environments experienced by many preschool children. The first set of studies look both at common literacy practices in community-based programs and the effect of teacher beliefs about literacy learning on the environment. The second set examines interventions addressing the preparation of staff and the enrichment of the literacy environment in preschool programs. These intervention studies include a redesign of the instruction of one preschool classroom as well as a long-term, large-scale professional development effort to increase teacher knowledge about appropriate literacy environments and practices.

LITERACY ENVIRONMENTS IN CHILD CARE SETTINGS

Center-Based Child Care

Beginning Steps in Literacy Quality Research.   Research on the everyday literacy practices in early childhood programs serving preschool-age children is a relatively recent phenomenon. When the first edition of this book was published, our study of child care centers in Indiana (Dunn, Beach, & Kontos, 1994) was one of the few available. Although dramatic evidence of the potential for child care programs to support and enhance young children's literacy learning had been available for some time (Neuman & Roskos, 1990, 1993), research on child care was heavily influenced by the Bermuda child care study (Phillips, Scarr, & McCartney, 1987). This landmark study defined program quality in general terms that did little to illuminate specific teaching practices. The typical research methodology was to combine structural or "regulatable" quality features, such as ratio, group size, and teacher qualifications, with a global observation of the environment. The Early Childhood Environment Rating Scale (ECERS; Harms & Clifford, 1980) quickly became the standard global quality assessment tool. The original ECERS and the more recent revised version (ECERS–R; Harms, Clifford, & Cryer, 1998) contain only a rudimentary representation of the literacy environment through the language and reasoning subscale that, as the title implies, focuses on language and cognition in a rather general way.

Our study (Dunn et al., 1994), as part of a larger study of child care quality, followed the methodological pattern already described. We sampled 30 child care classrooms serving 3- and 4-year-old children from 24 licensed child care centers and obtained both structural and global (i.e., ECERS) assessments of child care quality. Two scores derived from the 1980 version of the ECERS were used in data analyses: the language and reasoning subscale score and the developmentally appropriate activities factor score created by Whitebook, Howes, and Phillips (1989). The developmentally appropriate activities factor included items describing the availability of learning activities inviting exploration and experimentation. It had no items in common with the language and reasoning subscale.

In addition to these traditional tools of center quality we obtained more direct assessments of the literacy environment. The first was simply a record of the literacy-related activities available in the classroom during a free play or learning center period. No indication of how the materials were used was made during data collection. Duration of the play periods ranged from 15 minutes to 1 hour. The second literacy assessment tool was a 10-item, 5-point Likert scale (Hyson, Van Trieste, & Rauch, 1989) addressing the presence of functional print, children's access to books, writing materials, and story dictation experiences. An observer completed the instrument at the end of a 3-hour classroom observation. We used this instrument as an assessment of literacy quality.

Our assessments of the child care literacy environment revealed a situation far removed from the ideal. During classroom play periods startlingly few literacy-related activities were available ($M = .93$, $SD = .73$). Nine of the classrooms had no literacy activities present during playtime. The few activities available in the other classrooms were traditional library areas and writing and drawing materials. Note, however, that because our raw data provided only a list of materials available, we were unable to determine if the writing and drawing materials were actually used for literacy purposes or solely for art activities. The Hyson et al. (1989) scale revealed a slightly more encouraging situation with a mean in the moderate range ($M = 3.05$, $SD = .60$). These two literacy environment assessments were also found to be associated with the traditional measures of child care quality. More literacy-related activities were found in classrooms scoring higher on the ECERS developmentally appropriate activities factor. Overall literacy quality was better in classrooms scoring higher on both ECERS variables and when teachers were certified. In addition, the overall quality of the literacy environment positively predicted children's language development after family socioeconomic status was controlled.

Building on our 1994 study, Dunn and Norris (1999), using the Hyson et al. (1989) scale, found that the quality of the literacy environment was associated with a variety of child care quality assessments. Their sample included 71 child care classrooms, 25 of which were in centers accredited by the National Association for the Education of Young Children. The average item-mean score on the literacy quality scale was 3.28 ($SD = 1.02$), similar to that noted in the Indiana study. Also like our Indiana study, the quality of the literacy environment was positively associated with global and structural child care quality. Literacy environments were of higher quality in child care classrooms with higher ECERS scores and when directors and classroom teachers had higher levels of general education and specialized education in early childhood. Literacy quality was also higher in accredited programs with higher licensing capacities that were led by directors who held membership in an early childhood-oriented professional organization.

Associations with other measures of child care quality indicated literacy quality was better in classrooms staffed by teachers who engaged in sensitive interactions with children and who provided classroom experiences consistent with the field's definition of developmentally appropriate practices. Specifically, literacy quality was better when classroom activities and the classroom social-emotional atmosphere were developmentally appropriate.

A path analysis revealed a strong positive direct path from a composite variable representing program staff expertise to the quality of classroom literacy environments. A weaker positive path indicated families with more financial resources were likely to enroll their children in child care programs with better literacy environments. Surprisingly there were no direct or indirect paths from staff expertise or literacy quality to children's reading achievement as measured by the Test of Early Reading Ability (Reid, Hresko, & Hammill, 1989). Examination of the items on the literacy quality instrument indicated that, in the classrooms studied, the literacy teaching practices most critical to children's learning were often those occurring with the lowest frequency. Notable was the low level of teacher–child interaction during literacy-related experiences. The pattern of practices suggested by the item means may partially explain the lack of association between quality and children's achievement.

Recent Developments.   Recently additional research tools focusing specifically on the quality of the early childhood literacy environment have become available. The most comprehensive is the Early Language and Literacy Classroom Observation Scale (ELLCO; Smith, Dickinson, Sangeorge, & Anastasopoulos, 2002). The ELLCO consists of three main sections. The first is a literacy environment checklist describing the types of reading and writing materials available to children in the classroom. The second is a global classroom environment observation addressing more general aspects of the classroom such as organization of the environment, opportunities for child initiation, oral language facilitation, curriculum integration, and approaches to writing. The third section describes literacy activities, specifically book reading and writing practices, observed in the classroom. The availability of the ELLCO allows for a more detailed and comprehensive examination of literacy environments and practices in typical child care programs. Data from the Early Steps to Literacy[1] project provide an opportunity for such an examination of programs serving high concentrations of children in poverty.

Early Steps to Literacy.   The Early Steps to Literacy project, described in Beach et al. (2004), was a professional development intervention focused on improving the literacy environments and teaching practices experienced by preschool children living in poverty. Participants in the Early Steps to Literacy study ($N = 133$) were teaching staff (directors, lead teachers, assistants) from center child care and Head Start classrooms in both urban and rural areas. The teachers were mostly White (67%) and under 40 years old (78%). About one quarter of them (28%) were high school graduates, 46% had some college or an AA degree, 14% had a bachelor's degree, and 9% had some graduate school. Two thirds had not received any formal instruction in language and literacy. Of the rest, 16.5% had attended between 1 and 10 clock hours of formal instruction and 23% had attended more than 11 clock hours. The majority had been working in child care or Head Start for 5 years or less.

Pretest data from the Early Steps project were used to test a model of child care quality articulating the relationships between the traditional conceptions of quality described earlier (i.e., structural and global quality) and literacy quality (Dunn et al., 2005). Conceptually each of these forms of quality can be

[1]Early Steps to Literacy was funded by an Early Childhood Educator Professional Development Grant from the U.S. Department of Education awarded in 2001 to a team of collaborators at the University of Oklahoma in the College of Continuing Education and the College of Education. The views expressed are solely those of the authors and do not necessarily represent those of the U.S. Department of Education.

placed on a continuum representing their proximity to children's actual experiences in early childhood settings (see Dunn, 1993). Structural quality is often a social address variable and thus is the most distant of the three from children's actual experiences. Global quality is typically assessed with the ECERS and provides more detailed information about the setting and some indication of the processes that may actually occur therein. In the model tested, literacy quality was viewed as more detailed and specific than either structural or global quality. It is a more proximal indicator of children's experiences and provides greater detail about actual classroom events.

Path analysis was used to test the model. Two structural quality predictors comprised the first level of the path model: ratio and teacher characteristics. The latter included specialized education in early childhood, clock hours of formal instruction on language and literacy, and teacher beliefs. Teachers' beliefs often have a strong impact on practice (McMullen, 1999; Pajares, 1992) and have been associated with young children's conceptions of reading and writing (Wing, 1989); therefore, beliefs were included as a teacher characteristic under structural quality.

The next level of the model included global quality in the form of the ECERS–R and the sensitivity of teacher–child interactions (Arnett, 1989). Data on the quality of teacher–child interactions were made at the culmination of a 3-hour ECERS–R observation and represented the observer's overall judgment of interactions during that period. Thus, these data were deemed appropriate to include at the global quality level. Finally, the three scores from the ELLCO were used to measure the most proximal indicator of program quality, the literacy environment.

Findings from the path analysis validated the hypothesized model. Direct paths were found from ratio and teacher characteristics to global quality, and proximal quality of the literacy environment. The path coefficients indicated higher ratio (more children per teacher) was a negative predictor of ECERS and ELLCO quality. Teachers' specialized education in early childhood was a weak positive predictor of the ELLCO classroom observation. Likewise, teachers' hours of professional development in language and literacy had a minimal positive effect on ELLCO classroom literacy activities.

Teachers' beliefs about literacy had a significant effect on the observed quality of the literacy environment with more appropriate beliefs predicting all three ELLCO scores. Standardized beta coefficients for the direct paths between teachers' literacy beliefs and the ELLCO classroom environment, observation and literacy activities scores were just under .50. Direct paths were also found between global quality and proximal literacy quality scores. High levels of ECERS quality and sensitive teacher–child interactions were accompanied by higher quality literacy environments as assessed by all three ELLCO scores. These findings, together with the preceding studies, support the thesis we presented in the first edition of this book, namely that the quality of the language and literacy environment is a special case of child care quality.

Literacy in Family Child Care Homes

Although the literacy practices occurring in typical center-based child care programs are slowly becoming clearer, we still know very little about literacy in family child care home settings. As the name implies, these child care settings are in the home of the individual, usually a woman, providing the care. Many parents prefer this form of care for their young children as it is more "homelike" than a child care center. Typically the child care provider is the only adult present as she cares for a small group of children of mixed ages. Thus, she must juggle a multitude of responsibilities from greeting parents, facilitating children's play and learning, routine caregiving (e.g., diaper changing), and meal preparation. How family child care providers weave literacy experiences into events of the typical day is largely unknown.

Neuman and Roskos (2005) describe family child care homes wherein literacy learning is a part of a rich integrated curriculum. Activities in the homes spring from recent events in the children's lives and include meaningful content learning in literacy, science, and mathematics. However, recent self-report surveys of family child care home literacy environments suggest this ideal picture is not the norm. Cress (2000) studied 140 providers in one county in Indiana and Dunn and Norris (2002) examined 189 providers across the state of Oklahoma. Both found a variety of literacy materials available, but information on the quality and strategic use of these materials was not examined.

These two studies reported that family child care home providers owned at least 20 to 30 books that were available daily and readily accessible to children. Whether or not the books were rotated to maintain interest or used in ways to build literacy knowledge is unknown, however. Ninety-one percent of the Oklahoma providers reported they owned Little Golden Books, suggesting that at least some of the books were of less than optimal quality. On the other hand, the majority of Oklahoma providers owned books of multiple types (M = 9.24 types, SD = 1.19) including story books, information books, ABC and counting books, rhyming books, and chunky books. The lowest incidences of ownership (85%–88%) were found for wordless picture books, pop-up books, and touch and feel books.

Both family child care studies found that writing materials were regularly available to children. Providers in the Dunn and Norris (2002) sample reported having multiple types of writing implements available for children, with crayons and markers appearing most frequently (in more than 95% of the homes) and rubber stamps and magnetic letters least frequently (around 65%). Blank paper or scrap paper was available to children in almost all of the homes, however less than one third of the providers allowed children to use more formal writing papers, such as journals and stationery. Although most providers wrote words or statements for children (i.e., take dictation), it is unclear how this practice was used for learning. During quality observations children in 70% of the homes were seen engaging in some type of writing behavior in their play, but again data on the specific content and purpose of the writing were not collected. Negative correlations between family child care quality and the number of books and writing materials available (Dunn & Norris, 2002) raise concerns about the nature of writing experiences available to children in this setting.

A study by Walker (2004) provides some insight into the choices family child care providers make regarding literacy activities for children. Some providers view themselves as readers and writers, whereas others do not. Although most model reading and writing behaviors for children, they do not understand how their own literacy behaviors contribute to children's literacy learning. Further, even though they engage in explicit teaching tasks, they do not view themselves as teachers and therefore see no need to obtain professional development related to family child care. Most alarming, the providers in this study, who regularly read to children, did not believe this practice was an effective means of promoting children's literacy learning. Clearly, family child care providers are a population in need of significant assistance to maximize the literacy learning environments of their homes.

IMPROVING LITERACY ENVIRONMENTS

The research described earlier provides a picture of the challenges facing teachers if early childhood programs are to reach their potential in facilitating young children's literacy. Many child care staff lack training in how to support early literacy development, especially those with little preparation beyond high school. However, with more focus on the importance of preschool literacy environments for children's future literacy achievement, evidence is mounting that classroom environments can be improved, and that even small improvements in classroom practices can have an effect.

Short-Term Intervention

Beach and Kincade (1992) examined the connections between children's sense of being literate, defined by Young and Beach (1997) as their perceptions of their ability to participate in the literacy community, and the addition of more focused opportunities to interact with print. The study took place in a classroom for 4-year-olds in a university preschool. Although the classroom was not impoverished, there was no attempt to focus on literacy during the day other than to read a story aloud during whole-group time. Children seldom visited the library area and refused to pretend to read or write, although they would talk about story illustrations when prompted. The researchers, working with the classroom teacher, added literacy routines including rereading of a big book over the course of a week; interacting with the children about the pictures, making predictions, and connecting to their own experiences; composing their own variation of the story; and adding a writing center in the library area. At the end of the 4-week intervention, classroom observations indicated that more children were spending time in the library and writing area. They read to each other and the stuffed animals in the center and played with the letter stamps, reading to each other what they had written. When asked to read to an adult, most children would pretend to read the story using more book language and reading page by page from front to back. Several pointed to the print as they read the books or to their scribbles as they read their own writing. The researchers concluded that the children seemed to begin to see themselves as readers and writers, as participants in a literacy community instead of just observers of adults. They were able to demonstrate their knowledge about literacy by doing literate things and by engaging in literacy-related play. Whether this was attributable directly to the additional literacy activities or to children's perceived understanding that literacy had become more important in their classroom is unknown because there was no comparison group. However, the study does illustrate how literacy environments can support children's development of an understanding of their own literate possibilities.

This study underscored the need for teacher training about literacy development. The teacher in this study felt strongly about providing developmentally appropriate practices for the children. Yet her limited understanding of that concept and the policies of the program led to a less than optimal literacy environment. Professional development content needs to emphasize the importance of going beyond reading books to children and focus on how to include literacy practices in everyday life and in play, as well as how to support language and literacy interactions in all aspects of early childhood programs.

Long-Term Intervention

Intervention.   Early Steps to Literacy (Beach et al., 2004), introduced earlier, was one such project with a goal of changing the literacy environments and teaching practices experienced by preschool-age children living in poverty. In addition, the researchers examined the beliefs of the preschool teachers about literacy teaching and learning in preschool and the impact of the intervention on changes in their beliefs as well as on their classroom practices. Guided by research (cf. Showers & Joyce, 1996), the professional development intervention included two intertwined components: monthly classes and ongoing mentoring. The participants attended a college-level course in early literacy taught by an experienced early childhood educator. The course consisted of nine full-day sessions over the course of an academic year and included theory, practice, and implementation in teachers' own preschool classrooms. Topics for the course included supporting language learning, creating literacy-rich environments, interactive story reading, foundations of reading and writing, supporting phonological awareness and concepts about print, understanding the alphabet through writing, literacy and play across the curriculum, assessing early literacy understandings, literacy and diversity, and supporting family literacy. Requirements for the class included readings, journal entries, lesson implementations, lesson reflections, and quizzes. A more comprehensive description of the course is available in Beach, Wassner, and Stamps (2005).

The Early Steps evaluation design divided the preschool teachers into three groups. One group participated in the language and literacy class and was supported by mentoring for the duration of the class. A second group participated in the same class, had mentor support during the class, and had continued mentor support for approximately 5 months after the completion of the class. The third group acted as a no-treatment comparison group and received neither the class nor mentoring. Group membership was not randomized, but determined by geographic location of the teachers' work setting.

The mentoring component of the intervention was multipronged. First, each mentor attended the college course with her cohort of participants. Although each mentor was an experienced early childhood educator, knowledge about early literacy had not been a requirement for the job, so mentors learned along with the members of their cohort. In one intervention group, mentors visited their participants at least monthly, and sometimes more often. They observed their implementation of the concepts from the course, helped with homework, and gave feedback. These mentoring activities occurred during the time the course was in session and ended at its completion. In the other intervention group, mentors visited at least monthly, and sometimes more often; helped with homework; observed lessons; and gave feedback. In addition, they led monthly meetings for the participants during which they reflected on implementation of course concepts and activities and constructed literacy materials for their classrooms. These mentoring activities occurred during the time the course was in session and continued for 5 months following its completion.

Instruments and Data Collection.   Data were collected on teachers' beliefs and their actual classroom practices using four instruments. The Preschool Literacy Practices Survey (Beach, 2001), which was adapted from Burgess, Lundgren, Lloyd, and Pianta (2001), was used to assess teacher beliefs regarding how children learn about literacy, their beliefs about how literacy should be taught to young children, and their beliefs about the amount of time that should be devoted to specific literacy teaching practices. This self-report survey was rated on a Likert scale ranging from 1 (*least appropriate*) to 4 (*most appropriate*). Item scores were summed and divided to create a total score interpretable on the 4-point scale. Cronbach's alpha was above .80 on all three subscales.

The quality of the literacy environment was assessed using the 4-item Language and Reasoning subscale of the ECERS–R (Harms et al., 1998), the three ELLCO scores (Smith et al., 2002), and an observational measure of group time events (Dunn & Norris, 2001). The Group Time Events instrument consisted of 14 specific activities commonly used during large-group time, the majority of which included oral language interactions. Also represented were activities utilizing reading or writing tasks. Each activity was checked to determine if it was observed during group time. A factor analysis of the data revealed three different types of activities occurring during group time: activities focused on language and conceptual development, teacher-focused activities, and traditional group time activities.

Participants completed the Preschool Literacy Practices Survey (PLPS) before the intervention began and after its completion. Each participant was observed using the observation instruments three times: once before the intervention began, again at the conclusion of their class, and a third time several months after the completion of the class.

Findings.   The three subscales of the PLPS were examined through a repeated measures multivariate analysis of variance (MANOVA). The analysis resulted in a significant Time × Group interaction effect. Univariate analyses indicated significant interaction effects for each subscale. In each case, participants in both intervention groups outperformed the nontreatment comparison group. There were also differences between the two intervention groups. The highest average scores were seen in the intervention group with extended mentoring.

The same statistical analyses were applied to the ECERS–R, ELLCO, and Group Time Events with similar results. A repeated measures MANOVA resulted in a significant Time × Group interaction for each measure. Univariate analyses indicated the interaction effect was significant for all three scores computed for both the ELLCO and Group Time Events. The two intervention groups demonstrated better literacy practices at posttest than those seen in the no-treatment comparison group. Again, the group with extended mentoring had the most desirable findings. However, when all intervention groups (professional development delivery models, all cohorts) were combined and included with the no-treatment comparison group in a 3 (time: pretest, posttest, delayed posttest) × 2 (group) repeated measures MANOVA, the interaction effect was no longer significant. Delayed posttest scores for the treatment group declined somewhat. When combined, treatment groups did not have the more dramatic effect of the extended mentoring model of professional development.

Conclusions.   These findings point to the importance of sustained professional development that integrates instruction, application, reflection, and sustained support from a more knowledgeable other. After the Early Steps intervention, teachers' beliefs and practices matched more directly, especially for the group with the sustained mentoring. The intervention classrooms had richer literacy environments both physically in terms of literacy materials, and socially in terms of interactions between adults and children and among children. Intervention teachers were more likely to engage children in purposefully planned and challenging reading and writing activities that were balanced between child-initiated exploration and teacher-guided instruction.

The lack of a sustained effect at the delayed posttest is problematic. One explanation could be the high turnover in child care staff generally, and attrition in this sample specifically. One third of the participants dropped out of the first intervention group and one fourth dropped out of the second intervention group. This attrition was largely due to job changes, travel constraints, length of the class, and willingness to complete the requirements of a college class. Participants who were most successful exhibited conditions of readiness (i.e., had earned a child development associate credential or an associate's degree) that enabled them to persevere and commit to higher education. Because the delayed posttest occurred after the mentors had completed their work, a second explanation for the lack of sustained effect could be that these teachers needed continued support and encouragement to make the new literacy practices part of their teaching repertoire. Given their lack of prior professional development in literacy in particular, and early childhood education in general, it is logical that these teachers would need ongoing support and guided reflection to internalize the literacy practices and move beyond superficial implementation.

PROGRESS AND CHALLENGES

Progress

Since publication of the first edition of *Play and Literacy in Early Childhood,* our understanding of children's literacy experiences in typical community-based early childhood programs has advanced in multiple ways. The availability of research tools specifically designed to capture literacy events in early childhood programs has resulted in more literacy-specific descriptions of teaching and learning behaviors. Evidence supporting literacy quality as an important component of preschool program quality has been demonstrated by the studies reported earlier (Dunn et al., 2005; Dunn & Norris, 1999). Examinations of the literacy environments in family child care homes have joined the ongoing study of center-based preschool programs (e.g., Cress, 2000; Dunn & Norris, 2002; Walker, 2004). Policy initiatives at the federal level (e.g., Early Childhood Educator Professional Development Grants, Early Reading First) have provided opportunities to test professional development models based on extant research as seen in Early Steps to Literacy (Beach et al., 2004). The confluence of these events has resulted in greater communication and interaction between the literacy and early childhood research and practice communities as evidenced in this volume.

Continuing Challenges

Although signaling progress, the work described in this chapter also illustrates the continuing challenges facing the field in making high-quality preschool play and literacy environments the norm. The primary challenges are teachers' attitudes and beliefs, and their knowledge of effective literacy teaching practices. Enmeshed with these issues is the educational level of the typical preschool teacher in community programs, both center-based programs and family child care homes. As seen in the Early Steps to Literacy project (Beach et al., 2004) and in studies of family child care (Kontos, Howes, & Galinsky, 1996), the typical teacher or provider has only a few credit hours of college coursework, which may or may not be related to early childhood education, and typically are not related to children's language and literacy learning. Many have no formal education beyond high school. Yet, the findings described here, as well as existing literature (Bowman, Donovan, & Burns, 2001; Kontos et al., 1996), make it clear that specialized education in early childhood is a key predictor of global quality. More to the point, the most effective literacy teachers are those who have a deep knowledge of literacy and learning, and who are able to combine a variety of approaches to fit the child and the situation (Hall, 2003).

The knowledge and skills described by Hall (2003) are best mastered through professional development experiences characterized by both depth and intensity that occur over time allowing teachers to learn and accept unfamiliar ways of teaching. Although this type of professional development is not typical of that accessed by most child care staff (see Tout, Zaslow, & Berry, 2006), it has been effective in the interventions described here, as well as others in the literature (e.g., Kontos et al., 1996; Podhajski & Nathan, 2005).

Continuing support in adopting and improving new teaching practices appears to be essential (Beach et al., 2004; Podhajski & Nathan, 2005; Showers & Joyce, 1996). If a teacher's existing knowledge and practices are similar to that taught in a professional development experience, it will be relatively easy for that teacher to adapt his or her teaching and implement the new practice. If, on the other hand, the practices advocated in professional development are significantly different from the teacher's current knowledge, beliefs, and practices, change will be much harder to effect. Spillane, Reiser, and Reimer (2002) explain that teachers first view new ideas through the lens of old familiar ideas. Thus, to truly embrace the new practices the teacher must first accept that his or her existing beliefs may not be consistent with effective practices. Spillane et al. describe this process as a "loss ... [that] necessitates the discrediting of existing schemas and frameworks" (p. 415) and describe it as the most difficult type of change to achieve.

Fortunately, many teachers engage in practices that can be used as a foundation on which to build effective strategies for facilitating children's literacy development through play. In Kontos's (1999) study of Head Start classrooms, teachers used a variety of behaviors to facilitate children's play. Consistent with earlier literature (e.g., Christie & Enz, 1992) the teachers assisted children both inside and outside the play frame. Specifically, they helped children become involved in play as well as supporting and enhancing ongoing play (Kontos, 1999). However, the teachers rarely involved themselves in children's dramatic play, focusing instead on constructive and manipulative play. Moving teachers' support and enhancement of play into dramatic play episodes, which have rich potential for literacy learning, is therefore an important goal.

Professional development experiences that teachers see as directly related to their work with children are likely to be received positively (Taylor, Dunster, & Pollard, 1999). Therefore, coupling sound literacy teaching practices with familiar play facilitation strategies should have good potential for success and hopefully ease the change process described by Spillane et al. (2002). In addition, findings from the Early Steps intervention indicate teachers' beliefs and practices should also be addressed in professional development initiatives. Pulling these ideas together, the first topic in the Early Steps to Literacy class focused on children's language learning. The accompanying homework assignment required participants to purposefully engage in conversation with a child in their class. Thus, a familiar teaching practice was used to highlight the new information on literacy development.

Even though knowledge on effective and appealing professional development strategies is growing it is likely that engaging family child care providers in intensive professional development programs will be particularly challenging given that many do not view their work as teaching (Walker, 2004). This attitude is unlikely to motivate providers to seek professional development opportunities. Many providers view child care as a private family function similar to mothering. This is antithetical to the notion of child care as a profession with specific skills to be mastered (Taylor et al., 1999). This mindset intensifies the need to ensure that professional development provides immediate help in providers' work with children (Taylor et al., 1999; Walker, 2004).

Future Directions

Clearly, we need to continue to explore new models of professional development and their efficacy. Are there specific strategies that are more likely to be effective with specific populations? At what level must practices be implemented to result in real, lasting change that enhances children's literacy learning? Continuing attention should also be paid to the tools used to assess literacy environments and practices. We now have a better understanding of the literacy materials available in typical early childhood environments, but what are the teaching purposes for these materials? Are they used strategically or randomly? How can we help community-based early childhood teachers make consistent and effective use of current knowledge on children's literacy learning?

Makin (2003) boldly states that we are in greater need of ideas about how to translate research into practice than we are in need of additional research. As seen in the interventions described here and elsewhere in the literature (Podhajski & Nathan, 2005; Showers & Joyce, 1996), sustained mentoring or coaching approaches appear to have great promise. They are also consistent with theoretical ideas advocating the power of a more skilled other in effecting learning (Kozulin, Gindis, Ageyev, & Miller, 2003). In both the long and short run, professional development appears to be the key to high-quality literacy programs for young children.

REFERENCES

Arnett, J. (1989). Caregivers in day-care centers: Does training matter? *Journal of Applied Developmental Psychology, 10,* 541–552.

Beach, S. A. (2001). *Preschool Literacy Practices Survey.* Unpublished instrument, University of Oklahoma, Norman.

Beach, S. A., Ball, R. A., Biscoe, B., Dunn, L., Ferguson, A., Han, M., et al. (2004, December). *Early steps to literacy: The impact of professional development on preschool teachers and the children in their classrooms.* Symposium presented at the National Reading Conference, San Antonio, TX.

Beach, S. A., & Kincade, K. (1992, December). *The effects of structured literacy experiences on the perceptions of four years of themselves as readers and writers.* Paper presented at the annual meeting of the National Reading Conference, San Antonio, TX.

Beach, S. A., Wassner, M. (Writers), & Stamps, D. (Producer/Director). (2005). *Early steps to literacy: Courses for teachers and directors* [DVD]. (Available from Center for Early Childhood Professional Development, College of Continuing Education, University of Oklahoma, 1801 N. Moore Ave., Moore, OK 73160.)

Bowman, B., Donovan, M. S., & Burns, M. S. (2001). *Eager to learn: Educating our preschoolers.* Washington, DC: National Academies Press.

Bronfenbrenner, U., & Morris, P. (1998). The ecology of developmental processes. In W. Damon (Series Ed.) & R. Lerner (Vol. Ed.), *Handbook of child psychology: Vol. 1. Theoretical models of human development* (5th ed., pp. 993–1028). New York: Wiley.

Burgess, K., Lundgren, K., Lloyd, J., & Pianta, R. (2001). *Preschool teacher's self-reported beliefs and practices about literacy instruction* (Rep. No. 2–102). Ann Arbor, MI: Center for the Improvement of Early Reading Achievement.

Christie, J. F., & Enz, B. (1992). The effects of literacy play interventions on preschool play patterns and literacy development. *Early Education and Development, 3,* 206–220.

Cress, S. W. (2000). A focus on literacy in home day care. *Australian Journal of Early Childhood, 25*(3), 6–12.

Dickinson, D. K., & Neuman, S. (Eds.). (2006). *Handbook of early literacy research* (Vol. 2). New York: Guilford.

Dickinson, D. K., & Tabors, P. O. (Eds.). (2001). *Beginning literacy with language.* Baltimore: Brookes.

Dunn, L. (1993). Proximal and distal features of day care quality and children's development. *Early Childhood Research Quarterly, 8,* 167–192.

Dunn, L., Beach, S. A., & Kontos, S. (1994). Quality of the literacy environment in day care and children's development. *Journal of Research in Childhood Education, 9,* 24–34.

Dunn, L., Han, M., Ferguson, A., Beach, S. A., Tseng, S., Biscoe, B., et al. (2005, April). *Integrating the literacy environment into preschool program quality.* Paper presented at the annual conference of the American Educational Research Association, Montreal, Canada.

Dunn, L., & Norris, D. (1999, November). *Exploring the quality of literacy and mathematics environments in child care and their influence on children's achieve-*

ment. Paper presented at the annual conference of the National Association for the Education for Young Children, New Orleans, LA.

Dunn, L., & Norris, D. (2001). *Group time events.* Unpublished instrument, University of Oklahoma, Norman.

Dunn, L., & Norris, D. (2002). ["Reaching for the Stars" Family Child Care Home Validation Study]. Unpublished data, University of Oklahoma, Norman.

Hall, K. (2003). Effective literacy teaching in the early years of school: A review of evidence. In N. Hall, J. Larson, & J. Marsh (Eds.), *Handbook of early childhood literacy* (pp. 315–326). London: Sage.

Hall, N., Larson, J., & Marsh, J. (2003). *Handbook of early childhood literacy.* London: Sage.

Harms, T., & Clifford, R. (1980). *Early Childhood Environment Rating scale.* New York: Teachers College Press.

Harms, T., Clifford, R., & Cryer, D. (1998). *Early Childhood Environment Rating scale–Revised edition.* New York: Teachers College Press.

Hyson, M., Van Trieste, K., & Rauch, V. (1989, November). *What is the relationship between developmentally appropriate practices and preschool and kindergarten children's attitudes toward school?* Paper presented at the annual conference of the National Association for the Education of Young Children, Atlanta, GA.

Kontos, S. (1999). Preschool teachers' talk, roles, and activity settings during free play. *Early Childhood Research Quarterly, 14,* 363–382.

Kontos, S., Howes, C., & Galinsky, E. (1996). Does training make a difference to quality in family child care? *Early Childhood Research Quarterly, 11,* 427–445.

Kozulin, A., Gindis, B., Ageyev, V. S., & Miller, S. M. (Eds.). (2003). *Vygotsky's educational theory in cultural context.* Cambridge, UK: Cambridge University Press.

Makin, L. (2003). Creating positive literacy learning environments in early childhood. In N. Hall, J. Larson, & J. Marsh (Eds.), *Handbook of early childhood literacy* (pp. 327–337). London: Sage.

McMullen, M. (1999). Characteristics of teachers who talk the DAP talk *and* walk the DAP walk. *Journal of Research in Childhood Education, 13,* 216–230.

Morrow, L. M., & Schickedanz, J. A. (2006). The relationships between sociodramatic play and literacy development. In D. K. Dickinson & S. B. Neuman (Eds.), *Handbook of early literacy research* (Vol. 2, pp. 269–280). New York: Guilford.

Neuman, S. B., & Dickinson, D. K. (2001). *Handbook of early literacy research.* New York: Guilford.

Neuman, S., & Roskos, K. (1990). Play, print, and purpose: Enriching play environments for literacy development. *Reading Teacher, 44,* 214–221.

Neuman, S. B., & Roskos, K. (1993). Access to print for children of poverty: Differential effects of adult mediation and literacy-enriched play settings on environmental and functional print tasks. *American Educational Research Journal, 30,* 95–122.

Neuman, S., & Roskos, K. (2005). Whatever happened to developmentally appropriate practice in early literacy? *Young Children, 60*(4), 22–26.

Pajares, F. (1992). Teachers' belief and educational research: Cleaning up a messy construct. *Review of Educational Research, 62,* 307–332.

Phillips, D. A., Scarr, S., & McCartney, K. (1987). Dimensions and effects of child care quality: The Bermuda study. In D. A. Phillips (Ed.), *Quality in child care: What does the research tell us?* (pp. 43–46). Washington, DC: National Association for the Education of Young Children.

Podhajski, B., & Nathan, J. (2005). Promoting early literacy through professional development for childcare providers. *Early Education and Development, 16,* 23–41.

Reid, D. K., Hresko, W. P., & Hammill, D. D. (1989). *Test of Early Reading Ability.* Austin, TX: PRO-ED.

Richgels, D. J. (1995). Invented spelling ability and printed word learning in kindergarten. *Reading Research Quarterly, 30,* 96–109.

Roskos, K. (1997, April). *Through the bioecological lens: Some observations of literacy in play as a proximal process.* Paper presented at the annual meeting of the American Educational Research Association, Chicago.

Roskos, K., & Neuman, S. B. (2001). Environment and its influences for early literacy teaching and learning. In S. B. Neuman & D. K. Dickinson (Eds.), *Handbook of early literacy research* (pp. 281–292). New York: Guilford.

Shanahan, T., Cunningham, A., Lonigan, C., Escamilla, K., Molfese, V., Fischel, J., et al. (2004, December). *The National Early Literacy Panel: Findings from a synthesis of scientific research on early literacy development.* Paper presented at the annual conference of the National Reading Conference, San Antonio, TX.

Showers, B., & Joyce, B. (1996). The evolution of peer coaching. *Educational Leadership, 53*(6), 12–16.

Smith, M., Dickinson, D., Sangeorge, A., & Anastasopoulos, L. (2002). *Early Language and Literacy Classroom Observation: ELLCO toolkit, research edition.* Newton, MA: Brookes.

Snow, C. E., Burns, M. S., & Griffin, P. (1998). *Preventing reading difficulties in young children.* Washington, DC: National Academy Press.

Spillane, J. P., Reiser, B. J., & Reimer, T. (2002). Policy implementation and cognition: Reframing and refocusing implementation research. *Review of Educational Research, 72,* 387–431.

Taylor, A., Dunster, L., & Pollard, J. (1999). … And this helps me how? Family child care providers discuss training. *Early Childhood Research Quarterly, 14,* 285–312.

Tout, K., Zaslow, M., & Berry, D. (2006). Quality and qualifications: Links between professional development and quality in early care and education settings. In M. Zaslow & I. Martinez-Beck (Eds.), *Critical issues in early childhood professional development* (pp. 77–110). Baltimore: Brookes.

Walker, S. L. (2004). Emergent literacy in family child care providers: Perceptions of three providers. *Journal of Research in Childhood Education, 19,* 18–31.

Wenger, E. (1998). *Communities of practice: Learning, meaning, and identity.* Cambridge, UK: Cambridge University Press.

Whitebook, M., Howes, C., & Phillips, D. (1989). *Who cares? Child care teachers and the quality of care in America: Final Report, National Child Care Staffing Study.* Oakland, CA: Child Care Employee Project.

Wing, L. (1989). The influence of preschool teachers' beliefs on young children's conceptions of reading and writing. *Early Childhood Research Quarterly, 4,* 61–74.

Young, J., & Beach, S. A. (1997). Young students' sense of being literate: What's it all about? In C. K. Kinzer, K. A. Hinchman, & D. J. Leu (Eds.), *Inquiries in literacy theory and practice: 46th yearbook of the National Reading Conference* (pp. 297–307). Chicago: National Reading Conference.

7

Individual Differences in Play Style and Literacy: A Bioecological Perspective

Myae Han
University of Delaware

The play–literacy connection has been one of the most heavily researched areas of early literacy learning and instruction in the last decade (Yaden, Rowe, & MacGillivray, 2000). Much of this research reflects an ecological perspective where both the physical and social environments are thought to have considerable influence on children's play activities and literacy development (Neuman & Roskos, 2001; Smith & Connolly, 1980). This view prompted the design of literacy-enriched play settings strategy where classroom areas are equipped with materials that encourage children to engage in reading and writing activities. For example, the kitchen area of a housekeeping center might contain empty product containers (cereal boxes, soft drink cans, ketchup bottles), cookbooks, a telephone directory, food coupons, message pads, and pencils. Research shows that this design strategy stimulates increases in the frequency of emergent reading and writing in play activity (e.g., Neuman & Roskos, 1992), which has implications for literacy skill development. Other studies show that print-rich play settings provide a context for literacy interactions between teachers and children (Neuman & Roskos, 1993; Vukelich, 1994) and among peers (Christie & Stone, 1999; Neuman & Roskos, 1997).

Literacy-enriched play studies emphasized the importance of play as a context for learning in young children's development (Roskos & Christie, 2001), focusing on the one-way influence of environment (physical and social) on children's emerging reading and writing development. The research assumed unidirectional relationships between the player and the environment, with literacy-rich settings or more competent others exerting a press on children to incorporate literacy into their play.

Current developmental theories, however, espouse a more dynamic view of human development. Contemporary theories intersect aspects of human nature and ecology (Damon & Lerner, 1998), emphasizing the active role of human motivation. Bronfenbrenner's (1995) bioecological perspective, for example, proposes the need to examine the interaction between individual characteristics and environmental factors in the study of human development, stressing that individuals both shape and are shaped by their surroundings. Bronfenbrenner explains that human development takes place through the processes of progressively more complex reciprocal interaction between an active, evolving "biopsychological" human organism and the persons, objects, and symbols in its immediate environment.

Roskos and Christie (2001, 2004) also raise the point that the active role of individual intention may have been overlooked in literacy-enriched play research. Defining play as a system of activity that arises from individual intentions as well as from settings, they argue that children have an active role in deciding what they want to play and how they play, raising the possibility that individual differences in play behavior may impact the play–literacy interface.

More than two decades ago, Wolf and Gardner (1979) discovered that young children show a consistent pattern of preferences toward play. These researchers delineated two "styles" of symbolic play (see Table 7.1) that were consistent over time and across a range of settings and materials:

- Dramatists, or children who exhibit a strong interest in people and who prefer to engage in sociodramatic play, games, and storytelling.
- Patterners, or children who display interest in objects and their design possibilities and who like to engage in constructive play.

These play styles appeared to have a considerable influence on what children play with, where they play, how they play, and with whom they play.

Literacy-enriched play interventions typically focus on sociodramatic play settings, where children's play style may mediate the effectiveness of this intervention. Dramatists, who show a preference for dramatic play activity, for example, are more likely to choose literacy-enriched dramatic play settings

TABLE 7.1

The Definition of Patterners and Dramatists

Patterners	*Dramatists*
• Display considerable skill and interest in making patterns, structures, and spatial arrangements with objects and materials	• Exhibit a strong interest in human surroundings: what others do, feel, and how they can be known
• interest in an object's mechanical and design possibilities, rather than in communication or interpersonal events	• Prefer and do well in games, sociodramatic play, and story telling
• object-dependent	• Object-independent

and therefore may receive more exposure to the intervention. Patterners, on the other hand, may choose to spend most of their time playing in the block and art areas and thus experience less exposure to the literacy-enriched play settings. Focusing on these two broad patterns of play behavior, this study was designed to see how individual differences in play styles might influence children's play preferences in literacy-enriched settings. Additionally children's literacy levels were also examined as potentially influential in their literacy-enriched play activity. What children know and can do as emerging readers and writers can impact their interactions with teachers and peers.

In brief, the study sought to understand the interaction between individual differences and the environment during free-play time. To understand the dynamic role of individual differences in play and literacy, two child characteristics were examined: play style (patterners and dramatists) and literacy ability (low and high). Three environmental factors (Roskos & Twardosz, 2004) were investigated: play settings, teacher interaction, and literacy activities. The overview of bidirectional relationships between these two sets of variables is illustrated in Figure 7.1. The study addressed three research questions:

1. How do children's play styles and literacy abilities influence their choice of play setting and types of play during free play?
2. How do children's play styles and literacy abilities influence their literacy interaction with teachers in free play?
3. How do children's play styles and literacy abilities influence their literacy activities in free play?

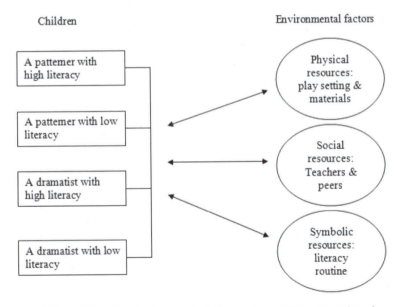

Figure 7.1.   Bidirectional relationship between target children and environment from the bioecological perspective. (Han, 2004, p. 24).

METHOD

The study was conducted in two phases. Phase 1 focused on identifying the focal children: patterners and dramatists with high and low literacy abilities. In Phase 2, focal children were observed for purposes of describing their play setting choices, the amount of interaction with teachers, and literacy activities.

Sample

Purposive sampling (Patton, 1990) was used to identify the focal children. This procedure depends on information-rich cases and a prolonged period of observation. The first phase of the study took place over a period of 3 months. The identification process was carried out in four Head Start preschools in a large metropolitan area in the Southwest. The four classrooms contained a total of 58 children, ages 3 to 5 years old, all from low-income families. Two classrooms had mixed populations of English- and Spanish-speaking children. The other two classrooms had dominant populations of English-speaking children with a few Spanish-speaking children. To identify the children's play styles, both the teachers and the researcher observed the children. The teachers were given an onsite informal lecture and discussion on play styles (definitions, characteristics, research background, etc.). Some teachers already recognized children's play styles as a result of this session. However, to collect rigorous data, the need for further observation was addressed. Therefore, teachers were asked to observe their children for 2 weeks. The teachers were asked to identify children in four categories during this observation: patterners, dramatists, mixed, and others or not sure. The play style record sheet with the list of children's names was given to the teachers. At the same time, the researcher observed each classroom and wrote field notes on each child's play activity in regard to play styles during the free-play time. Each child's play style was recorded on the same play style record sheet by the researcher. After 2 weeks, the teachers' and researcher's checklists were compared and each child's play style was identified. Among 58 children, 8 distinctive patterners and 6 distinctive dramatists were identified by both teachers and the researcher. The rest of the children showed "mixed" or were not observed for a long enough time.

To identify each child's literacy level, all 58 children were tested with three literacy-related assessments: (a) the Peabody Picture Vocabulary Test–III (Dunn & Dunn, 1997), a receptive vocabulary measure; (b) Get Ready to Read! (Whitehurst & Lonigan, 2001), a survey instrument that yields scores for early literacy abilities such as letter naming, phonemic awareness, and concepts of print; and (c) a modified version of the Concepts About Print test for preschoolers (Clay, 2000). Samples of the children's name writing were collected as well.

The results of literacy assessments were compared, and the children were categorized into high and low literacy-level groups. The children's play styles and literacy abilities were then cross-referenced, and 4 children were selected for further observation:

- A low-literacy dramatist.
- A high-literacy dramatist.
- A low-literacy patterner.
- A high-literacy patterner.

Literacy assessment results for these children are reported in Table 7.2. Both high-literacy-level children were able to write their first names correctly, whereas both low-literacy-level children were using invented spelling for their names using a few letters.

Three children were in the same classroom (Classroom A), and the high-literacy patterner was in another classroom (Classroom B). Classroom A had mostly English-speaking children and a few Spanish-speaking children. Classroom B had mixed population of bilingual, Spanish-, and English-speaking children. The low-literacy children were 4-year-olds; the high-literacy children were 5-year-olds. Literacy level and age were correlated. All 4 children were monolingual English speakers.

Data Collection

Phase 2 consisted of collecting qualitative data on the focal children during the free-play time over a 4-month period. Data sources included the following:

- *Video recording.* The researcher followed one child each day, videotaping his or her activities and interactions with others during the entire free-play time without stopping the camera. Each play session lasted

TABLE 7.2
The Results of Literacy Assessment of Target Subjects

Play Styles	Peabody Picture Vocabulary Test	Get Ready to Read!	Concepts About Print
The low literacy dramatist	77	3	3
The high literacy dramatist	107	17	7
The low literacy patterner	84	6	3
The high literacy patterner	98	11	4

between 30 to 60 minutes. The child wore a wireless microphone on the day of the video recording. The microphone was attached to a specially designed vest so that it did not disrupt play activities. A total of 1,277 minutes (21 hours, 17 minutes) of video recordings were collected from the four focal children. The total video recording time collected for each child was: (a) low-literacy dramatist, 335 minutes; (b) high-literacy dramatist, 300 minutes; (c) low-literacy patterner, 341 minutes; (d) high-literacy patterner, 301 minutes.

After the video recording, the digital videotapes were converted to movie files in a CD format for subsequent quantitative analysis, such as frequency counting, time sampling, and event sampling from the computer. A movie-capturing program and a compressing program were used to create MPEG files, and these files were then burned to CDs.

• *General transcripts and literacy incident transcripts.* These were developed from the video. These transcripts contained the description of the play activities in the different learning centers and interactions with other children and teachers. Literacy incident transcripts for each child were developed with only literacy-related activities, specifically reading and writing activities, phonological awareness activities, alphabet letter activities, and oral language experiences, such as dramatic play. This transcript contained conversations among children and teachers with actions being described in sentence statements.

Field notes, journals, member checking, document analysis, and peer debriefing were employed by the researcher. The researcher observed the children once a week (usually on Friday) as a nonparticipant observer, writing field notes and establishing rapport with the children. The researcher also wrote a journal with comments about the video data. These comments were shared with the teachers on a regular basis as a way of member checking. The researcher asked the teachers whether what the researcher had seen and learned from each child was correct or not. Each teacher's judgment was also added to the journal if the interpretation of the researcher was different from that of the teacher. The researcher also collected children's literacy products such as writing, drawings, paintings, and books that they had read. In addition, the researcher took pictures of artifacts during the free-play time.

Data Analysis

Data from the video were analyzed using time sampling, time measuring, frequency counting to measure children's use of play setting, and types of play displayed. Transcripts were coded and divided for each child to study quantity of interaction with a teacher and literacy activities.

Play Setting and Types of Play. To investigate children's choice of play settings, the amount of time that each child spent in a free-play area during play time was calculated from the CDs. When the child stayed in a certain play area for at least 1 minute engaging an activity, time was calculated based on setting entry and exit. If the child stayed at a certain center for less than 1 minute or was not engaged in an activity, it was coded as onlooking, wandering, or transition and excluded from the calculation.

Location is not necessarily a determiner of child activity. For example, children may engage in sociodramatic play in the writing center, play music in the manipulative center, or write at the block center. The cognitive level of play checklist was used to measure the frequency of different types of play, including functional play, constructive play, dramatic play, and games with rules (Piaget, 1962). In addition, Parten's (1932) social levels of play scale were measured, including solitary, parallel, and group play. These data are not reported in this chapter. A nonplay category was added to record academic activities such as reading, writing, doing worksheets, playing at the computer, and so on. The frequency of these types of play was measured from the video, using 5-minute interval time sampling.

Amount of Literate Interaction. To examine the amount of literate interaction with teachers and peers, the frequency of social contact with teachers was calculated from each child's literacy transcripts by counting speaker turns. For example, when a teacher said something to the child and the child responded to the teacher, it was counted as one turn. The number of teacher turns was counted as the frequency of literate interaction with teachers. The qualitative analysis was also performed, but not reported in this chapter (see Han, 2004, for a full description).

Proximal Literacy Activity. To examine the relationship between the play styles and proximal literacy activities, only literacy activities that occurred frequently or were enduring forms were considered. Children may show quick interest in certain literacy activity once, but then they never try it again. This kind of activity is not viewed as a proximal process nor does it seem to make significant contributions in the developmental process according to Bronfenbrenner (1995). To serve as a proximal process, certain interactions with the environment must have some degree of continuity, stability, and variation over time. To identify literacy activities as proximal processes, all literacy-related activities during play were identified from the videotapes, field notes, and children's documents. Literacy-related activities that occurred only once and for less than 3 minutes were eliminated from the list. Activities that lasted longer than 3 minutes without interruption or occurred more than one time in the field notes or videotape were selected. Six types of literacy activities were identified as proximal processes: emergent reading, interactive reading, narrative, phonological awareness activity, alphabet activity, and emergent writing (see Table 7.3).

Each episode was counted to see what types of literacy activities occurred and how often for the focal children. The number of proximal literacy activities was calculated from the literacy transcripts.

TABLE 7.3
The Definition of Proximal Literacy Activity Codes

Proximal Literacy Activity Codes	Definitions
Emergent reading	Children's attempt to read books or other types of print such as environmental (print independently).
Interactive reading	Interactive book reading with teacher or peers. It often includes discussion about the book or reading along with a teacher.
Narrative	Invented story telling without books. For example, children make up the story during the doll play or dramatic play. This ability to describe and tell a story is an important literacy skill (Paris, Wasik, & Turner, 1991).
Phonological awareness activity	Activities that increase children's awareness of the sounds of language such as rhyme, alliteration, sound matching.
Alphabet activities	Activities that promote identification of the letters of the alphabet including ABC books, alphabet blocks and puzzles, and alphabet charts.
Emergent writing	Writing activities using emergent forms of writing such as scribble writing, random letter strings, and/or conventional forms of writing.

RESULTS

The following reports the results from the choice of play settings and types of play, the amount of literacy-related social interaction with teachers, and proximal literacy activities.

Choice of Play Setting and Types of Play

Each child's choice of play setting and time spent in each setting is reported in Figure 7.2. Larger differences were observed between patterners and dramatists in setting choice in the computer, block, reading, and writing areas. Block and computer areas were more frequently used by the patterners than the dramatists, who spent little time in these settings. Dramatists spent more time at the art and dramatic play centers. They frequented the reading and writing centers more often than the patterners. Patterners, unexpectedly, spent con-

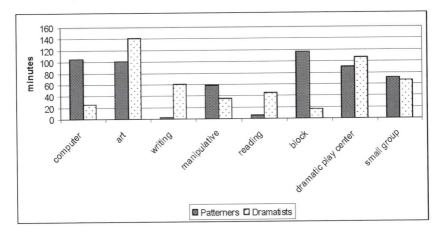

Figure 7.2.   The choice of play setting between the patterners and dramatists.

siderable time in the sociodramatic play area, although it was not clear whether they were engaged in dramatic play or other types of play.

Frequency of the cognitive play categories is described in Figure 7.3. Overall, patterners displayed constructive play and functional play, whereas dramatists exhibited dramatic play as expected. Considering this in light of the earlier finding, it can be inferred that even though these children played at the dramatic play center, their play was likely different from that of dramatists. For

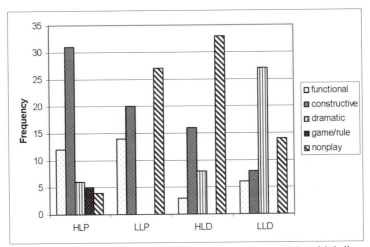

Figure 7.3.   The types of play in cognitive level. *Note.*   HLP = high-literacy patterner; LLP = low-literacy patterner; HLD = high-literacy dramatist; LLD = low-literacy dramatist.

example, a high-literacy patterner built a house with empty food containers in the dramatic play center instead of role playing.

The low-literacy patterner showed no instance of dramatic play during the period of the study, whereas the low-literacy dramatist showed the most dramatic play. The low-literacy patterner spent considerable time at the computer center, and nonplay was his most frequently recorded behavior. The high-literacy dramatist also showed a preference for nonplay activity, which was often performed at the reading and writing areas. The high-literacy dramatist was identified as a dramatist by both her teacher and a researcher during the first phase of the study because she spent a great deal of time at the dramatic play center pretending, interacting, and communicating with others. However, during Phase 2 of the study, the high-literacy dramatist engaged in less dramatic play and more reading and writing, and academic types of nonplay activity.

Amount of Literate Interaction With Teachers

The amount of literate interaction with teachers during the free-play was calculated by counting the frequency of literacy-related conversations (see Figure 7.4). The high-literacy dramatist had significantly more interaction with teachers during the literacy activities. Her dramatist tendencies combined with a high literacy level seemed to invite more interaction with the teachers. This increased interaction with the teacher may be one reason why the high-literacy dramatist showed more reading and writing activities during the second phase of the study.

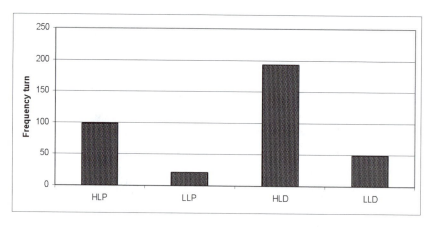

Figure 7.4.   Amount of literate interaction with a teacher.

Proximal Literacy Activity

Frequency of proximal literacy activity is reported in Figure 7.5. Overall, the two dramatists engaged in more proximal literacy activities than their peers with a patterner style. In addition, there were clear differences between the patterners and dramatists in terms of the types of literacy activities that children experienced during free-play time. Considering the fact that the data were collected during free play, where the choice of activities was given to the children, the activity choice may reflect children's interest and motivation.

The most striking differences between the patterners and dramatists were found on emergent reading versus interactive reading. Both dramatists experienced interactive reading with teachers or peers while the patterners showed no instance of interactive reading during free play within the time period of the study. Instead, the patterners preferred reading alone, which is categorized as emergent reading in this study. Interactive reading often involves teachers or peers who can scaffold their literacy knowledge and skills. Dramatists, it appears, engaged in more literacy-related interactions with teachers. Patterners engaged in more emergent types of reading such as reading environmental print.

Differences were also found in narrative activity. Both dramatists demonstrated narrative through invented storytelling, whereas both patterners showed no examples of narrative in the time of the study. Narrative activity usually occurred during dramatic play, such as telling a story to a doll. The low-literacy-level dramatist displayed frequent use of narrative during her play.

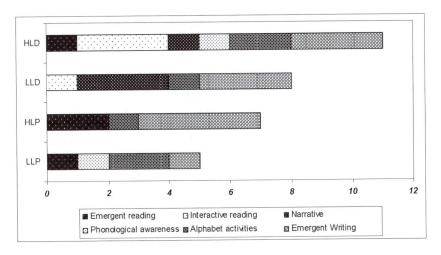

Figure 7.5.   Amount of proximal literacy activities during free-play time.

All the children were exposed to alphabet activities. Both classrooms had ample materials available for these alphabet-related activities, such as alphabet sorting toys, alphabet puzzles, ABC books, and alphabet letter pieces. Both dramatists and patterners chose to play with these toys occasionally.

Emergent writing took place in various play areas such as an art area, a writing center, a dramatic play center, and even a block center. The high-literacy patterner engaged in the most writing activities among the 4 children. The low-literacy patterner showed only one episode of writing activity.

It is also notable that all children, regardless of play style or literacy ability, rarely engaged in phonological awareness activity. Phonological awareness, the ability to attend explicitly to the phonological structure of spoken words, is one of the strongest predictors of future reading skills (Snow, Burn, & Griffin, 1998). The low-literacy patterner who often played at the computer, showed an interest in rhyming activity from the literacy software Miley & Bailey Preschool. The high-literacy dramatist's one incident of phonological awareness activity involved the sounds of letters at the writing center, where the teacher assisted the activity by encouraging, giving clues, and reinforcing the child's efforts.

DISCUSSION

This study described the influence of play style and literacy level on children's choice of activities in classroom play areas during free-play time. Results show that dramatists preferred more oral language activities, such as interactive reading and narrative activity, than their peers with a patterner style. Patterners, in turn, preferred solitary types of literacy activities, such as attempting to write and book browsing. In general the results show the active role of individual characteristics on play choices, and this should be recognized when planning an early literacy curriculum that is responsive to each child's characteristics, interests, and preferences. The 4 focal children in this study showed an active role in deciding how they would spend their time during free play.

The study does raise one word of caution, however. Dramatists seemed comfortable in the art, reading, and sociodramatic play centers where considerable language exchange and emergent reading took place. The patterners' favorite centers, such as the block center and the manipulative center, held fewer literacy materials, unless the teacher herself intentionally incorporated literacy materials into the area. In this respect, patterners may have lacked the opportunity to try out their literacy knowledge and skills during play time. Teachers, therefore, should support children's literacy exposure not only in traditional literacy-related areas, but also across play areas, thus creating a literacy-rich environment for all children in the classroom.

REFERENCES

Bronfenbrenner, U. (1995). Developmental ecology through space and time: A future perspective. In P. Moen, G. Elder, & K. Lúscher (Eds.), *Examining lives in context* (pp. 619–647). Washington, DC: American Psychological Association.

Christie, J., & Stone, S. (1999). Collaborative literacy activity in print-enriched play centers: Exploring the "zone" in same-age and multi-age groupings. *Journal of Literacy Research, 31,* 109–131.

Clay, M. (2000). *Concepts about print: What children have learned about the way we print language?* Portsmouth, NH: Heinemann.

Damon, W., & Lerner, R. (1998). *Handbook of child psychology* (5th ed.). New York: Wiley.

Dunn, L. M., & Dunn, L. M. (1997). *Peabody Picture Vocabulary Test–III.* Circle Pines, MN: American Guidance Publishers.

Han, M. (2004). *A bioecological view of play and literacy: Interaction between play predisposition and environment.* Unpublished doctoral dissertation, Arizona State University, Tempe, AZ.

Neuman, S., & Roskos, K. (1992). Literacy objects as cultural tools: Effects on children's literacy behaviors in play. *Reading Research Quarterly, 27,* 203–225.

Neuman, S., & Roskos, K. (1993). Access to print for children of poverty: Differential effects of adult mediation and literacy-enriched play settings on environmental and functional print tasks. *American Educational Research Journal, 30,* 95–122.

Neuman, S., & Roskos, K. (1997). Literacy knowledge in practice: Contexts of participation for young writers and readers. *Reading Research Quarterly, 32,* 10–32.

Paris, S., Wasik, B., & Turner, J. (1991). The development of strategic readers. In R. Barr, M. Kamil, P. Mosenthal, & P. Pearson (Eds.), *Handbook of reading research* (2nd ed., pp. 609–640). New York: Longman.

Parten, M. B. (1932). Social participation among preschool children. *Journal of Abnormal and Social Psychology, 27,* 243–268.

Patton, M. (1990). *Qualitative evaluation and research methods* (2nd ed.). Newbury Park, CA: Sage.

Piaget, J. (1962). *Play, dreams and imitation in childhood.* New York: Norton.

Roskos, K., & Christie, J. (2001). Under the lens: The play–literacy relationship in theory and practice. In S. Reifel (Ed.), *Early education and care, and reconceptualizing play* (pp. 321–337). New York: JAI/Elsevier.

Roskos, K., & Christie, J. (2004). Examining the play–literacy interface: A critical review and future directions. In E. Zigler, D. Singer, & S. Bishop-Josef (Eds.), *Children's play: The roots of reading* (pp. 95–124). Washington, DC: Zero to Three Press.

Roskos, K., & Twardosz, S. (2004). Resources, family literacy, and children learning to read. In B. Wasik (Ed.), *Handbook of family literacy* (pp. 287–303). Mahwah, NJ: Lawrence Erlbaum Associates.

Smith, P. K., & Connolly, K. (1980). *The ecology of preschool behaviour.* Cambridge, UK: Cambridge University Press.

Snow, C., Burn, M., & Griffin, P. (1998). *Preventing reading difficulties in young children.* Washington, DC: National Academy Press.

Vukelich, C. (1994). Effects of play interventions on young children's reading of environmental print. *Early Childhood Research Quarterly, 9,* 153–170.

Whitehurst, G., & Lonigan, C. (2001). *Get ready to read! An early literacy manual: Screening tools, activities, and resources.* Columbus, OH: Pearson Early Learning.

Wolf, D., & Gardner, H. (1979). Style and sequence in early symbolic play. In M. Franklin & N. Smith (Eds.), *Symbolic functioning in childhood* (pp. 117–138). Hillsdale, NJ: Lawrence Erlbaum Associates.

Yaden, D., Rowe, D., & MacGillivray, L. (2000). Emergent literacy: A matter (polyph-
ony) of perspectives. In M. Kamil, P. Mosenthal, P. Pearson, & R. Barr (Eds.),
Handbook of reading research (Vol. 3, pp. 425–454). Mahwah, NJ: Lawrence
Erlbaum Associates.

8

COMMENTARY:
Play, Literacy,
and Theories of Instruction

James E. Johnson
The Pennsylvania State University

This part includes three chapters on play and literacy relating to early childhood education (ECE) curriculum, teaching, and professional development. As a set, the chapters reflect theoretical, research, practice, and policy considerations very relevant to contemporary thinking about instruction in ECE; to varying degrees it may be fair to characterize them as a response to a perceived need to contribute useful information for transforming traditional ECE into state-of-the-art school readiness education.

A profound transformation has occurred in our field as we enter the 21st century. For the first time, 3- to 5-year-olds are widely viewed as intentional learners. As a result, there has been a shift away from traditional conceptions of developmentally appropriate practice toward the realization that we must develop, implement, and evaluate more deliberate and complex educative strategies in our attempts to foster learning and school readiness during the early years.

This commentary is framed by our theories of instruction—defined broadly to include present-day notions or best ideas about what and how to teach children enrolled in center-based pre-K and K programs. My approach is influenced by the current concerns about school readiness, but also by recent calls for an aligned and coordinated pre-K to Grade 3 (PK–3) ECE system of education (Bogard & Takanishi, 2005). Accordingly, after summarizing and commenting on the individual chapters, I briefly discuss each chapter's relation with school readiness concerns and make some general remarks relating to the proposed coordinated PK–3 ECE system, over and beyond the importance of these chapters for our theories of instruction for 3- to 5-year-olds. I believe that it is important to keep in mind longer term instructional goals and to encourage balanced expectations concerning readiness for children and schools, as opposed to only expecting children to be ready to achieve well academically at the next rung of the educational ladder.

Indeed, an important question nowadays when contemplating children's play and early literacy manifestations, ECE practices, and the aims of education may very well be this: How good is our eyesight? Even if we have good consensus on the targets of education during the early years, dialogues and debates about how to prioritize and achieve ECE goals remain contentious. For instance, although most would agree that ECE should be developmentally appropriate, enhancing, and responsive, many could take sides over whether emergent literacy trumps emergent personhood, or at least many could argue over whether this is a fair way to pose the question. Is our vision clear, or is it foggy due to the current sociopolitical educational climate following No Child Left Behind?

ECE is now at a very interesting and crucial three-way crossroads with its tremendous worldwide growth and expansion and public scrutiny. There is enormous pressure on ECE to be more accountable, standardized, and academic. An opposing response is to hold the line and insist on traditional child-sensitive practices. Yet a third way is to develop instructional theories and methods that are different from both of these extremes and recognize the need to unite the time-honored whole-child conception of the young learner with the view of the child as one who is an intentional learner who must be prepared for formal schooling.

ROSKOS AND CHRISTIE

Chapter 5 (this volume) by Roskos and Christie is a conceptual analysis of the implications of play and literacy research in our present-day educational policy context; it has as an organizing feature a look back at the past, an examination of the present, and suggestions for the future of ECE in general, and for instructional theories in particular. The authors present a cogent case for their argument that a considerable amount of classroom play by young children must now, in the 21st century, be connected with instructional goals in basic academic areas (new basics), and especially in the high-powered ones of math and literacy. Lengthy periods of stand-alone free play will no longer suffice in our era of developmental science, learning standards, and recognition that early literacy is a critical domain of childhood development.

In the section on the past, the authors review research and theory on the value of play in child development and for ECE curriculum planning and implementation—including some reference to the importance of play in ECE curricular models such as High Scope and the Creative Curriculum. Play is cherished in ECE because of its compatibility with the cardinal principle of teaching "the whole child" in a developmentally appropriate manner. Roskos and Christie review research linking play to physical, cognitive, social, and affective developmental domains and suggest that the strongest theoretical evidence of play's influence on the development of the whole child comes from Vygotsky and Elkonin's notion of play as a leading activity. Genuine play, they note, entails choice, self-awareness, and autonomous symbolic activity on the part of the child. When such is the case, play may be said to be at the heart of mental functioning and to be the parent of development, leading the child to the next level.

Roskos and Christie note that research on play and early childhood development has a long history and has generated considerable theoretical and empirical evidence for a positive connection between the two. This research tradition has led to many practical applications for curriculum and instruction in ECE. They discuss the uses of literacy-enriched play settings in pre-K and K programs as prime examples of fruitful pedagogy inspired by research on play and literacy development. Asserting play's value to other academic areas as well (e.g., math, science, and social studies), Roskos and Christie hint that elements of play (i.e., peer collaboration and heightened mental engagement) may benefit learning in general. Play's importance to self-awareness, reflection, and regulation are implicated as especially noteworthy and deserving of further research. Their hypothesis that play may have a mental engagement spillover effect that can foster acquiring new information in academic domains is a refreshing idea that should be followed up with more research. The notion signals that cognitive processes and operations, although difficult to measure and include in learning standards, are recognized as vital to ECE instructional theory—there is more to the curriculum and teaching than mere mastery of content.

The section on the present discusses why the 20th-century view of play as the "business of childhood" is being replaced by 21st-century reconceptualizations of play in ECE to meet new demands of our informational age. Currently new conceptualizations are coming about because of three megatrends that are having a profound impact on ECE in general, and play-based pedagogy in particular. Roskos and Christie's three megatrends are (a) early developmental science, (b) early learning standards and standards-based education, and (c) early literacy as a critical period of literacy development.

Developmental science, which combines neurobiological, behavioral, and social science research, is maturing to the point that sufficient evidence has accumulated to reject the view that infants, toddlers, and preschoolers are too young to learn. Accordingly, the child as an intentional learner is being increasingly accepted with important implications for ECE instructional practices and policies. Roskos and Christie illustrate this point by discussing Universal Pre-K and Early Reading First; the former is a policy vision of state-funded, high-quality ECE that is now gaining momentum in its realization, and the latter is a federal grant program that funds research applications that are taken to reflect a scientific approach to early literacy pedagogy.

Roskos and Christie assert that both these policy initiatives are underpinned by a skill begets skill premise that appears to be at odds with play activity. To the extent that these initiatives represent ultimate judgment on how ECE should be (perhaps a faulty vision?), I share this concern about the status of play in ECE. However, I believe that the skills beget skills premise as a base for ECE policy may have to make room for other principles from research. I predict that this will happen when the definition of what constitutes a scientific approach to the study of literacy broadens to include various methods of investigation of this complex educational topic.

The second trend concerning early learning standards and standards-based education also presents difficulties for play pedagogy in ECE. Two limitations of the standards movement in ECE are strong points of play. Both curriculum narrowing and what might be termed cognition narrowing are commonly heard criticisms of the educational standards movement. Standards-driven ECE tends to limit the scope of the curriculum with special focus on the high-powered academic areas of math and especially language and literacy, whereas play-based pedagogy focuses on the whole child and is usually expressed with an integrative and emergent curriculum entailing multiple curricular areas. Moreover, standards tap measurable overt performances and focus on declarative content knowledge and procedural knowledge; play is assumed to involve many covert cognitive processes that are difficult to assess empirically and so do not appear in the standards, although they are widely recognized to be important goals in ECE. Roskos and Christie give as an example of this the vital role of play in the development of self-regulation. Other complex cognitive and affective processes such as creativity and imagination could serve as further examples of this conflict between standards- and play-based approaches to ECE.

The third megatrend discussed in this chapter is the emergence and significance of early literacy as a recognized critical domain of early childhood development and education. As the authors note, an important reason why the new pre-K basics of math and language and literacy should nudge play off its privileged position in ECE is the extensive and intensive research that has been done, which has uncovered in considerable detail specific teachable and assessable components of early learning in these domains. Perhaps the value of play in ECE will be reestablished to its former position with more research. Applied research on the effects of play interventions may reveal important benefits for academic learning in different subjects, and practice-embedded research in classroom contexts may lead to more understanding about how effective play-based interventions work and their effects on academic, cognitive, and social-affective child outcomes. Then we would have a balanced appreciation of play and the basics and academic learning.

In the section "Looking Ahead," the authors advocate keeping educational play in the ECE curriculum through amplifying efforts to network it with the new pre-K basics. The demands of new early learning standards for basic skills that are needed for school readiness force ECE teachers to find new and better ways to tie play to specific educational aims. Roskos and Christie describe in some detail an Early Reading First project, the Arizona Centers for Excellence in Early Education, as an example. The different ways that this program uses the *Doors to Discovery* commercially published curriculum with English language learners are enlightening and also reveal how play can complement learning basic literacy and language skills during the early years. Roskos and Christie end by arguing that the basics should be extended to include self-regulation. Self-regulation development is served by mature play and it is critical for academic and social school readiness.

DUNN AND BEACH

Dunn and Beach (chap. 6, this volume) pose two questions: What literacy instructional practices are present in ECE center-based programs found in the community? How are these practices related to teachers' beliefs about literacy learning during the early years? Revisiting a 1994 study in which 30 preschool classrooms were assessed for the general quality of the centers and for literacy environment quality, these researchers lament the fact that nine classrooms had no literacy activities at all during free play and that few literacy-related activities were available across the 30 classrooms. A positive relationship was found between overall quality as measured by the Early Childhood Environment Rating Scale (ECERS) and the quality of literacy activities available, with literacy quality being significantly associated with teachers' certification status.

Dunn and Norris (1999) built on the 1994 study by assessing 71 ECE classrooms, 25 of which were accredited by the National Association for the Education of Young Children (NAEYC). Again a positive relation was found between literacy quality and general quality, with literacy quality higher in accredited programs and when directors and teachers had higher levels of general education and more specialized professional preparation in ECE. In addition, Beach and Dunn (chap. 6, this volume) review investigations that have used new assessment tools and more sophisticated analytic procedures such as path analysis. For instance, they describe findings from a number of studies that employed the Early Language and Literacy Classroom Observation scale (ELLCO), an instrument that allows for a finer and more complete assessment of literacy-related teaching practices and classroom settings. Finally, they review recent studies using assessments of teacher beliefs about literacy that are generally reported to be associated with ELLCO scores. Overall, the evidence presented in this part of the chapter supports Beach and Dunn's thesis that the quality of the language and literacy environment is a special case of general ECE quality, and furthermore that ECE quality depends on certain teacher characteristics such as education level, certification status, and specialized ECE professional preparation. Teachers' beliefs and knowledge about children's literacy learning, literacy environmental provisions, and instructional practices are also important.

Beach and Dunn then discuss a second set of studies on improving ECE literacy environments. Although not as bleak as at the time of the first edition of this volume, there is still a great need for improvement, especially in family child care programs. Intervention studies are presented having to do with either short-term redesign of preschool classroom instruction or with long-term, large-scale professional development efforts aimed at increasing teacher knowledge and judgment concerning optimal literacy environments and practices.

Beach and Kincade (1992) is an example of a short-term classroom intervention to change literacy practices and settings through working with the teacher. This study evaluated children's literacy behaviors in a university preschool following a 4-week intervention that consisted of adding various literacy routines. Beach and Dunn use this study to illustrate how teachers can help children begin to see themselves as participants in a literacy community. The authors suggest that often teachers need professional development to learn how literacy activity can be integrated with play and other learning activities in ECE settings. Long-term intervention studies reviewed by Dunn and Beach support the claim that teachers need professional development to make new literacy practices part of their teaching repertoire. To improve play and literacy instructional practices, teachers need to develop a balanced appreciation of research and theory on the one hand, and the value of personal experiences and learning from role models and mentors on the other hand.

The authors are correct to stress the need for quality teacher preparation and development in the literacy and play area of ECE pedagogy. However, it is also important to keep in mind that quality teacher education programs should aim to graduate new teachers who realize that they do not have to limit themselves to definitions and formulations given to them by their teachers, researchers, or policymakers. ECE practitioners should be professionally prepared to conceptualize and employ play pedagogies within their own evolving theory of practice (Wood & Attfield, 2005). Moreover, teachers need freedom and administrative support to try out their own new ideas as well as those suggested by cutting-edge research in the play and literacy curricular area.

There are currently available in the ECE literature a number of innovative intervention techniques related to literacy and play that can provide content for preservice and in-service professional development in addition to the ones noted by Dunn and Beach. One example is the aforementioned Paley model, which is becoming increasingly influential in ECE (McNamee, 2005; Wiltz & Fein, 1996). Paley's storytelling/story-acting methods represent a formal classroom procedure designed to generate social, multimodal literacy through play. Her techniques focus attention on promoting children's literacy-making behaviors that support the development of a classroom narrative culture (Groth & Darling, 2001; Nicolopoulou, 2002).

Three additional play-based pedagogies related to literacy are (a) workshop pedagogy (Trageton, 1994), (b) Playworlds (Baumer, Ferholt, & Lecusay, 2005; Lundqvist, 1995; Rainio, 2005), and (c) improvisational play intervention (Lobman, 2003, 2006). These strategies are designed for older children in kindergarten and the primary grades. In simplified form, they are suitable for use with preschool children as well.

Workshop pedagogy, developed by teacher educator and play researcher Arne Trageton, has been used in Norway for more than 25 years and is now used in many other countries as well. Children in small groups work and play with concrete art and craft materials such as blocks, flexible materials, paper, clay, and rigid materials; their activities center around a common theme such as "our village." In social constructive play children make two- and three-dimensional representations of aspects of the theme, such as people, cars, shops, and houses. Children then dramatize what might happen in their constructed thematic environment. Next, from their experiences the children have had so far doing the workshop activities, they are asked to make up a story related to their special theme, about which they write narratives or draw pictures depending on their ability. Finally, the teacher can guide the group to do math around what they have made in the earlier stages of the workshop pedagogy that entailed work with concrete materials or based on their story narratives or play enactments. The teacher is a discussion facilitator during all the phases of the workshop pedagogy. More recently, Trageton (2002a, 2002b) advocated the use of word processors so that children can publish books, classroom newspapers, and magazines in a collaborative manner, doing their reading and writing as purposeful pursuits assisted by technology.

Playworlds was developed in Finland by Lundqvist (1995). Children and adults co-create a fantasy world based on fables and folk tales and children's literature. For an extended period of time part of the classroom is turned into an imaginary world with teachers and children role playing characters and commentators. Teachers scaffold the children in their creative behaviors and lead them from free play to more organized school activities involving academic subjects (Baumer et al., 2005; Rainio, 2005). A related technique was used by Tyrrell (2001) in her first-grade classroom. She successfully used fantasy figures to develop literacy in her students, sustaining over the entire school year an imaginative classroom environment in which literacy learning flourished and children's imaginations were extended and enriched.

Improvisational play intervention is a method whereby teachers and children create a playful and imaginative world together without employing prescripted material, as is the case in Playworlds (Lobman, 2003, 2006). Lobman has explored the use of improvisation as a cultural art form that can be used in the ECE classroom to enhance responsive teaching and teacher–child relations. In this method teacher–child interactions are viewed as an ensemble where teachers pick up on children's cues and find ways to enhance and extend their activity using various improvisational principles such as "Don't negate," and "Yes and" (Lobman, 2006). Mutual responsiveness and choice making are used to generate successful scenes and play episodes from scratch—using whatever materials are available. Teachers are urged to create classroom environments and to allow for enough time to support spontaneous child–child narrative activity, but to be skillful partners themselves when needed during improvisational play. This technique helps teachers learn how to play better with children, a worthy goal in itself, and one often neglected in teacher education. Improvisational play, like the other methods already mentioned, rests on a social and multiple symbol system view of literacy (Bearne, 2003).

HAN

Han (chap. 7, this volume) begins by noting the considerable attention given by ECE researchers and practitioners over the years to the use of literacy-enriched play settings as an instructional strategy to foster emergent literacy and play development. Han then raises the important concern that children do various actions and have different experiences with the same materials and play settings and that we need to learn more about how individual difference variables interact with environmental setting variables. She argues that we need to become more informed and sensitive to individual differences among young children to make more suitable arrangements that are responsive to them as we seek to promote higher levels of play and literacy during the early years.

Three theoretical underpinnings of this research are Bronfrenbrenner's (1995) bioecological model that posits there is a complex reciprocal interaction between the person and the objects and symbols in the person's immediate environment, Roskos and Christie's (2001) emphasis on individual intentions influencing a person's actions in play–literacy settings, and Wolf and Gardner's (1979) work identifying two styles of pretend play—person-oriented dramatists and object-oriented patterners—as an important personality dimension affecting the play of young children.

Han designed and implemented a two-phase, multiple methods small sample size investigation to explore young children's play and literacy behaviors as a function of their individual play styles and level of literacy ability. She focused on four preschoolers who were deemed, after careful Phase 1 research assessments, to be either high or low in literacy, and to be either a play dramatist or a play patterner. In the second phase she analyzed 5 or more hours of video recordings of free-play observations per child to score each child's preferences for play setting and behavior as well as to estimate the extent of each child's literate interaction with a teacher during free play. She also assessed each child's amount of proximal process literacy activity during free play (i.e., emergent reading, interactive reading, alphabet activity, emergent writing, narrative making, and phonological awareness activity). Following Bronfenbrenner's definition of proximal process behavior, a given type of literate activity had to happen more than once and each occurrence had to last for at least 3 minutes without interruption to count. A number of findings supported her general argument that individual differences in early play style and literacy ability exert an active influence on opportunities for play and nonplay activities in the classroom. These opportunities, in turn, relate to literacy experiences.

A good example of how person and environmental variables interact was the finding that the child who was judged to be a high-literacy patterner stacked empty food containers to make a house in the literacy-enhanced dramatic play center instead of role playing. Hence, a different type of play, constructive, was manifest, yet one not without significance for emergent literacy. Although oral vocabulary probably is not stimulated in this play episode, other components of literacy were stimulated, such as letter and word knowledge. Noteworthy also is that this child tried to read the print on the wall of the dramatic play center and on puzzles. The solitary nature of these literacy activities during play should not go unnoticed.

Of further significance is the fact that the two patterners in Han's study also showed no occasion of interactive reading with peers or with teachers. Rather they did their reading alone during free play. Not experiencing this form of literacy in a social context precluded peer or teacher scaffolding of their literacy knowledge and skills. Han discussed this finding by noting that oral language development can suffer for patterners as a result—compared to the dramatists who are doing much of their literacy actions with others. This finding alerts ECE practitioners that some children, due to their play propensities, may not be deriving as much benefit as do other children from literacy opportunities in the classroom. Patterners may not be as receptive to teachers' attempts to build an inclusive community of literate players, such as in the tradition of Paley's narrative approach to the curriculum (McNamee, 2005; Wiltz & Fein, 1996). As yet research tells us little about individual differences in children's response to group-based teaching strategies for narrative and play expression in the classroom.

Another significant observation in the Han study was that the high-literacy patterner was seen doing the most writing of the four children—and usually in the writing, art, or literacy-enhanced dramatic play centers. On the other hand, the low-literacy patterner showed writing only once and it occurred in a block center. This child sat for 20 minutes on the floor using a chair as a table on which to write on a paper letters and various drawings. He brought the literacy materials over to the block center to do this. Han speculates that the child must have felt more comfortable doing writing in the block center than in the writing center and applied attachment theory in her interpretation that this may have been a form of affective self-scaffolding. The child may have had a strong emotional tie to the blocks.

Another compatible explanation for this episode is suggested by Renninger (1990, 1992) who has theorized that individual interest is a potent regulator of psychological activity in young children. Interest here refers to stored knowledge and value for a class of events or activities and as such can serve as a powerful organizer for intentional and goal-directed behaviors. Renninger has found that individual interest can increase attention and memory for tasks and can increase persistence when under stress, as well as positively influence social and object play. Young children's play with an identified object of interest, such as blocks, can lead their play with other objects for which they have some knowledge but perhaps less interest. Objects of interest are used to explore new possibilities for an activity, make challenges, and construct a repertoire of actions that can transfer to other tasks or play situations (Renninger, 1990). Further research should examine in addition to general play styles how particular objects of interest are involved in literacy and play development.

DISCUSSION AND CONCLUSIONS

This commentary's introduction noted ECE's current preoccupation with school readiness and how the three chapters in this part may be viewed as a response to this national trend in the field. Roskos and Christie's (chap. 5, this volume) conceptual and policy analysis chapter traces the history of theory and research on play and child development, presents an explanation for why play is now threatened, and then proposes ways to improve how play can be used in ECE. Roskos and Christie, it would appear, are arguing that we can best help young children get ready for school by accepting the premises of the policy shifts that have resulted in the 21st century due to the standards movement and due to a new perspective on early reading instruction that has come about from "scientifically based reading research." However, it is also critical that we should not abandon play. Play serves the growth of self-regulation and self-awareness and symbolic reflection during the early years, and it can and should be effectively networked with other instructional methods across learning domains and activity centers.

Dunn and Beach's (chap. 6, this volume) research review also relates directly to the theme of school readiness. Their interest in the correlates and determinants of literacy quality and in interventions to foster this quality is based on the belief that promoting emergent literacy in young children is very important in helping children be prepared for school. Although they do not make explicit their reasons for advocating professional development in relation to literacy beliefs and knowledge, one can surmise that this goal looms large in importance because of its connection to school readiness. One way to reduce the number of poorly prepared students who do not take to reading automatically is to increase the number of quality ECE programs that focus on emergent literacy.

School readiness is an urgent concern today given the pressing social problems in our country; there are enormous achievement gaps relating to social class and minority group status. School readiness is aided by having widely available high-quality ECE programs. We know that such programs are characterized by developmentally responsive teaching, appropriate and engaging materials, literacy curricular activities, parent involvement, and most important of all, having high-quality ECE teachers. Excellent teachers are essential for helping children overcome pervasive and persistent educational shortcomings. To obtain this workforce we need the professional development of teachers in the special areas of child development and ECE (Bowman, Donovan, & Burns, 2001; Shonkoff & Phillips, 2000), including teacher training in play and literacy instruction.

Good teacher education programs are needed to prepare high-quality ECE teachers. This mandate is supported by a position paper by the Association for Childhood Education International (ACEI, 2004) and by a white paper by the American Association of Colleges for Teacher Education (AACTE, 2004). Support is also provided by revised and improved standards for ECE teacher preparation from the NAEYC and the National Council for Accreditation of Teacher Education (Hyson, 2005). These standards and recommendations recognize that there are new challenges marked by cultural and linguistic diversity and changing family structures, geographic locations, and values. Achieving good teacher education programs to prepare teachers to help children get ready for school is one side of the coin; the other side of the coin is to have these programs set to produce teachers to work in the newly proposed aligned and coordinated PK–3 educational settings.

Han's (chap. 7, this volume) tie-in to school readiness is implied or indirect. One implication of her research is the need to better prepare teachers to provide more developmentally responsive learning arrangements in play and literacy centers, with special attention to young children who seem more object-oriented or person-oriented. This work is a welcomed reminder that individually appropriate education entails attention to personal traits such as ability level and play style, and not just consideration of molar attributes such as children's ethnicity, socioeconomic status, or exceptionality. Children will be more ready for their subsequent schooling when they are afforded play and emergent literacy experiences in the classroom that take into account child characteristics on both the molecular and the molar levels.

This commentary's introduction also mentioned that the current PK–3 initiative in the public schools is an important backdrop when discussing school readiness and can also be a useful framework for discussing the three chapters in this part. School reform based on an aligned and coordinated PK–3 educational system is based on research in ECE and child development and convincing logical arguments (Bogard & Takanishi, 2005; Kauerz, 2006). The Foundation for Child Development in New York is promoting the PK–3 initiative, which is gaining increasing attention in state departments of education across the country.

The PK–3 vision is developmental at its core and as such is a hopeful and humanistic vision that can serve as tonic for hard-line school readiness discourse that is prevalent in the United States today. Externally, this vision encompasses universal availability of the full range of state-funded programs for 3- and 4-year-olds (e.g., school- and community-based prekindergartens, Head Start, and family child care), all-day kindergarten, and small adult–child ratios in the primary grades. More significantly, this vision presumes that school readiness is a two-way street. Not only must the preschool years include developmentally enriching experiences to enable young children to gain the most from their first classroom learning encounters, but schools must also be responsive to the individual variation that young students bring to the classroom. Teachers need to be sensitive and responsive to differences in the needs and interests of specific children in their class, as well as being knowledgeable about child development in general, and about specific curriculum content (Graue, 2006).

Another defining feature of the PK–3 initiative as an attempt to create an aligned and coordinated ECE system is a major emphasis on the alignment of curriculum and learning, standards, and assessment—horizontally, vertically, and temporally (Kauerz, 2006). Horizontal alignment refers to matching up standards, curriculum, and assessments within a single grade level; vertical alignment refers to the same across grade levels; and temporal alignment concerns the child's learning over the entire calendar year, which then also includes learning in the summer between grade levels. Continuity of learning experiences is needed for education to be developmentally sound. PK–3 aspires to provide such education for children and their families during the crucial formative years. The PK–3 initiative aims for a seamless system of curriculum, assessment, and teacher preparation.

The PK–3 movement challenges ECE researchers and practitioners to maintain a holistic and contextualized view of the young child. As Roskos and Christie (chap. 5, this volume) suggest, the days have passed when we would ask whether play and socializing goals or learning and academic goals should be included in programs for young children. ECE in the 21st century does not operate in such an either–or mode. Both play and learning are important, just like what happens to the child at home and at school are both important. "Learnful" play and playful learning are both critical factors for successful curricular planning and implementation from prekindergarten through third grade. Having this outlook on play and learning is especially important for successful realization of the PK–3 approach because play and learning have often been dichotomized in the past with play as something preschoolers do and learning as something school-age children do. Play and learning need to be combined for ECE to be developmentally appropriate, responsive, and engaging over the range of years represented by the PK–3 approach. In general, the PK–3 vision requires that we foreground learning as taking place in a dynamic system that includes multiple and interacting dimensions of development-affective, cognitive, social, physical, and spiritual. Networking play with learning should help us meet this requirement.

For many years the field of ECE has accepted the view that playing well and developing well go together. Educational standards and mastering basic skills especially in the area of emergent literacy are new emphases in ECE that influence instructional theorizing about play. The pedagogical notions and techniques found in the play and literacy movement seem to be on the right path to serve ECE in the 21st century. Blended curriculum such as found in the Arizona ECE model is a good example of adopting the play and literacy movement's both–and as opposed to an either–or stance when it comes to academic goals and social-emotional goals. Later on hopefully the graduates of such ECE programs will do well academically and also be able to make friends readily.

However, I believe that ECE should not be turned into merely school readiness education. ECE should be valued for its own sake first and foremost. ECE is more than a transition from home to school, and more than a way to get ready to achieve academically at the next grade level. We must ask this: Are we paying sufficient attention to the needs and interests of young children in the here and now? Even if a child for some reason would not go on in school, a certain amount of attention should be given to literacy and the new basics anyway. However, excessive, misdirected focus on the child's future in school can cost too much. Sadly, one child who wanted to be a teacher at the start of the kindergarten year said at the end of the school year to my wife (who is a child mental health professional who works with young children in their homes, schools, neighborhoods and communities), "I don't like school anymore."

Later on we thought how awful that the kindergarten experience over the year somehow killed this child's enthusiasm for school and education. We suspect the culprits are narrow curriculum, too much testing, and direct instruction.

We cannot let standards for content and basic skills learning dictate our instructional theories, policies, and practices in ECE. Too much is left out. We would be forgetting about the complex cognitive-affective processes that underlie the various performances we can assess. For example, child choice and perceived control promote child concentration and support eagerness to learn. We need ECE classrooms that are wholesome social-affective systems. Sensitive and nurturing teachers are the *sine qua non* of high-quality ECE. These teachers also need to support imagination and creativity and playfulness in young children.

To reiterate, clearly we need a balanced appreciation for literacy and other basics on the one hand, and for playfulness, imagination, and creativity on the other hand. To achieve these aims, programs following the path of the play and literacy movement should consider incorporating to some extent the playful pedagogies cited and briefly described in this chapter (i.e., Paley's narrative model, workshop pedagogy, Playworlds, and play improvisation). Professional development of teachers is a key ingredient to turn play and literacy research and theory into better ECE policies and practices.

Finally, I recommend that we fix our gaze on PK–3 as a catalyst for meaningful educational reform that is based on developmental research and a progressive agenda. We need research to learn more about how to influence play so that it helps growing literacy and introduces and models literacy concepts appropriate across these grade and age levels. Recognizing the changing meaning of play and literacy throughout the PK–3 span is necessary for supporting a seamless, coherent, and aligned system of ECE. Literacy and play research in the years ahead must attend to building an empirical base for constructing informed instructional theories that can help us back the right educational policies for fostering the best practices.

REFERENCES

American Association of Colleges for Teacher Education. (2004). *The early childhood challenge: Preparing high-quality teachers for a changing society.* Washington, DC: Author.

Association for Childhood Education International. (2004). *Preparation of early childhood teachers.* Olney, MD: Author.

Baumer, S., Ferholt, B., & Lecusay, R. (2005). Promoting narrative competence through adult-child joint pretense: Lessons from the Scandinavian educational practice of Playworld. *Cognitive Development, 20,* 576–590.

Beach, S., & Kincade, K. (1992, December). *The effects of structured literacy experiences on the perceptions of four-years of themselves as readers and writers.* Paper presented at the annual meeting of the National Reading Conference, San Antonio, TX.

Bearne, E. (2003). Rethinking literacy: Communication, representation and text. *Reading Literacy & Language, 37*(3), 98–103.

Bogard, K., & Takanishi, R. (2005). PK-3: An aligned and coordinated approach to education for children 3 to 8 years old. *Social Policy Report: Giving Child and Youth Development Knowledge Away, 19*(3), 1–23.

Bowman, B., Donovan, M., & Burns, M. (Eds.). (2001). *Eager to learn: Educating our preschoolers.* Washington, DC: National Academy Press.

Bronfenbrenner, U. (1995). Developmental ecology through space and time: A future perspective. In P. Moen, G. Elder, & K. Luscher (Eds.), *Examining lives in context* (pp. 619–647). Washington, DC: American Psychological Association.

Dunn, L., & Norris, D. (1999, November). *Exploring the quality of literacy and mathematics environments in child care and their influence on children's achievement.* Paper presented at the annual conference of the National Association for the Education of Young Children, New Orleans, LA.

Graue, E. (2006). This thing called kindergarten. In D. Gullo (Ed.), *K today: Teaching and learning in the kindergarten year.* Washington, DC: National Association for the Education of Young Children.

Groth, L., & Darling, L. (2001). Playing "inside" stories. In A. Goncu & E. Klein (Eds.), *Children in play, story, and school* (pp. 220–237). New York: Guilford.

Hyson, M. (Ed.). (2005). *Preparing early childhood professionals: NAEYC's standards for programs.* Washington, DC: National Association for the Education of Young Children.

Kauerz, K. (2006, January). *Ladders of learning: Fighting fade-out by advancing PK-3 alignment* (Issue Brief No. 2). New York: New America Foundation Early Education Initiative.

Lobman, C. (2003, May). The BUGS are coming! Improvisation and early childhood teaching. *Young Children, 58,* 18–23.

Lobman, C. (2006). Improvisation: An analytic tool for examining teacher–child interactions in the early childhood classroom. *Early Childhood Research Quarterly, 21,* 455–470.

Lundqvist, G. (1995). *The aesthetics of play: A didactic study of play and culture in preschools.* Uppsala, Sweden: Uppsala Studies in Education.

McNamee, G. (2005). "The one who gathers children:" The work of Vivian Gussin Paley and current debates about how we educate young children. *Journal of Early Childhood Teacher Education, 25,* 275–296.

Nicolopoulou, A. (2002). Peer-group culture and narrative development. In S. Blum-Kulka & C. Snow (Eds.), *Talking to adults: The contribution of multiparty discourse to language acquisition* (pp. 117–152). Mahwah, NJ: Lawrence Erlbaum Associates.

Rainio, P. (2005). *Emergence of a playworld: The formation of subjects of learning in interaction between children and adults* (Working Paper No. 32). Helsinki, Finland: Center for Activity Theory and Developmental Work Research.

Renninger, A. (1990). Children's play interests, representation, and activity. In R. Fivush & J. Hudson (Eds.), *Knowing and remembering in young children* (Emory Cognition Series, Vol. III, pp. 127–165). Cambridge, MA: Cambridge University Press.

Renninger, A. (1992). Individual interest and development: Implications for theory and practice. In K. A. Renninger, S. Hidi, & A. Krapp (Eds.), *The role of interest in learning and development* (pp. 361–395). Hillsdale, NJ: Lawrence Erlbaum Associates.

Roskos, K., & Christie, J. (2001). Under the lens: The play–literacy relationship in theory and practice. In S. Reifel (Ed.), *Early education and care, and conceptualizing play* (pp. 321–337). New York: JAI/Elsevier.

Shonkoff, J., & Phillips, D. (Eds.). (2000). *From neurons to neighborhoods: The science of early childhood development.* Washington, DC: National Academic Press.

Trageton, A. (1994). Workshop pedagogy—From concrete to abstract. *The Reading Teacher, 47,* 350.

Trageton, A. (2002a). *Creative writing on computers and playful learning: Grade 1.* Paper presented at The Association for the Study of Play annual meetings, Santa Fe, NM.

Trageton, A. (2002b). *Creative writing on computers and playful learning: Grade 2.* Paper presented at The Association for the Study of Play annual meetings, Santa Fe, NM.

Tyrrell, J. (2001). *The power of fantasy in early learning.* New York: Routledge Falmer.

Wiltz, N., & Fein, G. (1996, March). Evolution of a narrative curriculum: The contributions of Vivian Gussin Paley. *Young Children, 51,* 61–68.

Wolf, D., & Gardner, H. (1979). Style and sequence in early symbolic play. In M. Franklin & N. Smith (Eds.), *Symbolic functioning in childhood* (pp. 117–118). Hillsdale, NJ: Lawrence Erlbaum Associates.

Wood, E., & Attfield, J. (2005). *Play, learning and the early childhood curriculum* (2nd ed.). London: Chapman.

THE PLAY–LITERACY
SOCIAL CONTEXT

9

Social Contexts for Literacy Development: A Family Literacy Program

Susan B. Neuman
University of Michigan

Virtually unknown a decade ago, the concept of family literacy has come of age (Auerbach, 1995; Benjamin & Lord, 1996; Taylor & Dorsey-Gaines, 1988). Increased interest and awareness in the family as educator has sparked a proliferation of programs, publications, and public policies, all designed to broaden access to education and to enhance family skills in reading, writing, and communication. Although different definitions exist (Morrow, 1995; Nickse, Speicher, & Buchek, 1988), most programs are designed to improve the education of the mother or other caregivers to improve the quality of family life and the achievement of the child. Consequently, these programs address not only the parent or the child as literacy learners, but the parent–child relationship. It is presumed that the skills learned and practiced by the adult and the child produce an intergenerational and reciprocal transfer of skills.

A primary challenge for family literacy researchers, however, has been to understand the transfer process, particularly as it applies to families from diverse economic, educational, and cultural backgrounds (Connors, 1993). For example, although many program developers support a family strengths model that recognizes the importance of respecting cultural differences in childrearing practices (Darling, 1989), still, Auerbach (1989) argues, programs continue to perpetuate a transmission of school practices model. She suggests that the unifying assumption underlying these programs is school based: Parents are taught to transmit the culture of school literacy through the vehicle of the family.

Yet what characterizes the homes of successful literacy learners, both of middle and lower income, is the sheer range of opportunities to use language and literacy-related practices as an integral part of daily family life (Anderson & Stokes, 1984; Auerbach, 1989; Hart & Risley, 1995). Children and adults experience reading and writing not as isolated events but as part of the social activities with family and friends in their homes and communities. Literacy-related activity, therefore, often occurs in cultural contexts for action that are constructed by people in interaction with one another (Laboratory of Comparative Human Cognition, 1983). Teale's (1986) ethnographic study, for example, reported that for almost 90% of all reading and writing activities observed in 22 households, the focus of the activities was not on literacy itself; rather, literacy occurred as aspects of activities that enabled family members to organize their lives.

For young children in particular, these activities are likely to consist of talking, drawing, or playing, rather than adult-like behaviors like reading a book or writing a letter. Vygotsky (1978) argued, for example, that such activities as make-believe play, drawing, and writing can be viewed as different moments in an essentially unified process of developing written language. Studies by Dyson (1982) and Gardner (1980) among others suggest that the beginnings of literacy occur in all kinds of symbolic inventions, marks on paper, and gestural language. It is in these symbolic activities that the beginnings of writing and reading can be found.

Thus, it could be argued that the training of school-like behaviors overlooks the everyday routine involvement in literacy-related activity (play, conversations, drawing, writing) that is not captured in models of interaction based on didactic school practices. Rather, these everyday events involve children and their caregivers in a collaborative process of learning that must be adapted to the specific activity at hand. From Vygotsky's (1962) sociohistorical approach, the social context is viewed as an integral aspect of learning and development.

Revising the zone of proximal development to include these everyday processes, Rogoff's concept of guided participation emphasizes the active role of the learner. As the more skilled partner, caregivers in the course of routine activity guide children's participation in relevant activities, help them adapt their understanding to new situations, and assist them in assuming responsibility for managing problem solving (Rogoff, 1990). From their active involvement in the activity, children are thought to appropriate an understanding that may carry to future occasions and new situations that resemble those in which they have participated. Such communication is thought to occur through two focal processes: creating bridges of understanding from the known to new ideas, and structuring children's participation in activities through opportunities that both support and challenge their involvement (Rogoff, Mosier, Mistry, & Goncu, 1993).

From this perspective then, literacy learning for families may occur across a variety of situations, each of which may require mutual adjustments that provide the basis of intersubjectivity between adults and children (Neuman & Gallagher, 1994). This includes the implicit rules and demands and patterns of interaction that may either support or constrain literacy learning (Bloome & Green, 1984). For example, Tizard and Hughes (1984) reported that the home learning contexts of imaginative play, storybook reading, and games with rules created different expectations and adjustments by both parents and children to meet the demands of the specific situations.

In this chapter, I describe an intervention program designed to enhance guided participation and intersubjectivity between adolescent mothers and children. I argue that literacy learning for young children occurs across a variety of different contexts and interactions. From these findings, I posit that other mutual activities, including play and instructional projects, in addition to book reading may offer the richest potential for supporting children's early literacy development.

METHOD

Setting and Participants

The setting for this research was in a school-district-sponsored Adult Basic Education (ABE)/Graduate Equivalency Diploma (GED) program serving adolescent mothers or pregnant teenagers in an urban metropolitan area. The program was designed for 30 women to attend a literacy program, and a parenting education class, two or three mornings a week for a 3-month period, with accompanying day care provided for their young children (ranging in ages from 3–4 years old). Most of the mothers in the program were African American, averaging 19 years old, and all were on public assistance.

Infants and toddlers of adolescent mothers were provided free day care in a center located two blocks away from the school site. The center consisted of a large room (see Fig. 9.1), staffed by five paraprofessional women. Half of the room was devoted to cribs, playpens, and strollers, and the other half of the room was reconstructed as part of a collaborative effort between parents and staff to accommodate toddler play and literacy-related activities (Neuman, Hagedorn, Celano, & Daly, 1995). This included a large table for small-group activities and two sociodramatic play areas based on principles derived from previous studies (Neuman & Roskos, 1992, 1993): a fully stocked kitchen and a grocery store. Labels of common objects and environmental print were prominently displayed throughout the play spaces and literacy-related objects (i.e., egg cartons, cereal boxes, cash register) were included in each area. A small library of books along with dolls, pillows, a rocking chair, and a fish tank were designed to provide a homelike atmosphere for toddlers' explorations with language and literacy. Six toddlers (3 boys and 3 girls) and 6 infants (4 boys and 2 girls, ages 3–5 months) attended the center on a regular basis. The average age of toddlers was 2.4 years, ranging from 1.5 years to 4 years old.

Along with providing day care, the center was also designed to serve as a demonstration program, helping to enhance adolescent mothers' knowledge about child growth and development. Led by a home visitation worker, occasional parenting education classes provided mothers with opportunities to observe, through a two-way mirror and videotape monitors, child developmental patterns, typical play activities, and effective disciplinary approaches as demonstrated by the child care workers. Prior to our intervention, however, mothers were not encouraged to participate or interact with children in the center itself.

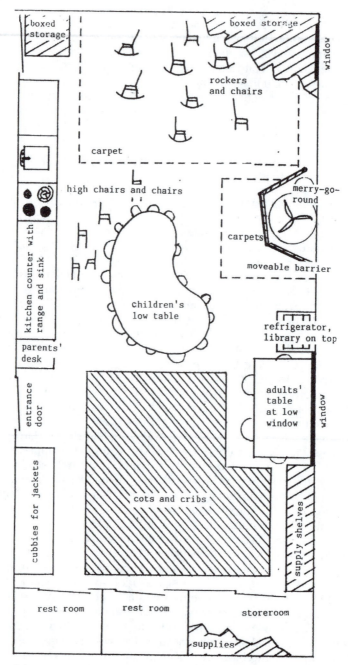

Figure 9.1. The day care environment: Before (this page) and after (facing page) intervention.

154

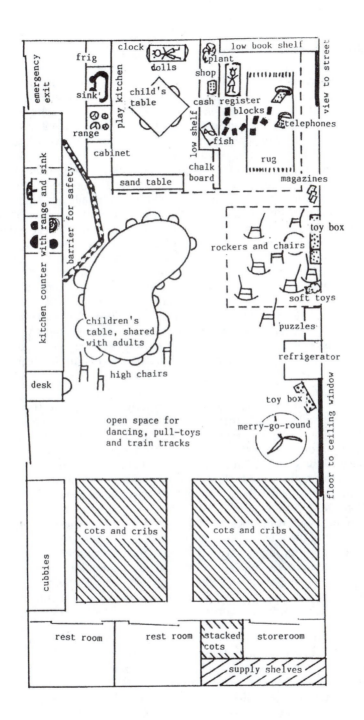

The Family Literacy Program

Our program was designed to more closely align mothers' literacy and parenting education classes to provide for ongoing opportunities for parent–child interaction. Much of the literature (Berlin & Sum, 1988; Landy & Walsh, 1988; Williams, 1991) has focused on the difficulties adolescent mothers experience when their children become toddlers (see review in Neuman & Gallagher, 1994); Thormann (1985), for example, identified a nontalking style of interaction, and a denial of childbearing concerns between teen mothers and their children. Further, Furstenberg, Brooks-Gunn, and Morgan (1987) reported that a large percentage of these children eventually need foster care. Therefore, the overriding objective of this program was to encourage mother–child communication through developmentally appropriate tasks and activities in the day care center. Language and literacy-related behaviors were seen as the tools through which these communication processes might occur for engaging children in close communication in a variety of tasks.

We constructed a model of the processes that seemed to reflect varying phases of support and responsibility on the part of the caregiver and child. Sharing much in common with the concepts of guided participation (Rogoff, 1990), and scaffolding (Wood, Bruner, & Ross, 1976), our aim was to describe these processes in a manner that might be used as strategies for parents as they engaged in the verbal and nonverbal exchanges of daily life. This model included four basic components (see Table 9.1).

Get Set.   In collaborating with children, caregivers need to consider the arrangement and structuring of the activity, so that children may participate at a challenging, but comfortable level (Lidz, 1991; Rogoff et al., 1993). Such arrangements require a degree of intentionality on the part of the caregiver to actively involve the child. Further, the caregiver needs to provide some level of metacognitive support, controlling and taking primary responsibility for higher level goals as the child engages at a level of which he or she is capable at the time (Diaz, Neal, & Vachio, 1991). This process of getting set, then, is dynamic, with caregivers adjusting their level of involvement to the level of perceived competence of the child. It involves an effort by the caregiver to recruit the child's attention (through nonverbal, verbal, and environmental cues), to focus, and to maintain the child's attention and goal orientation. Behaviors to enhance getting set might include orienting a child that it is now time to do the activity, communicating and giving the child a reason to pay attention, and encouraging him or her to focus on a particular topic of interest.

Give Meaning.   Within the context of joint activity, caregivers may accentuate certain features of the activity as being more relevant and meaningful than others. Through this process, children learn the attributed cultural values of what is important and what can be ignored. Part of this process includes the labeling of common objects (Neuman & Gallagher, 1994). Further, it involves an understanding of the relationships among objects and events through com-

TABLE 9.1

Definitions of the Four Processes in Guided Participation

Get Set

- Recruits the child's interest in an activity
- Gives child a reason to become involved in an activity
- Focuses children's attention on something observable, "Look at this ..."
- Attempts to keep their attention throughout an activity

Gives meaning

- Helps the child understand what is important to notice and the values associates with
- Labels objects that are seen in the environment
- Adds descriptive comments or elaborations about an object
- Adds animation or affect to objects to make the activity come alive and provoke interest
- Demonstrates or models a behavior

Builds bridges

- Makes connections to child's past or future: "Do you ever ..."
- Elicits connections from a child: "Tell me if ..."
- Encourages imagination: "Can you imagine if ..."
- Induces hypothetical, cause–effect type thinking: "What if ..."

Step back

- Gives the child a strategy for completing a task: "This is a way you an make it work ..."
- Encourages turn taking on the part of the child
- Provides elaborative feedback: "No ... it works this way ..." "How about trying ..."
- Responds to the child's initiatives: "So you are building a train?"

parison and contrast (Azmitia & Perlmutter, 1989). When they give meaning, caregivers share the importance and value of an interaction, as well as communicate through affect and explanation, how this information may promote further understanding (Lidz, 1991). Behaviors associated with giving meaning, therefore, might include the labeling of objects, adding affect to make the objects more understandable to the child, and elaborating on actions or objects.

Build Bridges. Once the context and meaningfulness of an activity is conveyed, caregivers may extend children's understanding by linking the activity to something that is either within or beyond the children's own experiences. This task is seen as essential for intellectual growth (Tizard & Hughes, 1984) by helping children make sense of present experiences by relating these issues to the past. It may also facilitate children's understanding of events that cannot be actually be perceived by encouraging them to employ their imagination to anticipate further activities. Sigel and his colleagues (McGillicuddy-De Lisi, Sigel, & Johnson, 1979; Sigel & McGillicuddy-De Lisi, 1984), for example, have described this concept as distancing, and have documented the association of these parental behaviors to cognitive development of preschoolers. Behaviors that build bridges may include making connections between what is going on now and other experiences either past or present, inducing cause-and-effect relations, and moving the experience from what caregivers and children can actually see in front of them to what they can imagine.

Step Back.   A crucial feature of participation is the transfer of responsibility for the managing of joint problem solving from caregiver to child (Rogoff, 1990; Wertsch, 1984). This includes facilitating the mastery of the task and providing encouragement and prompts so that the child can work toward independence and self-regulation. It requires caregivers to carefully limit their support when they see that the child is able move ahead or beyond his or her current level of ability (Rogoff & Gardner, 1984). Caregivers enable children to take over responsibility when they give children strategies and practice for completing tasks, encourage children to seek out activities on their own for their novelty and complexity, and help them to overcome their feelings of insecurity and anxiety associated with the unfamiliar (Lidz, 1987). Behaviors associated with stepping back include helping the child understand a principle so that he or she can take control of the task, encouraging turn taking, and providing elaborated feedback to induce strategic thinking.

Using this model, we structured an individually based intervention that followed a three-part cycle of instructing, coaching, and analysis. The first part of the cycle was to provide individualized instruction on one phase of the model. For example, we first discussed with the mother the importance of getting set, and then described different ways to recruit and maintain children's interest in an activity. We would use various examples from children's activities in the center, and then encourage the mother to describe common activities of their own in the home or community.

The second step involved inviting the mother to try out some of these suggestions with the children in the center. We asked the mother to read to the children from concept books or narratives in the library, to instruct them in a goal-directed task provided by the staff (e.g., writing a letter, building a tower with blocks, making shapes with dough), and to facilitate play with the children in sociodramatic play settings. Considering the age of the young children, activities were organized in 15- to 20-minute time blocks, and structured throughout the sessions in a counterbalanced fashion. During each session, one or two of us would observe and coach the mother, as necessary. Such efforts on our part included suggesting favorite books that the children might enjoy, taking aside a child who was being disruptive to others, helping the mother to employ a strategy with children, and debriefing informally together.

The third part of the intervention was an analysis of the activities. Here, one of the researchers and the parent viewed segments from videotapes of their observations together and made suggestions for helping the parent with the different tasks. Three hour-long sessions with each mother were scheduled over the course of the intervention, following a similar pattern. Segments were selected to highlight certain features of a particular phase of the model. The mother was then asked to recall the incident, to evaluate herself and the child's activity, and then to discuss what she might want to do differently if she were to do it again. Sometimes these sessions were merely confirmatory, highlighting certain practices of the mother; at other times, however, they were quite directive, as noted in the following session on building bridges.

(with Deria)

Researcher:	This is a great session. At the time you were concentrating on building bridges which was connecting what the children were reading with their experiences. Did you see how you did that?
Mother:	It just came out. I didn't know I was actually doing that.
Researcher:	You were saying things like, "Do you play with trains at home. Have you ever been on a train?" Then you asked him how come he liked trains so much. What was he going to do when he grew up? That's what we mean when we say you take the ideas in the book, and you move away from the book itself to the things that connect with their lives. Sometimes, ideas from the book put them in mind with an experience they already know.

(with Ramona)

Researcher:	What do you think of the session?
Ramona:	I was kind of rushing.
Researcher:	Why were you rushing?
Ramona:	I guess cause I'm older and I get it and I know what it is.
Researcher:	If you wanted to relate the book to the child's own life, what kind of questions could you ask?
Ramona:	Do you like to play like this? Have you ever tried this before?
Researcher:	So you can see to go through this book and teach them to treat it like flashcards, is to miss a lot of nice things about it. Slow down a little bit. Really, it's not sufficient for us to have children simply recognize the pictures in a book. That's important but it's also important that what is here is related to their lives and experiences. That way they can see that it fits into the world as they know it in some special way.

This three-step cycle was repeated over 12 one-hour sessions, beginning in January and running through June. In some cases, mothers interacted with their own children; however, on many occasions, they engaged in these activities with one or two other toddlers in the center. All sessions were videotaped, yielding approximately 12 hours of videotape transactions with children and researchers for each mother.

Data Analysis

To examine mothers' ability to guide children's participation and the potential variation across contexts, each taped session was divided according to the context of interaction (storybook reading, instruction, and play). Within each context, taped sequences were segmented into 2-minute intervals, equaling 7 to 10 intervals for each context per session. Two of these 2-minute intervals were then selected at random and transcribed verbatim. Transcriptions included verbal and nonverbal, or gestural exchanges. These data represented a total of 24 two-minute intervals of interaction within each context, representing 72 transcribed intervals in all for each mother.

Next, we coded the mothers' exchanges (verbal and gestural) in these segments using the definition of the processes within guided participation: get set, give meaning, build bridges, and step back. Each exchange was read holistically for gist rather than clause by clause. For example, "Look Kalief, see the fireman (in the book). He's rolling up the hose," was coded as helping the

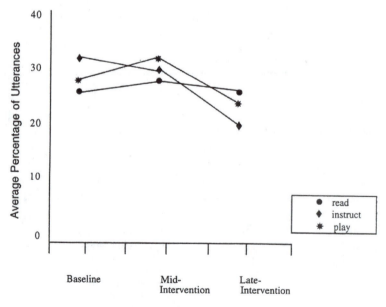

Figure 9.2.   Maternal exchanges in getting set.

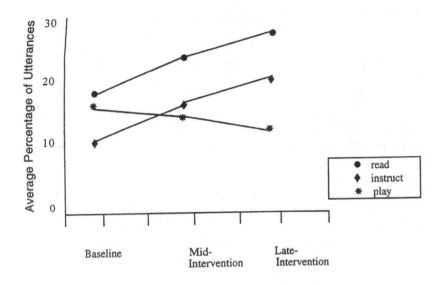

Figure 9.3.   Maternal exchanges in giving meaning.

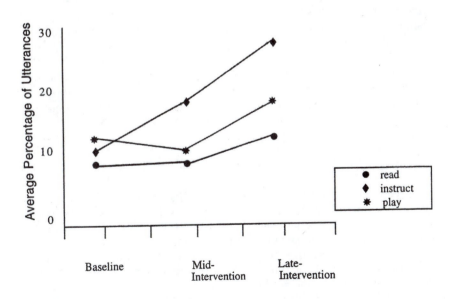

Figure 9.4.   Maternal exchanges in building bridges.

child give meaning. We then derived a percentage for each type of exchange from the total number of exchanges in the transcript.

To establish reliability, several transcripts were examined by myself and a research associate to refine the coding scheme. Transcripts were then coded by one of us and reviewed by the other. Disagreements were resolved through discussion, review of informal notes, and the judgment of the researcher most familiar with the context of the interaction. This procedure resulted in a high level of consistency in the coding of the transcripts.

We then calculated the average percentage of maternal exchanges (both verbal and gestural) for each context independently according to the processes in guided participation.

RESULTS

As reported in Figures 9.2 through 9.5, mothers' exchanges in getting set were slightly higher at the outset of the study for instructing than for reading or play. More exchanges were devoted to initiating and maintaining children's attention in a goal-directed activity (e.g., building a tower) and children's play than were observed in storybook reading. Toward the latter part of the intervention, however, although the pattern for storybook reading remained essentially the same, fewer exchanges of this type were observed in the instructional and play context, suggesting children's enhanced receptivity to the intentions of the mother.

Maternal exchanges of giving meaning were observed with greatest frequency in the reading situation throughout all phases of the study. A typical illustration involved Daria and her son, Barrington, as they read the story, "Harry and the Dirty Dog":

Daria:	Who's in the tub?
Barrington:	Harry
Daria:	Harry, that's right. [points] That's Harry getting scrubbed up. Do you see scrub brush? Do you see Harry? What's that? [points]
Barrington:	The bathtub?
Daria:	That's right, and Harry's mom is giving him a bath.

This context provided continuous opportunity for mothers to label objects and pictures, and to extend their meaning with additional elaboration of descriptive characteristics and related information. The instructional context, to somewhat lesser extent, also provided occasions for mothers to focus on what aspect of the task was important in the activity and the frequency of this type of exchanges appeared to be maintained throughout the study. Unlike the reading and instructional contexts, however, mothers' meaning exchanges in the play situation declined, probably reflecting children's increasing familiarity with the play objects and their meaning in the play setting.

As shown Figure 9.3, it appears that mothers' exchanges in the play context turned increasingly to building bridges. For example, Kalima and her daughter Delores are playing in the kitchen:

Kalima:	What are you making?
Delores:	Toast.
Kalima:	What do you like on your toast?
Delores:	[Running around through cabinets] I like bananas and peanut butter and raisins, and jelly. [Holds up a block] Want some?
Kalima:	That tastes good!

As the objects became known, exchanges with children appeared to reflect events outside the perceptual field, to encourage children's imagination in dealing with objects, events, and actions or symbolic activity. Increases in going beyond the events in the story to those in the past or anticipated in the future was also observed in the book context, but these exchanges declined in the latter phases of the study. No changes were observed in the instructional context throughout the intervention, suggesting that this particular situation may not have provided as much occasion for making demands on the children to infer from the observable present.

However, the instructional context clearly provided the richest opportunity for exchanges that encouraged stepping back, or the transfer of responsibility from mother to child. Kimberly (the mother) and Edward, a 4-year-old, are building with blocks:

Kimberly:	Are you going to build me a tower?
Edward:	Yup, and it's going to get higher and higher?
Kimberly:	Start with the large blocks, and then use the small blocks.
Edward:	I'm using these blocks [the larger ones], and I'm going to build you a big, big tower. Here go the window, so you can look out.

In this context, mothers' interactions seemed to provide for feedback and self-regulating strategies so that the child could increasingly take on aspects of the tasks. To a lesser extent, mothers' exchanges in the play context also appeared to be designed to facilitate children's independence and activity. As one might expect, the reading context did not seem to accommodate as many opportunities for stepping back as did the other contexts.

In sum, these graphic representations indicated that the frequency of mothers' exchanges was likely to be related to the situation created by reading, instructing, and play. Differences in the frequencies of mothers' exchanges were small in helping children to get set through involving and maintaining their involvement in the interaction. However, these differences were more striking for the other three processes. Although clearly not exclusive, the reading context seemed to provide the greatest opportunity for giving meaning, sharing with children the perceived value of objects and relationships, whereas mothers in the play context were more likely to engage children in building bridges, helping them to employ their imaginations in dealing with objects, events, and people. Finally, the instructional context seemed to provide a situation for mothers to hand over responsibility to children, assisting them in mastering particular skills and reducing their levels of support when the children seemed able to function independently.

IMPLICATIONS FOR LANGUAGE AND LITERACY DEVELOPMENT

Observations of language and literacy learning in the context of family and community relations suggest that children learn the values and the uses of these cultural practices through their everyday experiences of family life (Anderson & Stokes, 1984; Heath, 1983; Teale, 1986). In the process of arranging and guiding children's participation, caregivers support and facilitate children's growing understanding and problem-solving capabilities in learning (Rogoff, 1990). Consequently, we have argued that the process of guided participation, which involves the tacit forms of communication between caregivers and children in everyday joint activity, may more aptly describe the transfer of educational beliefs and behaviors from parent to child and children to parent than the prevailing school-based model found in many family literacy programs (Nickse et al., 1988).

Our study was designed to provide experiences and coaching to teenage mothers to enhance their communicative interactions in ways that might guide children's participation toward greater independence and responsibility. To do so, we developed a four-part model reflecting the processes of initiating, giving meaning, transcendence, and transference. The results of our analysis indicated that the young mothers were able through interpersonal communication to effectively encourage children from the perceptual toward the conceptual, as they engaged in tasks that required strategic thinking and planning. These results suggest that the model of getting set, giving meaning, building bridges, and stepping back may be a useful metaphorical device for structuring children's participation in challenging tasks. Taken together with our previous research, it indicates that through coaching, teen mothers are highly capable of establishing intersubjectivity through language.

As indicated in this study, however, the processes of interpersonal communication are clearly influenced by the social context. In this study, two of these situations involved the rather well-defined, goal-directed tasks of storybook reading and a learning task, whereas the play situation represented a less constrained setting. In each of these settings, we found that mothers' exchanges tended to be adjusted to meet the demands of the situation. Storybook reading appeared to best support interactions around the development of meaningful relations among objects and experiences. In this setting, children seemed to have the greatest opportunity to perceive or experience what culturally defined experiences were most important to note, to compare and to categorize based on perceptions and explanations of how events and objects relate. On the other hand, the play context supported interpersonal communication of events beyond the children's own experiences. More than any other setting, this context supported distancing strategies, described by Sigel and his colleagues (McGillicuddy-De Lisi, 1982; Sigel, 1985) as those classes of behavior that demanded the child to employ his or her imagination in dealing with objects, events, and people, and to plan and anticipate future events. In contrast to the other two settings, the instructional task seemed to create a climate where the adult could organize opportunities for children to develop mastery. In this setting, children's expectancies of success appeared to enhance their willingness to explore on their own, and to take increasing responsibility for the task demands. These results further extend the work of Rogoff and Lave (1984) and their colleagues (Lave & Wenger, 1991), examining the adjustments of adult–child interactions that occur within different task settings.

These results have important implications for language and literacy learning in family literacy programs as well as early childhood settings. If certain interpersonal interactions are supported or constrained in different situational contexts, it suggests that a range of activities and practices are critical for literacy learning (adult and child). Specifically, a broad array of activity in varying contexts may constitute the richest resource for literacy development. In this study, for example, play activities involved children in using language to express meaning, in symbolically transforming objects to create imaginary situations, and in making connections between their immediate personal world and activities that are important in the larger social world of family and community. All of these activities are central for literacy development. Therefore, as we have broadened the definition of what constitutes emerging literacy (Teale & Sulzby, 1986), so too, must we reconceptualize how literacy learning occurs among families to include the practical activity that may be adjusted to contextual variations. As Rogoff (1982, 1990) has reported in her extensive research, as have others (Lave & Wenger, 1991; Neuman & Roskos, 1997; Newman, Griffin, & Cole, 1989), rather than assume broad generality in cognitive activity, we must attend to the contexts in which this knowledge and these skills may develop (Rogoff, 1982).

Finally, our results suggest that caregivers' interactions emphasizing bridge building and transference were accompanied by the co-occurrence of children taking greater control of the activity at hand. These changes may reflect characteristics associated with active responses on the part of children's reading and play activities as noted in previous research (Neuman & Gallagher, 1994; Ninio & Bruner, 1978). It suggests that through such child-centered activities like play, children may come to feel a sense of ownership and control of their world. Such feelings of competence and control are likely to nourish children's interests and expectations about learning and about becoming accomplished writers and readers.

REFERENCES

Anderson, A., & Stokes, S. (1984). Social and institutional influences on the development and practice of literacy. In H. Goelman, A. Oberg, & F. Smith (Eds.), *Awakening to literacy* (pp. 24–37). Portsmouth, NH: Heinemann.

Auerbach, E. R. (1989). Toward a social-contextual approach to family literacy. *Harvard Educational Review, 59,* 165–181.

Auerbach, E. (1995). Critical issues: Deconstructing the discourse of strengths in family literacy. *Journal of Reading Behavior, 27,* 643–661.

Azmitia, M., & Perlmutter, M. (1989). Social influences on children's cognition: State of the art and future directions. In H. W. Reese (Ed.), *Advances in child development and behavior* (pp. 89–144). Orlando, FL: Academic.

Benjamin, L. A., & Lord, J. (1996). *Family literacy.* Washington, DC: Office of Educational Research and Improvement.

Berlin, G., & Sum, A. (1988). *Toward a more perfect union: Basic skills, poor families, and our economic future.* New York: Ford Foundation.

Bloome, D., & Green, J. (1984). Directions in the sociolinguistics study of reading. In P. D. Pearson (Ed.), *Handbook of reading research* (pp. 395–422). New York: Longman.

Connors, L. J. (1993). *Project Self Help: A family focus on literacy* (No. 13). Center on Families, Communities, Schools & Children's Learning.

Darling, S. (1989). *Kenan Trust family literacy project and program model.* Louisville, KY: Kenan Trust Family Literacy Project.

Diaz, R., Neal, C., & Vachio, A. (1991). Maternal teaching in the zone of proximal development: A comparison of low- and high-risk dyads. *Merrill-Palmer Quarterly, 37,* 83–108.

Dyson, A. H. (1982). The emergence of visible language: Interrelationships between drawing and early writing. *Visible Language, 16,* 360–381.

Furstenberg, F., Brooks-Gunn, J., & Morgan, S. P. (1987). *Adolescent mothers in later life.* New York: Cambridge University Press.

Gambrell, L., & Heland, V. (1993). *Increasing young children's access to books: A school, home, and community involvement project.* Paper presented at the National Reading Conference, Charleston, SC.

Gardner, H. (1980). *Artful scribbles: The significance of children's drawings.* New York: Basic Books.

Heath, S. B. (1983). *Ways with words: Language, life, and work in communities and classrooms.* New York: Cambridge University Press.

Laboratory of Comparative Human Cognition. (1983). Culture and cognitive development. In P. H. Mussen (Series Ed.) & W. Kessen (Vol. Ed.), *Handbook of child psychology: Vol. 1. History, theory and methods.* New York: Wiley.

Landy, S., & Walsh, S. (1988). Early intervention with high-risk teenage mothers and their infants. *Early Child Development and Care, 37,* 27–46.

Lave, J., & Wenger, E. (1991). *Situated learning.* New York: Cambridge University Press.

Lidz, C. (Ed.). (1987). *Dynamic assessment.* New York: Guilford.

Lidz, C. (1991). *Practitioner's guide to dynamic assessment.* New York: Guilford.

McGillicuddy-De Lisi, A. (1982). Parental beliefs about developmental processes. *Human Development, 25,* 192–200.

McGillicuddy-De Lisi, A., Sigel, I., & Johnson, J. (1979). The family as a system of mutual influences: Parental beliefs, distancing behaviors, and children's representational thinking. In M. Lewis & L. A. Rosenblum (Eds.), *The child and its family* (pp. 91–106). New York: Plenum.

Morrow, L. M. (1995). *Family literacy: Connections in schools and communities.* Newark, DE: International Reading Association.

Neuman, S. B., & Gallagher, P. (1994). Joining together in literacy learning: Teenage mothers and children. *Reading Research Quarterly, 29,* 382–401.

Neuman, S. B., Hagedorn, T., Celano, D., & Daly, P. (1995). Toward a collaborative approach to parent involvement in early education: A study of teenage mothers in an African-American community. *American Educational Research Association, 32,* 801–827.

Neuman, S. B., & Roskos, K. (1992). Literacy objects as cultural tools: Effects on children's literacy behaviors in play. *Reading Research Quarterly, 27,* 202–225.

Neuman, S. B., & Roskos, K. (1993). Access to print for children of poverty: Differential effects of adult mediation and literacy-enriched play settings on environmental and functional print tasks. *American Educational Research Journal, 30,* 95–122.

Neuman, S. B., & Roskos, K. (1997). Literacy knowledge in practice: Contexts of participation for young writers and readers. *Reading Research Quarterly, 32,* 10–32.

Newman, D., Griffin, P., & Cole, M. (1989). *The construction zone: Working for cognitive change in school.* New York: Cambridge University Press.

Nickse, R., Speicher, A. M., & Buchek, P. C. (1988). An intergenerational adult literacy project: A family intervention/prevention model. *Journal of Reading, 31,* 634–642.

Ninio, A., & Bruner, J. (1978). The achievement and antecedents of labeling. *Journal of Child Language, 5,* 1–16.

Rogoff, B. (1982). Integrating context and cognitive development. In M. E. Lamb & A. L. Brown (Eds.), *Advances in developmental psychology* (pp. 125–161). Hillsdale, NJ: Lawrence Erlbaum Associates.

Rogoff, B. (1984). Adult assistance of children's learning. In T. R. Raphael (Ed.), *The contexts of school-based literacy* (pp. 27–42). New York: Random House.

Rogoff, B. (1990). *Apprenticeship in thinking: Cognitive development in social context.* New York: Oxford University Press.

Rogoff, B., & Gardner, W. (1984). Adult guidance of cognitive development. In B. Rogoff & J. Lave (Ed.), *Everyday cognition: Its development in social context* (pp. 95–116). Cambridge, MA: Harvard University Press.

Rogoff, B., & Lave, J. (1984). *Everyday cognition.* Cambridge, MA: Harvard University Press.

Rogoff, B., Mosier, C., Mistry, J., & Goncu, A. (1993). Toddlers' guided participation with their caregivers in cultural activity. In E. Forman, N. Minick, & A. Stone (Eds.), *Contexts for learning: Sociocultural dynamics in children's development* (pp. 230–253). New York: Oxford University Press.

Sigel, I. (1985). A conceptual analysis of beliefs. In I. Sigel (Ed.), *Parental belief systems* (pp. 345–371). Hillsdale, NJ: Lawrence Erlbaum Associates.

Sigel, I. E., & McGillicuddy-De Lisi, A. (1984). Parents as teachers of their children: A distancing behavior model. In A. Pellegrini & T. Yawkey (Eds.), *The development of oral and written language in social contexts* (pp. 71–92). Norwood, NJ: Ablex.

Taylor, D., & Dorsey-Gaines, C. (1988). *Growing up literate: Learning from inner-city families.* Portsmouth, NH: Heinemann.

Teale, W. H. (1986). Home background and young children's literacy development. In W. H. Teale & E. Sulzby (Eds.), *Emergent literacy* (pp. 173–206). Norwood, NJ: Ablex.

Teale, W., & Sulzby, E. (1986). *Emergent literacy: Writing and reading.* Norwood, NJ: Ablex.

Thormann, M. S. (1985). Attitudes of adolescents toward infants and young children. In S. Harel & N. Anastasiow (Eds.), *The at-risk infant psychological-social-medical aspects.* Baltimore: Brookes.

Tizard, B., & Hughes, M. (1984). *Young children learning.* Cambridge, MA: Harvard University Press.

Vygotsky, L. S. (1962). *Thought and language.* Cambridge, MA: MIT Press.

Vygotsky, L. S. (1978). *Mind in society: The development of higher psychological processes.* Cambridge, MA: Harvard University Press.

Wertsch, J. V. (1984). The zone of proximal development: Some conceptual issues. In B. Rogoff &. J. Wertsch (Ed.), *Children's learning in the "zone of proximal development"* (pp. 7–17). San Francisco: Jossey-Bass.

Williams, C. W. (1991). *Black teenage mothers.* Lexington, MA: Lexington.

Wood, D., Bruner, J., & Ross, G. (1976). The role of tutoring in problem solving. *Journal of Child Psychology and Psychiatry, 17,* 89–100.

10

Literacy, Play,
and Authentic Experience

Nigel Hall
Manchester Metropolitan University

In recent years literacy has been rediscovered as a social phenomenon. Of course *rediscovered* is a misleading word, as literacy itself has never been anything other than a social phenomenon. It would be truer to say that it has finally been recognized by the academic community as a more comprehensive notion than had hitherto been the case. If all the articles, books, pamphlets, and pieces on literacy were piled up, most of them would be seen to be associated with school literacy. It is probably the most exhaustively studied curriculum area, and as every reader of newspapers and viewer of television programs can attest, it is still the curriculum area that features most predominantly in people's minds. However, alongside the seemingly inexhaustible studies of classroom literacy has been developing a new range of studies from historians, anthropologists, and sociologists that position literacy rather differently from how it is normally conceived within schooling. It is a view of literacy that is often at odds with the conventional school notions of literacy, and when the two perspectives are examined it is schooling that is left having to answer the biggest questions. Barton (1991) pointed out, "Most theories of literacy start out from the educational settings in which literacy is typically taught ... These views of what literacy is are often at odds with what people experience in their everyday lives" (p. 3).

Perhaps the easiest way of illustrating this is to do something that for a century literacy researchers failed to do, and that is consider literacy in use in people's everyday lives. What characterizes the experience and use of literacy beyond and outside of school? A growing body of research (including Barton, 1994; Finders, 1997; Fishman, 1988; Heath, 1983; Prinsloo & Breier, 1996; Street, 1993; Voss, 1996) suggests that in everyday life, literacy:

- Is almost always highly meaningful to people's lives and often results from personal choices.
- Is both initiated by users and responded to by users.

- Is used to make things happen; it is means-ended and success is measured by whether it achieves these ends.
- Is located in a social past and future; it comes out of prior experience and connects to future experience.
- Is used for a very wide range of purposes, involves a wide range of sources and audiences, and varies in the demands it makes on users.
- Is often highly social.
- Is often a highly enjoyable experience, is sometimes challenging, and sometimes defeats everyone.
- Is used in different ways by different communities who have different values for and beliefs about literacy.

Street (1984) uses the term *ideological literacy* to characterize the ways in which literacy occurs in daily life. Ideological literacy refers to types of literacy that draw their meanings and use from being situated within cultural values and practices. Because cultures differ in the things they value and practice, literacy will differ both at a deep level and at a manifested level. An ideological model of literacy suggests that there are multiple literacies rather than a single literacy and that the use of these literacies creates engagement, involves wider networks, and is consistently related to the everyday lives of people in their communities.

Literacy in schools has a quite different character. In schooling, literacy:

- Is seldom meaningful and relevant to children's lives as people.
- Is almost always imposed on children, forcing them to be responders and seldom initiators.
- Is seldom used to make things happen in the world; exercises are treated as ends in themselves—as here and now activities—and success is measured by performance on the task.
- Only has a past and future in relation to difficulty; in other words, connections across literacy practices are not related to previous or future meanings or uses, but simply to being easier or more difficult.
- Is usually experienced within exercises that focus on narrow aspects of literacy, involves a limited range of specially privileged purposes and audiences, and makes relatively constant demands on users.
- Is usually experienced as individual practice.
- Is seldom situated within the social practice of literacy.
- Is defined in narrow and decontextualized ways that govern interpretations, choices and modes of practice, and assessment.

Street (1995) refers to these kinds of practices as representing an autonomous model of literacy. *Autonomous literacy* refers to literacy that is separated from the wider social world of actual use and that is treated as a neutral object to be studied, analyzed, and mastered as a technical device. In schools, literacy itself is treated as an autonomous phenomenon, one that has a life-world of its own, unconnected to the ways in which it is actually used by people in their lives. Schools, as a principal agency for maintaining the autonomous model of literacy, engage in pedogogization of literacy through a range of instructional processes (Street, 1995).

Juliebo (1985) vividly highlighted the contrasts between these two models of literacy (although not naming them as ideological and autonomous) when she compared the literacy experiences of very young children at home with their experiences in kindergarten. She commented:

- In the home the child was the main initiator of literacy learning whereas in school the teacher was the initiator and the children's attempts to initiate were not accessed.
- At home sharing and reciprocity were constantly manifest. In the kindergarten, in general, the children had to reciprocate in the predetermined programme, the construction of which was not mutually shared between the teacher and learner.
- Many activities in kindergarten were only concerned with the here and now and precluded transcendence. This was particularly true of work time and art activities. At home transcendence was present in most children's literacy interactions.
- At school literacy activities were not grounded in the children's own life worlds, and as a result often lacked meaning. This was in strong contrast to the home where literacy was a part of everyday life. Interactions in the home were almost always accompanied by a joyful sharing. (pp. 132–133)

If this level of contrast exists for children in the usually less formal world of kindergarten, then it must be much greater as children move through school. Yet, the almost tragic irony is that the primary justification for teaching literacy in school is to enable people to use it in the ways associated with life outside of and beyond schooling. How exactly is the autonomous model of literacy supposed to result in success in the world of ideological literacy usage? Why does schooling operate a mode of literacy so distinct from everyday usage? Are they necessarily opposites or is it possible for schooling to incorporate more of the real-worldness into its own practices? Is it perhaps time, as Ivanic and Moss (1991) ask about writing, that "Educational institutions contribute to, rather than detract from, people's experience of writing and learning to write in the community" (p. 194)?

For as Reither (1993) comments:

What is missing from these classrooms are the circumstances that make possible and (thus) motivate writing as a social process—the very conditions that make collaboration and cooperation appropriate, even necessary, in many business, governmental, and professional work places. What is missing are the rhetorical needs and moves that drive the production of written knowledge. (p. 196)

Clearly these questions extend beyond writing to literacy itself, and the un-reflective, largely unresearched view that success in school literacy practices is a guarantee of literacy success in life beyond school has itself begun to be subject to challenge both historically (Graff, 1995) and empirically (Barton & Hamilton, 1998; Varenne & McDermott, 1986).

The result of all this is the separation between literacy in schools and literacy in life beyond.

The major problem with reducing this drift toward separation is that the autonomous use of literacy is so firmly institutionalized within and beyond schooling, and is currently being reinforced so strongly by recent narrow political moves in many countries (the adoption of the National Curriculum in the United Kingdom, and the creation of statewide curriculums in both the United States and Australia) that major structural change is unlikely. Does this mean that it is impossible to present young children with a more realistic experience of literacy, or is there a place within conventional schooling where this can be done?

What I want to argue in this chapter is that sociodramatic play is a perfect vehicle for providing the rhetorical needs identified by Reither (1993), for providing literacy and literacy-related experiences that are more ideologically situated than is normally the case in classrooms, and can allow schools, as requested by Ivanic and Moss (1991), to contribute to children's understanding of the role of literacy in community life.

THE INTERRELATIONSHIP BETWEEN PLAY AND LITERACY

What is it about sociodramatic play and the way children use it in school that makes it so appropriate for this task? Very simply, it shares many of the underlying characteristics of ideological literacy.

Play is almost always highly meaningful to children, and what happens in play is usually the personal choice of the players. "At some point between three and four the children learn that even though powers do exist beyond their ken, they can nonetheless order a universe that makes sense and is under control" (Paley, 1988, p. 29).

Within play, children initiate events and as co-players respond to other people's initiations. Play is often structured in events, thus the elements of the play are grounded in the events. These elements are not played for their own sake—they are means to ends. Within these events, the action is coherent, and the success of play is not measured by performance in the elements but by the satisfaction of the players about the whole event.

Play frequently emerges out of wider preoccupations of children and relates to their lives as young human beings with a past, present, and future.

> The children were actors on a moving stage, carrying on philosophical debates while borrowing fragments of floating dialogue. Themes from fairly tales and television cartoons combined with social commentary and private fantasy to form a tangible script that was not random or erratic. (Paley, 1988, p. 12)

Within play a huge range of topics occur, and those topics draw on a wide range of sources and involve a range of roles. The demand on players is not a constant but will vary according to role, situation, and event.

> Boys play in sandboxes or in backyard locations declared by them to be specific settings; in these appropriately named scenes, they play at being fishermen, mechanics, heavy equipment drivers, firemen, policemen, etc. They also play at being monsters, flying saucers, and Buck Rogers. Girls designate areas of the yard or their room to be kitchens, churches, stores, bedrooms, etc., and in these places they pretend to be mothers, babies, church leaders, "fancy ladies," and experts in other female dominated activities. They also play at being monsters, Wonder woman, and wild animals. (Heath, 1983, p. 162)

Although sociodramatic play can be individual, it is often social, allowing all life to be constructed within its parameters. Because it is social and sociable, it is usually enjoyable and challenging.

Finally, the meanings of play are not historically and politically determined by the institutions of schooling but relate to concerns of the lives of people as lived outside schooling.

> Images of good and evil, birth and death, parent and child, move in and out of the real and the pretend. There is no small talk. The listener is submerged in philosophical position papers, a virtual recapitulation of life's enigmas. (Paley, 1988, p. 6)

Thus children's play, like everyday literacy practices, draws meaning from being situated within cultural histories, values, and practices and thus generates engagement, involves networks, and is consistently related to the everyday lives of people in their communities.

LITERACY IN ASSOCIATION WITH PLAY INSIDE THE CLASSROOM

The experience examined here was an attempt to set up a context in a classroom of 5- to 6-year-old children in which literacy occurred within an ideological framework rather than within one that treated literacy as an autonomous object. This required experiences that did not distance the children from real-world purposes for literacy, that did not use language and literacy solely for analytic purposes, and that situated experience within a complex social situation rather than the narrow ritualistic performance demands of conventional school literacy tasks. It set out to privilege a wide variety of written genres, to involve the children with texts that were problematic and confronted their beliefs about the world and their roles and rights, and to treat the children as competent users of literacy rather than unskilled, ignorant, and passive users of literacy. For this to happen, the experiences had to transcend the artificial barriers of school and classroom walls.

The mechanism for achieving this was to be an association with socio-dramatic play. Although, as becomes clear later, the literacy experiences mostly occurred outside of the play itself, it was the commitment and engagement of the children toward the sociodramatic play that provided the impetus for the literacy work, sustained it across a considerable amount of time, and generated an intense level of engagement by the children.

The school was a small British school. The class contained 35 children in a rather small classroom. A third of the children had recently arrived in the class from the nursery class and were either just 5 or about to turn 5 years of age. Another third had been in the class for one term (roughly a semester), and the rest for two terms. A cross-school theme on transport was in existence and the teacher decided that for one term her sociodramatic play area would be a garage. Despite the small area of the classroom, this was considered sufficiently important that it would occupy a substantial space.

The intention was that the children would visit a real garage, and then, using various materials (for craft, design, and technology experience), would build equipment and furnish the garage area, which was to have a workshop space and an office. Once the area was built, the children would then be free (subject to normal management procedures relating to noise and numbers) to play as they wished in that area without adult interference. Described in that way, the garage was not significantly different to most other play experiences for these young children. It has become common practice within such play for a range of literacy resources to be available in play areas, and for relevant signs, notices, and labels to be developed within such areas (Hall & Robinson, 1995), the expectation being that children will make use of these by incorporating them into their play.

What was to be different about this experience was that most of the literacy was associated with the play, but outside of it. Inside the play area, the children could play as they wished, but that play provided the social context and motivation for external engagement in a range of relevant, complex literacy events.

A couple of important principles were to guide this external experience. The first was that it was to be event based. Most of the literacy experiences associated with the garage were intended to be situated within events in which literacy was a means to an end, not the end in itself. They were not going to be literacy events, but life events within which literacy had a role. The second was that the children's experience with the garage was to be associated with problematicity in ways that impinged on the children's experiences with the play area. Only through facing problematicity would they be personally engaged with responding to situations. The events or problems were introduced in a variety of ways. Some were simply announced by the teacher, some came by way of letters arriving in the classroom, and some were introduced by other individuals.

An extensive range of events was experienced by the children, three of which are examined briefly in the rest of this chapter.

Getting Permission   Given that the children had already visited the real garage, had started to think about what items they would need to have and build, and had even started collecting things for the building process, the teacher introduced the first event and made the children's world a little more problematic. In a discussion, the teacher suddenly told the children that people could not simply build anything whenever or wherever they wanted; permission had to be obtained and this permission had to come from the Town Hall Planning Department. The class discussed what they needed to ask, and several of them wrote letters (see Example 10.1). Of course, the teacher had previously arranged with someone at the Planning Department that a response would be sent.

Dear the tothul wiy wot To Bld a garig Jan wiy hav sum Spahns and str uv figs and sum and a ofs and sum lods win waprs and sum pmd ishn and Sum plan Love from Lydia	**Example 10.1** Translation Dear the Town Hall. We want to build a garage. Can we have sum spanners (wrenches) and some other things and some ladders and an office and some windscreen wipers and some planning permission?

From phrases such as "Dear the Town Hall" and asking for "some planning permission" it is clear that the children have only a vague idea of what is involved here. Planning permission is seen as an object, as are ladders and spanners (wrenches). This did not deter the teacher; as long as most things were within the children's understanding, she felt that some new and difficult concepts could be tolerated. The response from the Town Hall was to send an application form. The form was far too difficult for these children to read for themselves but, surprisingly, the concepts needed to understand the form were mostly comprehensible at some level to the children. As a consequence, with some help and discussion about what was being asked for, some of the more able writers were eager to have a go at providing the information required (see Example 10.2).

Example 10.2

See next page for
Example 2

In addition to the forms, all the children drew plans that were also sent. The contact at the Town Hall immediately sent back a letter agreeing to the garage. Preparation for the garage did not stop during the week that this event was talking place. The teacher had let the children know that she was sure that permission would be granted so long as they made the application.

Planning
Application Form

Please read the guidance notes which
will help you to complete this form.
4 copies of the form and 4 sets of
plans should be submitted.

PART ONE

1

Name and Address of Applicant and Agent

Name and Address of Applicant

Name Clare

Address Hazel grove
Chapul street
Hazel grove
stokpot

Postcode SK7 4EB   Daytime Tel No. 483 437

Name and Address of Agent (if any)

Name

Address INFant school

Postcode   Daytime Tel. No.

Person to contact

2

Proposed Development

A Location or Address of Proposed Development

Hazel grove INFant school

B Description of Proposed Development (specify the number of units in the case of housing development)

Garage

12 Fust eps Long   9 Wad

C Size of Site (edge in red on submitted site plan)   hectare

D Is the proposal for a temporary period? Answer YES or NO [Yes] If yes, for how long un tol easter

E Do you own or control any adjoining land? (edge in blue on submitted site plan) Answer YES or NO [Yes]

3

Type of Application

Please tick one box

A This is an outline application   □ If so go to Question 4

B This is a reserved matters application   □ If so go to Question 4

Outline Application No.

Date of Outline Permission

C This is a full application for

(i) Building or engineering operations only □

(ii) Change of use without any building or engineering operations at present □

(iii) Change of use and building or engineering operations   ✓

(iv) Mining operations or waste disposal □ Complete additional form

(v) This is an application for renewal of a temporary permission   □

Application No. of existing permission

(vi) This is an application for removal or variation of a condition of a previous planning permission □

Condition No.   Application No.

Now go to Question

4

Outline Applications and Reserved Matters Application

If you have ticked A or B in Question 3, please tick the relevant boxes

Do you wish to seek approval for any of the following matters as part of this application?   Answer YES or NO □

If yes, please tick the relevant boxes.

Siting □   Design □   External Appearance (including materials) □   Means of Access □   Landscaping □

The function of this event was getting permission. It was not an exercise in form filing or letter writing. The literacy experiences were needed simply to achieve the overall aim of the event. Because it was a life event, it contained much more than literacy. Probably for the first time in their lives these 5-year-olds became aware of a notion of authority that lay outside the family, the school, and the police. They began to see that a bureaucracy is involved and that work, and in this instance workplaces, do not have freedom to exist and do whatever they want. On a more practical level, not many 5-year-olds have begun to understand that the builder of workplace has to have concern for drainage, hazardous substances, and so on. The children were gaining insight into important forms of social control and were experiencing work as something considerably more complex than they could have possibly conceived.

It was important to the children to get this permission. Their visit and the preparation had excited them, and they were really looking forward to having the garage up and running. Thus the activities involved in getting permission were part of overcoming a problem that stood in the way of achieving their personal goals. It is difficult to conceive of 5-year-olds wanting to write and get permission to do math. It was the commitment to play and the intensity of that experience for young children that constituted their motivation and engagement.

Applying for a Job   Within a relatively short period of time, permissions were obtained, the garage was approaching completion, and the children were wanting to play in it. The teacher then introduced another factor derived from the real world of work: People have to apply for a job. Before one can apply for a position there has to be an advertisement and before there can be an advertisement, there has to be a job description. Example 10.3, an advertisement for a secretary for the garage office, was written by a child for this play area. The discussion that surrounded the writing of these advertisements serves an important function related to the role play. The visit to the garage and the related talk provided a chance to consider who does what and what each job involved. However, creating advertisements also requires careful thought about the detail of each role and about the characteristics needed. The discussion about deciding what to put in the advertisement enables everyone to learn about the roles. It is not that the children will have to follow a predetermined script when they go to play in the area, but they will be better informed about some of the possibilities. This adds to the richness of the play and increases the level of understanding about the overall theme. Thus a reciprocity is established. The sociodramatic play motivates engagement in the events occurring outside of the play, and these external events inform and sustain the play within the area.

Example 10.3
Translation
Wanted

A good secretary, must do typing, a good writer can answer the phone, a hard worker, nice to customers.

Further reinforcement of what the roles involved was provided when children chose to apply for the jobs, which provided experience of writing in response to an explicit request for precise information. If the job requires particular things, the applicant needed to say something about those things.

The children had to read the advert carefully and address points in their own letters or application forms.

The teacher was aware that within the activities provided there had to be scope for all levels of ability. The applications for jobs provides a good example of the various levels of writing experience in this class and how the activity allowed each child to offer his or her distinctive contribution regardless of competence. Example 10.4 shows a child who is at the very beginning of his writing development. He can barely write his own name and, on this occasion, is having his writing translated by the teacher on the application forms. The second child (Example 10.5) is already quite competent at putting her message onto paper.

Example 10.4
Pipe's garage application form

Pipe's Garage Application form

Name. a d A M v v M T o
Address. L o h o n d a d y o o y s

Phone number.

Job. m e c a d h i c

Why I will be good at the job.

I u W y h d s O s

I will do it at my house.

Example 10.5
Translation

I will be the boss because I will be good at the job and make sure the people work hard. I would be kind to the customers.

Pipe's Garage Application form

Name. Heather
Address.
Phone number. 4823828
Job. m a n i j e r

Why I will be good at the job.
I will be the boss
becos I will be good at
the job mayk sur the pilpy
Werk hard + mud le kid to
the kusterm

Again, the experience changed and developed the children's understanding of the garage as a socially positioned phenomenon, and provided a means-ended experience of a number of literacy structures not usually encountered by very young children.

Repairing the Nursery Bike   As play areas in this school became established, teachers talked to each other about what was happening, and sometimes they decided to get involved in each others' areas. When one of the bikes belonging to the nursery (for 3- and 4-year-olds) broke, the staff thought it was a good opportunity to ask the garage for an estimate for a repair. First, the children in the nursery were encouraged to write letters on their own asking the mechanics to come and fix the bike, and then some of them visited the class with the garage and read their letters to the 5-year-olds.

A group of the garage mechanics then visited the nursery to examine the bike, but before they went, the whole class discussed what they were going to do when they got there. There had already been some discussion about estimating, looking at broken things and deciding what was wrong with them. They thought that they might be able to fix it on the spot, and they decided to take some tools. They also realized that they might need to test the bike to see what was wrong. It was important to make notes so that they could bring the information back with them to use when producing the estimate; for this they took a clipboard and pencils.

On return to the classroom the children discussed the problem and tried to decide how much to charge for the repairs. A brief but interesting discussion took place that highlights the dilemma of "playing for real." At this age, the children had little understanding of the difference between pennies and pounds and did not yet have a clear grasp of the larger numbers. They were aware that the nursery did not have much money to pay for the repair.

T: Now you be thinking, don't write it down yet, how much do you think it's going to cost?

C: 20 pence.

T: Does it cost just pennies in the garage? I know whenever I go to the garage it's pounds and pounds and pounds. It costs pounds to have a car repaired. You've got all the little parts that cost quite a lot of money.

C: How much was it?

T: I think mine might have been about 60 pounds.

C: It might be 44 pence.

C: It's going to cost 100 pounds.

T: You think it would be 100 pounds, do you?

C: No, they haven't got that much.

The compromise was for 44 pounds and a number of children in their role as mechanics wrote estimates that were sent to the nursery (see Example 10.6).

mr pipe   garage

the hahal bos
twis Bay is sef
is hie hiw uyl
is Robly sit
the fels cem of
is scwi kicg
44 pas tiw Fis the
Bac

Example 10.6
Translation

The handlebar twists by itself. It needs
new oil. Has a wobbly seat. The
pedals come off. It is squeaking.
Forty-four pounds to fix the bike. The
children received the following reply.
To the mechanics Forty-four pounds is
a lot of money. Could you make it
cheaper for us? From The Nursery

To take the children's understanding of costs a little further, a small group of
children were taken back to the garage by the teacher. Every car in the United
Kingdom over 3 years old has to have an annual road-worthiness test, and the
teacher's car was due for one, and she took it to Mr. Pipe's garage. When they
arrived, they discussed with Mr. Pipe why things cost so much to be mended.
The conversation, mainly between the teacher and Mr. Pipe, covered elementary economics of the cost of materials, having to pay for labor and electricity,
and needing to make a profit.

T: Where do you think Mr. Pipe might get the money from to pay for the
       electricity and the lights? How will he get the money?
C: From the bank.
T: From the bank. Well, how does he get his money in the bank? Where does
       he get his money from?
C: Someone sends it to him.
Mr. P: Oh yes ... aye, yes, ha ha.
T: Who gives it to him? Who gives Mr. Pipe his money?
C: The bank.
T: Well, he has to put it in the bank first. The bank doesn't just give money
       away.
C: His boss.
Mr. P: Ha ha. I've been doing it wrong all these years.
C: Does he have to pay his customers?
T: Oh, no he doesn't.
Mr. P: It feels like it.
C: The customers have to pay Mr. Pipe.

Later in the classroom the discussion continued.

T: What does he pay for in the garage?
C: He has to pay for the building.
T: Right, the building.

C: And he has to pay for the lights.

T: The lights and the …

C: The equipment in the garage.

As a result of the visit and the discussion with the real Mr. Pipe, the children were able to give the nursery some reasons for the high cost of their initial estimates. They were able to explain and justify their charges, as shown in Example 10.7.

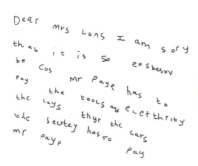

Example 10.7
Translation

Dear Mrs. Lomas. I am sorry that it is so expensive because Mr. Pipe has to pay for the tools and electricity, the lights and the cars. The secretary has to pay Mr. Pipe

As in the other two events, the event structure meant that literacy was only one concern among many. The event could much more accurately be characterized as one about economics than about literacy. The work in the garage was helping the children in many ways, not the least in beginning to understand how the world actually works. The discussion about money and payment, although probably not clearing up many misconceptions, was at least able to confront the assumptions of some of the children about economic facts of life. It also meant that the play repertoire of the children was extended. Play events could now become more complex and involve an additional layer of knowledge about garages and how they worked.

Other Events   Across the whole time (some 13 weeks) that the children were preoccupied with the garage, a range of events occurred, all of which involved literacy as a means to an end, and also demanded that the children think about something to do with the garage. The biggest challenge for the children was probably the neighbor who objected to them building a garage, but all the events meant new knowledge, new experiences, and ways of sorting out the situations that resulted. Almost all the writing associated with meeting the needs of these events took place outside the physical space of the play area, and took place in other curriculum time. Within the play area, the children played as determined by themselves, sometimes completely ignoring the fact that it was a garage.

But there were many other times when the free play in the area was clearly based on the ideas developed through the experiences discussed in the groups. Part of this acting in role involved the literacy associated with these roles, and the supply of literacy materials was important in enabling this to happen. Constantly new notices were added, clipboards were used to make notes of jobs to be done, and letters were written in the office.

There were times when the children began play episodes that involved changing wheels or welding parts on cars. Noticing this, the teachers invited some of the players to draw up rules or instructions relating to some of the garage operations. The production of such things as lists of rules and instructions arose more directly out of the play in the area and created yet more opportunity to discuss what happens in such a place and what the various roles involve. For example, the list of rules for welding derives from a clear understanding of what welding is and what is involved when doing it (see Example 10.8). To write this, the group of children had to think of what they had seen at Mr. Pipe's garage and think carefully about the safety features involved in the activity.

Rules For Welding

Example 10.8

1 Rules. You must wear gloves.
2 You must wear a welding mask.
3 You must wear a helmet.
4 Don't be silly.
5 Don't be naughty.
6 You must wear overalls.
7 Be sensible.
8 Don't touch the flame.

But in addition, they would take with them into the play area a more informed view of how to be a welder.

CONCLUSION

Too often in play areas children's understanding is not developed beyond the everyday procedural activities of the related real-life participants. Too often in play the baker bakes, the policeman arrests or directs traffic, the nurse takes temperatures, and the mechanic mends the cars; these tend to get repeated over and over again as the children play. In contrast, the events experienced by the children in this classroom allowed them to do those things but also developed their understanding of the garage as a situated social phenomenon in which people have wider concerns and competing goals.

Throughout the study, the children engaged in the writing with considerable intensity and purpose. The children were not particularly conscious that they were engaged in a literacy learning experience. This was living rather than learning. When someone says you cannot have your garage because you do not have permission, you do not stop and think "I must learn how to fill in a form." You intuitively call on your knowledge and skill to develop an appropriate response. When the teacher talks about it with you, the conversation helps you think of things you might not have known or had forgotten about. However, when you come to write, you do so not because that is the set exercise, but because you want your garage! In the process, a whole range of skills are developed and the result is a more experienced and competent writer.

The constant association with the sociodramatic play meant that all the writing experiences were meaningful, were used to make things happen, were means-ended, were linked to a past and future that had real significance, involved a wide range of audiences and purposes, were highly social, and reflected the children's values and beliefs about how to use literacy appropriately—in short, all the things characteristic of genuine literacy use. It is, of course not fully real literacy use—it was not a real garage. Nevertheless, from the children's perspective, they were engaged in literacy practices that achieved real ends; they secured their garage, they got the jobs they wanted, and they defended their judgments about costs for repairing the bike.

I have left for last one vital point. During the entire course of the play theme, the children demonstrated total enjoyment of the experience. Enjoyment is often frowned on in learning, but people—all people, not just 5-year-old people—learn more efficiently, with greater intensity, and with more purpose when the learning is fun. Enjoyment keeps learners going when those moments arrive that require patience, perseverance, and application. Sociodramatic play not only gave meaning to the literacy learning, it made literacy an enjoyable, immensely satisfying experience for young children.

REFERENCES

Barton, D. (1991). The social nature of writing. In D. Barton & M. Hamilton (Eds.), *Writing in the community* (pp. 1–13). London: Sage.

Barton, D. (1994). *Literacy: An introduction to the ecology of written language.* Oxford, UK: Blackwell.

Barton, D., & Hamilton, M. (1998). *Local literacies: Reading and writing in one community.* London: Routledge.

Finders, M. (1997). *Just girls: Hidden literacies and life in junior high.* New York: Teachers College Press.

Fishman, A. (1988). *Amish literacy.* Portsmouth, NH: Heinemann.

Graff, H. (1995). *The labyrinths of literacy: Reflection on literacy past and present* (Rev. & exp. ed.). Pittsburgh, PA: University of Pittsburgh Press.

Hall, N., & Robinson, A. (1995). *Writing and play in the early years.* London: David Fulton.

Heath, S. B. (1983). *Ways with words: Language, life, and work in communities and classrooms.* Cambridge, UK: Cambridge University Press.

Ivanic, R., & Moss, W. (1991). Bringing community writing practices into education. In D. Barton & M. Hamilton (Eds.), *Writing in the community.* London: Sage.

Juliebo, M. (1985). The literacy world of young children. *Reading-Canada-Lecture, 3,* 126–136.

Paley, V. (1988). *Bad guys don't have birthdays.* Chicago: University of Chicago Press.

Prinsloo, M., & Breier, M. (1996). *The social uses of literacy.* Amsterdam: John Benjamins.

Reither, J. (1993). Bridging the gap: Scenic moves for collaborative writing in workplace and school. In R. Splika (Ed.), *Writing in the workplace: New research perspectives* (pp. 195–206). Carbondale: Southern Illinois University Press.

Street, B. (1984). *Literacy in theory and practice.* Cambridge, UK: Cambridge University Press.

Street, B. (1993). *Cross-cultural approaches to literacy.* Cambridge, UK: Cambridge University Press.

Street, B. (1995). *Social literacies: Critical approaches to literacy in development, ethnography and education.* London: Longman.

Varenne, H., & Mcdermott, R. (1986). Why Sheila can read: Structure and indeterminacy in the reproduction of familial literacy. In B. Schiefflelin & P. Gilmore (Eds.), *Literacy: Ethnographic perspectives* (pp. 188–200). Norwood, NJ: Ablex.

Voss, M. (1996). *Hidden literacies: Children learning at home and at school.* Portsmouth, NH: Heinemann.

11

Play and Early Literacy: A Vygotskian Approach

Elena Bodrova
Mid-continent Research for Education and Learning

Deborah J. Leong
Metropolitan State College of Denver

Although by now, Vygotsky is universally recognized as one of the giants in the field of education, the impact of his theories on classroom practices outside Russia is negligible compared to that of his contemporaries Piaget, Montessori, and paradoxically, even of Pavlov. Strangely enough, although this might be attributed to the difficulty of translating Vygotsky's metaphoric language into practical recommendations or to the fact that most of the work done by generations of his students in Russia has not yet been translated, the real reason may lie in an idea that constitutes the very core of Vygotsky's cultural historical theory. We are referring to the idea of the social situation of development being the basic source of development that "determines wholly and completely the forms and the path along which the child will acquire ever newer personality characteristics, drawing them from social reality" (Vygotsky, 1984/1998, p. 198).

A logical consequence of this idea is to admit the futility of importing instructional practices (no matter how effective in their original implementation) to be applied in a new context, as according to Vygotsky, these practices will not match the social situation of development specific to children growing up in this new social context. In fact, this is exactly what has happened when elements of highly successful Vygotsky-based early literacy program were applied in Western schools. In the best case, the integrated system of instruction was reduced to a collection of isolated teacher tricks as happened with the Elkonin blocks widely used in remedial reading programs (e.g., Clay, 1993) and in the worst case, Vygotsky-based instructional strategies failed to impact children's learning altogether (see, e.g., Wilder, 1972).

An alternative route for those who are intrigued by Vygotsky's ideas and want to apply them in Western classrooms is to design new and original practices that are based on these ideas but that also address the unique social situation of development facing young children on this side of the ocean. Following this very route, in our work we tried to distill those principles of the Vygotskian theory that were successfully translated into instructional practices by several generations of post-Vygotskians and then apply these principles in U.S. early childhood classrooms. In this chapter, we discuss several of the main principles of Vygotsky's cultural historical theory that we found most important for our understanding of the relationship between play and literacy. We also discuss a set of new instructional practices based on these principles that we developed to promote play and literacy development in preschool and kindergarten-aged children.

LITERACY INSTRUCTION AS "ARMING CHILDREN WITH TOOLS"

For Vygotskians, the purpose of learning and teaching is more than acquiring and transmitting a body of knowledge; it involves the acquisition of mental tools. Varying from culture to culture—from the first scratches on cave walls representing numbers to the complex categories and concepts used in modern science and mathematics—all mental tools share the same function: to expand the capacity of mind beyond the limits set by human biology. Tools evolve (both in phylogeny and ontogeny) so that a tool used to support one's memory can be as simple as a string tied around one's finger or as complex as a shopping list organized according to the aisles in the supermarket. They also progress from being completely external (think of young children's use of their fingers to count) to the ones that can be internalized such as mathematical formulas that a student has memorized that simplify complex calculations.

Although similar to mechanical tools, like a hammer or saw, in the sense that mental tools, too, make it possible for humans to carry out more challenging tasks and to do them with greater ease and efficiency, mental tools also have one unique characteristic: Even when the tools themselves exist outside the human organism they nevertheless have an impact on its internal functioning. Mental tools transform the human mind. "Man introduces artificial stimuli, signifies behavior, and with signs, acting externally, creates new connections in brain," writes Vygotsky (1983/1997, p. 55). The changes in the human mind that Vygotsky associated with the use of mental tools include the transition from "reactive" behavior consisting of a response to the environment to behavior that is intentional and deliberate.

Vygotsky considered language to be a primary mental tool because it facilitates the acquisition of other tools and supports the transformation of many mental functions from reactive to intentional. Oral speech, specifically in the form of private speech, was credited by Vygotsky with the power of transforming the perception-driven concrete thinking of toddlers into the abstract symbolic thinking of schoolchildren and adults (Vygotsky, 1934/1987). Compared to oral speech, written speech presents an even more powerful tool, being "connected with the mastery of an external system of means developed and created in the process of cultural development of humanity" (Vygotsky, 1983/1997, p. 133) and leading to formation of such critical competencies as "conscious awareness and volition," nowadays commonly referred to as metacognition and self-regulation. Written speech further propels the mind toward abstract, reflective thinking and the mastery of subjects such as science, philosophy, and mathematics.

However, unlike oral speech, which most children master quickly and seemingly effortlessly, learning to read and write requires special instruction and even when this instruction is provided, many children still struggle with this task. Vygotsky (1934/1987) presents a convincing case for why children experience difficulties learning to write even though they are already proficient in expressing themselves orally. Vygotsky argues that similar to other school subjects, mastery of written speech relies on children's having competencies that they, in fact, do not possess at the time they are first introduced to letters and words. He compares the mental processes involved in speaking and writing and concludes that written speech requires higher levels of abstraction (both abstraction from intonation and expression inherent in oral speech and abstraction from the audience) and different, "voluntary" use of semantics, syntax, and phonetics—metalinguistic awareness in today's language. In addition, by the time literacy instruction commences, children typically have not developed the need to communicate in writing. Thus mastering written speech requires more than just being able to use oral speech. It requires that children possess an additional complex set of cognitive and metalinguistic skills.

Vygotsky then uses this apparent disconnect between the demands of literacy instruction and children's existing capabilities to introduce his now famous idea of the zone of proximal development (ZPD)—the idea that when properly designed and timed, instruction "moves ahead of development" and "impels or wakens a whole series of functions that are in a stage of maturation" (Vygotsky, 1934/1987, p. 212).

Over a half-century since the Vygotskian concept of the ZPD became known to Western educators, multiple attempts have been undertaken to apply this idea to classroom instruction. Most of these attempts, however, have not been successful, the reason for this being an apparent incompatibility between uniqueness of each child's zone and the school's need to provide instruction to many children with their diverse ZPDs at the same time. One possible answer to this dilemma is to identify conditions that will enable not one but many children to function at the highest levels of their respective zones. Fortunately, Vygotsky (1933/1967) himself identified one of these conditions in his article "Play and Its Role in the Mental Development of the Child."

MAKE-BELIEVE PLAY AS THE UNIVERSAL ZONE OF PROXIMAL DEVELOPMENT FOR PRESCHOOL[1] AND KINDERGARTEN-AGED CHILDREN

Vygotsky (1933/1967) examined different components of play and the way they affect the young child's emerging mental functions and concluded that play "is not the predominant form of activity, but is, in a certain sense, the leading source of development in preschool years" (p. 6). When analyzing play into its components, Vygotsky limited the scope of play to the dramatic or make-believe play typical for preschoolers and children of primary school age. Thus, Vygotsky's definition of play does not include many kinds of other activities such as movement activities, object manipulations, and explorations that were (and still are) referred to as play by most educators as well as non-educators. Real play, according to Vygotsky, has three components:

- Children create an imaginary situation.
- Children take on and act out roles.
- Children follow a set of rules determined by specific roles.

Although imaginary situations and roles in make-believe play are its commonly accepted features, the very idea that play is not totally spontaneous but is instead contingent on players abiding by a set of rules may sound completely counterintuitive. However

> whenever there is an imaginary situation in play, there are rules—not rules that are formulated in advance and change during the course of the game, but rules stemming from the imaginary situation. Therefore, to imagine that a child can behave in an imaginary situation without rules, i.e., as he behaves in a real situation, is simply impossible. If the child is playing the role of a mother, then she has rules of maternal behavior. The role the child plays, and her relationship to the object if the object has changed its meaning, will always stem from the rules, i.e., the imaginary situation will always contain rules. In play the child is free. But this is an illusory freedom. (Vygotsky, 1933/1967, p. 10)

Each of these three components of play has an important role in the formation of the child's mind, in the development of the child's abstract thinking and the development of conscious and voluntary behaviors, the necessary prerequisites for successful mastery of content children will encounter in school. Play creates the conditions in which the prerequisites for reading and writing develop.

---

[1]At the time of Vygotsky as well as at the time when most of his students conducted their research on play, formal school in Russia started at age 7. Considering this age difference along with the difference in the instructional methods in preschool and school settings, it would be valid to extend Vygotsky's use of the term *preschool* to U.S. children the now attend both preschool and kindergarten.

Role-playing in an imaginary situation requires children to carry on two types of actions simultaneously—external and internal. In play, these internal actions—operations on the meanings—are still dependent on the external operations on the objects. However, the very emergence of the internal actions signals the beginning of a child's transition from the earlier forms of thought processes—sensorimotor and visual-representational—to more advanced abstract thought:

> A child learns to consciously recognize his own actions and becomes aware that every object has a meaning. From the point of view of development, the fact of creating an imaginary situation can be regarded as a means of developing abstract thought. (Vygotsky, 1933/1967, p. 17)

For example, when Marcella uses a toy block as a telephone to order pizza at the restaurant, she is aware that the block is being used as a pretend telephone as she holds it up to her ear and starts talking. By using the block in this way she imposes another meaning on the object by her actions.

Another way make-believe play contributes to child development is by promoting intentional behavior. It becomes possible because of the inherent relationship that exists between roles children play and rules they need to follow when playing these roles. For preschoolers, play becomes the first activity where children are driven not by the need for instant gratification, prevalent at this age, but instead by the need to suppress their immediate impulses. In play

> at every step the child is faced with a conflict between the rule of the game and what he would do if he could suddenly act spontaneously. In the game he acts counter to what he wants ... [achieving] the maximum display of willpower in the sense of renunciation of an immediate attraction in the game in the form of candy, which by the rules of the game the children are not allowed to eat because it represents something inedible. Ordinarily a child experiences subordination to a rule in the renunciation of something he wants, but here subordination to a rule and renunciation of acting on immediate impulse are the means to maximum pleasure. (Vygotsky, 1933/1967, p. 14)

Summarizing multiple ways make-believe play impacts child development Vygotsky concludes that

> The play–development relationship can be compared with the instruction–development relationship, but play provides a background for changes in needs and in consciousness of a much wider nature. Play is the source of development and creates the zone of proximal development. Action in the imaginative sphere, in an imaginary situation, the creation of voluntary intentions and the formation of real-life plans and volitional motives—all appear in play and make it the highest level of preschool development. (Vygotsky, 1933/1967, p. 16)

Although Vygotsky was the first one to recognize the power of make-believe play to move the child forward, most empirical evidence of this power was collected by his students after Vygotsky's death. In his defining book *Psycholo-giya Igry* [The Psychology of Play], Elkonin (1978) enriched his mentor's idea that play creates a child's ZPD with concrete details about the mechanisms involved in elevating a preschool child to the level where this child is a head above himself.

According to Elkonin (1978), the center of make-believe play is the role that a child acts out. Because children act out not the exact actions of their role models but rather a synopsis of these actions, they, in fact, generate a model of reality—something that requires abstract thought. Elkonin argues that in make-believe play, children begin to apply abstract thought in two different ways: when they use objects in their symbolic function and when they act out a symbolic representation of relationships that exist between the roles. In both instances, the use of symbols is first supported by toys and props and later is communicated to play partners by the means of words and gestures. Elkonin sees this evolution of play as a reflection of the universal path of cognitive development: from object-oriented actions accompanied by social or private speech to thinking aloud with no objects involved to mental actions proper, abstract and abbreviated (Elkonin, 1978).

The power of play to support development of intentional, self-regulatory behaviors was attributed by Elkonin (1978) to the fact that the roles children choose to play are often the roles of adults (doctors, drivers, chefs, etc.) engaged in socially desirable behaviors. By imitating these behaviors in play, children learn to adjust their actions to meet the norms associated with the behaviors of these modeled roles, thus practicing planning, self-monitoring, and reflection essential for intentional behaviors. Elkonin cites a study where preschool children were found to be able to stand still significantly longer when playing "a guard" than when they were simply asked to do so by the teacher. Interestingly, no differences between these two conditions were found either for toddlers or for school-aged children, which led Elkonin to the conclusion that during the preschool years (not earlier and not later) play provides the greatest support for emerging self-regulation.

Elkonin (1978) has identified four principal ways for play to influence child development. All four expected outcomes of play activity are important for preparing the foundations for subsequent learning that takes place in primary grades. Elkonin describes four major mechanisms involved in play's impact on the child's development:

1. Play impacts the child's motivation. In play, children develop a more complex hierarchical system of immediate and long-term goals where immediate goals can be occasionally forgone to reach long-term goals. Through the process of coordinating these short-term and long-term goals, children become aware of their own actions, which make it possible for them to move from reactive behaviors to the intentional ones. To play "airplane," children have to stop and make tickets and passports and set up a security line. They have to postpone the airplane play to make props and set up the environment.

2. Play facilitates cognitive decentering. The ability to take other people's perspectives is critical for coordinating multiple roles and negotiating play scenarios. In addition, in play, children learn to look at objects through the eyes of their play partners, a form of cognitive decentering. Think of a child playing patient who is given a "shot" with a pencil: To act according to his role, this child needs to put himself or herself in the shoes of the child playing doctor, for whom this pencil is a pretend syringe. Later, this ability to coordinate multiple perspectives and to decenter will be turned inward, leading to the development of reflective thinking.

3. Play advances the development of mental representations. This occurs as a result of a child's separating the meaning of objects from their physical form. First, children use replicas to substitute for real objects (toy telephone), then proceed to use objects that are different in appearance but can perform the same function as the object prototype (a block held as a telephone), and finally, most of the substitution takes place in a child's speech or gestures with no physical objects present (gesture and a change in speech indicate the phone). Learning to operate not with real objects but with their symbolic substitutes contributes to the development of abstract thinking and imagination. It is important to note that for Vygotskians, imagination is not a prerequisite for play but an expected outcome.

4. Play fosters the development of deliberate behaviors, physical and mental voluntary actions. The development of deliberateness in play becomes possible due to the child's need to follow the rules of the play. In addition, as children constantly monitor each other's following these rules, they engage in other-regulation—a process that involves comparing observed behaviors with the "planned" ones. Planning and monitoring are essential features of deliberate behaviors. Practicing other- and self-regulation in play prepares the foundation for more advanced deliberate behaviors including planning and monitoring of one's mental processes—the metacognition.

Elkonin's detailed analysis of play's impact on child development supports Vygotsky's insight that make-believe play is the source of development for young children. Because one of the major lines of development in Vygotsky's theory involves children's mastery of cultural tools that results in subsequent transformation of their mental functioning, play can be viewed as the context that facilitates children's acquisition of these tools, including written language.

Our observations in a variety of kindergarten, preschool, and Head Start classrooms reveal a generally low level of make-believe play with 4- and 5-year-old children playing in a way one can expect to see in toddlers. These children rarely attempt to try a new theme, preferring instead to act out the same familiar scenarios of family, school, and doctor. Even books and videos filled with information about realistic as well as fantasy settings and characters often fail to inspire children to turn their housekeeping area into an aquarium or a castle. In their play, children often depend on realistic toys and props, having a hard time when they need to use their imagination to make up a substitute for a prop they do not have. Although the subject of the reasons for such decline of play go beyond the scope of this chapter (see, e.g., Bodrova & Leong, 2003a, 2003b, for a discussion on this topic), suffice it to say that we do not consider this immature level of play sufficient to afford children all the potential benefits of play. To remedy this situation, interventions are needed to raise the level of play (Bodrova & Leong, 2001), if children are to be able to take advantage of the benefits of play for literacy and cognitive development.

PLAY–LITERACY CONNECTIONS: THE VYGOTSKIAN PERSPECTIVE

Vygotskians consider play as a precursor to literacy in more than one way. First, play can be viewed as a general precursor to all academic learning including learning to read and write. Unlike the incidental learning that occurs in multiple contexts throughout childhood, academic learning takes place in a formal school setting and imposes specific demands on children's social and cognitive functioning. In the years prior to school entry, learning follows the child's own agenda in the sense that children learn what they wish at the pace they wish, to the degree that they wish. To succeed in the formal school setting children have to make a transition to the learning that follows the school agenda (Vygotsky, 1956). In terms of the mental processes that have to be engaged during learning, it means making a transition from behaviors that are "spontaneous, involuntary, and without conscious awareness" to those that are "abstract, voluntary, and characterized by conscious awareness" (Vygotsky, 1934/1987, p. 205). Children must now learn what the teacher says is important at the pace the teacher sets and to the degree that the teacher wants (enough to pass a test). Although most of the restructuring of children's mental functioning takes place during school years, make-believe play appears to be the context where these abstract, voluntary, and conscious behaviors are first practiced.

Similar to academic learning in general, learning to read and write also requires children to engage in abstract, voluntary, and conscious behaviors. As is evident from our earlier review of Vygotsky's perspective on the differences between oral speech and written speech, the latter requires higher levels of abstraction, intentionality, and conscious awareness:

> When learning to spell words that are spelled phonetically, the child gains conscious awareness that a word such as "fast" contains the sounds F-A-S-T, that is gains conscious awareness of his own activity in the production of sound; he learns to pronounce each separate element of the sound structure voluntarily. In the same way, when the child learns to write, he begins to do with volition what he has previously done without volition in the domain of oral speech. (Vygotsky, 1934/1987, p. 206)

All of the features of make-believe play identified by Vygotsky and Elkonin make their own specific contributions to the development of the abstract, voluntary, and conscious behaviors necessary for children's mastery of written speech, thus providing multiple supports for this emerging competence. Therefore, it could be said that make-believe play creates a ZPD for the development of early literacy.

PLAY AND WRITING

In addition to its general impact on academic learning, Vygotsky identified specific ways make-believe play prepares the foundation for young children's writing. In fact, he considered make-believe play along with drawing two major sources of children's ability to write. In both these activities, children learn to associate sign and the meaning of this sign. In play it occurs through the use of gestures indicating the new or changing function of a play prop. In drawing, a gesture results in making a mark that later becomes a representation of a word or a phrase:

> [A] child symbolic play may ... be understood as a very complex system of speech aided by gestures that supplement and indicate the meaning of individual toys. Only on the basis of indicating gestures does the toy gradually acquire its meaning precisely as drawing, supported at first by a gesture, becomes an independent sign. (Vygotsky, 1983/1997, p. 135)

Repeated naming and renaming toys in play helps children master the symbolic nature of words as the child first "unconsciously and spontaneously makes use of the fact that he can separate meaning from an object" (Vygotsky, 1933/1967, p. 13). It leads to children's eventual realization of the unique relationship that exists between words and the objects they signify—in other words, the emergence of metalinguistic awareness that is frequently associated by contemporary researchers with children's mastery of written language.

Whereas play makes young children conscious of the words they use, drawing provides them with a means to make a tangible record of their own stories and messages. Vygotsky finds many indications that early drawings are linked to the child's oral speech, from the frequent rise in self-directed speech observed as children were engaged in drawing to the similarities between children's drawings and their verbal concepts, both conveying only essential and constant characteristics of objects. From that, Vygotsky concludes that young children's drawings are "a unique graphic speech, a graphic story about something ... more speech than representation" (Vygotsky, 1983/1997, p. 138).

Even before learning to use conventional letters to record their messages, young children begin to use their "proto-writing" for the same function as they will eventually use mature writing: They employ the instrumental function of written speech to expand their mental capacities. Studies conducted by Vygotsky's colleague and student Luria demonstrated a gradual progression in children's ability to use written symbols as memory aids (Luria, 1929/1998). He discovered that written symbols used by young children often fall between schematic drawings and writing representing not the words in the oral message but rather the objects this message was about. For example, the sentence

"There are five pencils" was recorded with more scribbles than the sentence "There are two plates," although these two sentences had the identical number of words in them (Luria, 1929/1998). Some of Luria's findings (e.g., ability of 3-year-old children to reliably "read" and "reread" their idiosyncratic scribbles) made their way into Western literature, initiating research of the early forms of writing that appear prior to the onset of formal schooling (see, e.g., Ferreiro & Teberosky, 1982).

Learning letters supplies the final component to move the child from idiosyncratic forms of "drawing speech" to a conventional way of recording speech in written words. Early writing (as well as early reading) still depends on oral speech—dependence that is later overcome by experienced readers and writers:

> The initial written symbols serve as a sign of verbal symbols. Understanding written language is done through oral speech, but gradually this path is shortened, the intermediate link in the form of oral speech drops away, and written language becomes a direct symbol just as understandable as oral speech. (Vygotsky, 1983/1997, p. 143)

LEARNING TO WRITE IN THE EARLY CHILDHOOD CLASSROOM: PLAY PLANNING AS A VYGOTSKIAN-BASED STRATEGY THAT INTEGRATES PLAY AND LITERACY

Underscoring the instrumental function of written speech and its symbolic nature, Vygotsky advocated early instruction in reading and writing as a way to foster young children's cognitive development. True to his own belief that good instruction should lead development and not follow it, Vygotsky explains the value of learning to write early not in the context of preparing children for formal schooling, but in the broader context of using cultural tools for supporting the development of higher mental functions.

Although not specifying the exact pedagogy of this early instruction, Vygotsky outlined its general path, emphasizing that "teaching must be set up so that reading and writing satisfy the child's need" and that the goal of the instruction should be "to teach a child written language and not writing the alphabet" (Vygotsky, 1983/1997). Focus on letter formation and learning of the alphabet leads in Vygotsky's view to children merely mastering the "writing habit" as opposed to using written language the way it is supposed to be used in the culture: as a means of communication with others and with oneself and as a mental tool.

Play planning was designed as a complex strategy that simultaneously supports several aspects of play as well as several aspects of emergent literacy. The relative importance of each of these aspects varied as children were making progress toward more mature play and more mature writing. It is important to note that play planning is first of all a strategy that promotes higher level play and that its benefits for literacy development are contingent on the quality of play in which children engage. With play that remains nonimaginative and short-lived, children have little to plan for and the activity might turn into a mere exercise in writing devoid of meaning and carried out in a mechanical way. Needless to say, such use of play planning defeats its purpose, having no effect on either play or literacy.

Over several years, we have developed a number of protocols to implement play planning that we have adapted to the specific characteristics of a classroom. Typically, a play planning session takes place immediately prior to center time (also called choice time). First, children review yesterday's plans and read them to the teacher and to each other, then they choose a center in which they want to play, verbally state their plan, make a mark on a piece of paper to represent this plan, and read this mark to the teacher and to each other. The entire session takes about 10 minutes followed by 30 to 50 minutes of center time. The centers children play in are the ones typically found in most early childhood classrooms—art, manipulatives, blocks, and so on. All of the centers, however, have additional materials that allow children to engage in pretend play no matter which center they choose. For example, the manipulatives center may have miniature animals so that children can play farm or zoo, the block center has toy trucks and people that can fit in them, and so on. Thus, the term *play plan* would accurately describe the plan a child makes even if this child chooses a center other than dramatic play.

To encourage the communicative and instrumental function of written marks even when the marks themselves are idiosyncratic, we have children make their play plans using a colored marker or pencil that matches the color of the sign that designates a specific center (see Fig. 11.1). Thus, even at the early stages of play planning children are able to use their own and each other's plans as memory aids or as supporting evidence in resolving

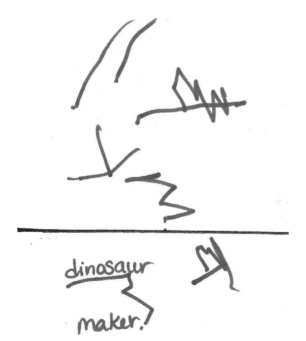

Figure 11.1. The child made a scribble and said that he was going to be a dinosaur maker.

conflicts. The latter happens frequently as many children find themselves in one center interfering with the play of those who had planned to play in this very center. After some initial teacher modeling and prompting, children quickly learn to ask the "trespassers" if the color of their plans matches the color of the center they "intruded." Such positive redirecting (as children are reminded of what they wanted to do and not of what they are not supposed to be doing) virtually eliminates fights and arguments, creating a friendly atmosphere in a classroom. As children use their colored scribbles to remind themselves and others about their plans, they practice self-regulation and other-regulation, essential components of intentional behavior.

As children progress from scribbles to representational drawing, they move to the next level of using written marks for self- and other-regulation (see Fig. 11.2). Now, with some teacher prompting and modeling, children include more details in their play plans including the props they will be using or making, the setting in which they will be playing (e.g., a castle), or their play partners. As drawing becomes more detailed, play plans provide more opportunities for the teachers to support make-believe play without intervening in and disrupting the play as it is occurring. The teachers suggest to children ahead of time how they can try out new roles, add new twists to the play scenario, or think of a way to substitute for lacking props. Potential conflicts caused by children not knowing how to coordinate the roles or share the props are worked out in advance, which further reduces the number of fights and arguments and allows children to engage in extended planning characteristic for mature play. Although at this stage (as well as at the previous one) teachers take dictation and write down what children say, children rarely pay attention to the teacher writing, using color and pictures as primary cues in "reading" their plans.

As the quality of play and experience in using written marks to communicate to

Figure 11.2.   The child made a picture and dictated to the teacher: I am going to cook.

themselves and to others grows, many children start discovering the function of teacher's writing (that represents exact words of the child's plan rather than its general meaning) and many children attempt to write on their own. Because carrying out multiple tasks involved in writing still presents a great challenge to young children, we developed a specific kind of scaffolding designed to assist children in remembering the words that comprise the oral message as they are "writing." Called scaffolded writing (Bodrova & Leong, 1996, 1998), this strategy is based on Vygotskian ideas of external sign mediators and private speech being the first mental tools acquired by young children. When using scaffolded writing, a child draws lines as placeholders for the words prior to dictating or writing these words. Isolating the planning stage (drawing the lines) from the writing process makes the entire task more manageable for young children, freeing enough memory and attention resources to allow them to concentrate on each individual word.

In early attempts to "write" down their play plans, many children produce lines on their own, dictating to the teacher words that are represented by each of the lines (see Fig. 11.3). Because play plans at this stage start with the same stem ("I am going to ...," "Today I will ...," etc.), children soon discover that there is the same word that is always written on the first line (*I*), on the second (*am*), on the fourth (*to*), and so on. At this point, it is common to see play plans with many empty lines standing for the words children cannot write with occasional letters or words written on one or two lines for the words the child knows how to represent. The point at which children start attempting to write individual words is an opportune time for the teachers to introduce additional tools that help children establish correct correspondence between the sound they hear in a word and a letter that represents this sound. Picture alphabet charts provide an excellent tool and so do the name tags of children's classmates, especially if the teacher makes sure that children practice name recognition in multiple contexts and has pointed out the fact that Tommy starts with a

Figure 11.3. The child made the lines and dictated to the teacher: I am going to get some groceries.

T. The alphabet chart and the name tags help children to establish sound-to-symbol correspondence so that they can represent the word with a letter.

With play planning implemented on a regular basis and make-believe play maintained at a high level, many children approach the end of their preschool year being able to write down their entire message using a combination of sight words and phonetic spelling (see Fig, 11.4). They can also read their messages without relying on their memory or the pictures, as they accurately reread their old messages or messages with no illustrations. At this point, children also make a transition from recognizing words and letters in their own writing to reading messages of their friends and finding familiar words and letters in various kinds of print. Encouraging children to read each other's messages "on the words" provides them with an additional motivation to represent as much of each word as possible to avoid confusions (e.g., does *c* stand for *castle* or *computer*?).

Analysis of play plans as well as the results of literacy assessments (see, e.g., Bodrova & Leong, 1998, 2001, 2003a, 2003b) indicate that preschoolers and kindergartners (including those initially classified as at-risk for future reading failure) can meet or exceed literacy expectations when they are introduced to writing in a context that is meaningful to them and are systematically scaffolded along the way. It can be concluded that these children had mastered the internal aspect of written language and became aware of their behaviors as writers and readers. This combined with higher levels of intentionality and awareness displayed in play as well as in writing makes these children well prepared for the beginning of formal schooling.

EARLY LITERACY IN THE SOCIAL CONTEXT: WHAT WE CAN LEARN FROM VYGOTSKY

The Vygotskian approach helps us to see literacy development in a broader context and to understand why chil-

Figure 11.4. The child made the lines and wrote on these lines: I am going to be the third little pig and I will build.

dren have difficulty transitioning from oral language to reading and writing. Literacy from the Vygotskian perspective is more than just being able to read and write; it is part of the development of mental tools—tools that are vital for cognitive development. Learning literacy is more than alphabet knowledge or phonemic awareness, it requires a complex set of underlying cognitive skills that many children, particularly at-risk children, do not have at the entry of first grade.

Moreover, this approach shows us why the dropping down of the first-grade curriculum into kindergarten and preschool will be doomed to failure, if all we do is make sure that children memorize their letters or practice phonemic awareness. The Vygotskian approach argues that make-believe play is, in fact, the best context for developing the important underlying skills necessary for both learning literacy and creating the conditions in which teachers can support the development of mental tools. Using make-believe play allows teachers to maximize their impact on their students' developing literacy skills, at the same time supporting their other critical competencies in cognitive, linguistic, and social-emotional areas. With the imminent danger of play disappearing from preschool (it has already all but disappeared in kindergarten) it is more important than ever to make sure that play that takes place in an early childhood classroom is the kind of play where "a child is always above his average age, above his daily behavior; in play it is as though he were a head taller than himself" (Vygotsky, 1933/1967, p. 107).

REFERENCES

Bodrova, E., & Leong, D. J. (1995). Scaffolding the writing process: The Vygotskian approach. *Colorado Reading Council Journal, 6,* 27–29.

Bodrova, E., & Leong, D. J. (1998). Scaffolding emergent writing in the zone of proximal development. *Literacy Teaching and Learning, 3*(2), 1–18.

Bodrova, E., & Leong, D. J. (2001). *The Tools of the Mind Project: A case study of implementing the Vygotskian approach in American early childhood and primary classrooms.* Geneva, Switzerland: International Bureau of Education, UNESCO.

Bodrova, E., & Leong, D. J. (2003a). Chopsticks and counting chips: Do play and foundational skills need to compete for the teacher's attention in an early childhood classroom? *Young Children, 58*(3), 10–17.

Bodrova, E., & Leong, D. J. (2003b). Learning and development of preschool children: The Vygotskian perspective. In A. Kozulin, B. Gindis, V. Ageev, & S. Miller (Eds.), *Vygotsky's educational theory in cultural context* (pp. 156–176). New York: Cambridge University Press.

Bodrova, E., & Leong, D. J. (2005). Vygotskian perspectives on teaching and learning early literacy. In D. Dickinson & S. B. Neuman (Eds.), *Handbook of research in early literacy development* (pp. 243–256). New York: Guilford.

Bodrova, E., & Leong, D. J. (2006). *Tools of the mind.* Columbus, OH: Merrill/Prentice-Hall.

Clay, M. (1993). *Reading recovery: A guidebook for teachers in training.* Portsmouth, NH: Heinemann.

Elkonin, D. (1978). *Psikhologija igry* [The psychology of play]. Moscow: Pedagogika.

Ferreiro, E., & Teberosky, A. (1982). *Literacy before schooling.* Exeter, NH: Heinemann.

Luria, A. (1998). The development of writing in the child. In M. K. De Oliveira & J. Valsiner (Eds.), *Literacy in human development* (pp. 15–56). Norwood, NJ: Ablex. (Original work published 1929.)

Vygotsky, L. S. (1956). *Obuchenije i razvitije v doshkol'nom vozraste* [Learning and development in preschool children]. *Izbrannye Psychologicheskije Trudy* [Selected psychological studies]. Moscow: RSFSR Academy of Pedagogical Sciences.

Vygotsky, L. S. (1967). Play and its role in the mental development of the child. *Soviet Psychology, 5*(3), 6–18. (Original work published 1933.)

Vygotsky, L. S. (1987). Thinking and speech. In R. W. Reiber & A. S. Carton (Eds.), *The collected works of L. S. Vygotsky: Vol. 1. Problems of general psychology* (N. Minich, Trans., pp. 39–285). New York: Plenum Press. (Original work published 1934.)

Vygotsky, L. S. (1997). The history of the development of higher mental functions. In R. W. Reiber (Ed.), *The collected works of L. S. Vygotsky: Vol. 4.* (M. J. Hall, Trans.). (Original work published 1983.)

Vygotsky, L. S. (1998). Child psychology. In R. W. Reiber (Ed.), *The collected works of L. S. Vygotsky: Vol. 5* (M. J. Hall, Trans.). (Original work published 1984.)

Wilder, G. (1972). *Analysis training: Failure to replicate Elkonin.* Technical report #202. Madison, WI: University of Wisconsin Center for Cognitive Learning. ERIC # ED070067.

12

COMMENTARY:
Play, Learning, and Teaching

Peter Hannon
University of Sheffield

Underlying this chapter is dissatisfaction that, despite many years of research in education, we still have a rather restricted vocabulary and set of concepts for addressing two of its central issues, namely teaching and learning. Insofar as this is true it makes it difficult to assess, from a sociocultural perspective, the contribution of play to literacy learning and literacy teaching.

If we take teaching to be any purposeful activity to promote learning, and if we accept there are many ways of doing it, it is surprising that there are so few terms, and so few concepts behind those terms, for understanding the activity. In addition to teaching, we also have the terms instructing, tutoring, coaching, training, drilling, schooling, and, recently, guided participation. There are not many more. Some of those in use are imprecise, some overlap, and some may simply be synonyms for others. Sports such as baseball or cricket may well have a more extensive and precise vocabulary for describing ways of throwing a ball than does education for describing one of its central activities.

Regarding learning, no line of educational enquiry has done more than literacy research to uncover and document ways in which children, particularly young children, learn. It is now two decades since a simplistic account of literacy as a cognitive skill acquired only through school instruction had to yield to a broader, sociocultural account that recognizes literacy is also a social practice in which children learn to participate through a combination of their own efforts at meaning making and others' willingness to involve them (Ferreiro & Teberosky, 1982; Goelman, Oberg, & Smith, 1984; Hall, 1987; Hannon, 1995; Heath, 1983; Meek, 1982; Roskos & Christie, 2000; Teale & Sulzby, 1986). One of the ways in which children make meaning is through play, and chapters in this book provide ample testimony to there being links between play and literacy. Yet we are, perhaps, still at an early stage in understanding how best to exploit those links educationally. That is partly due to the fact that the word *play* covers a wide range of children's activities and consequently there are many ways—not yet fully characterized—by which educators can enable the kind of play likely to promote literacy learning. A further challenge is that institutional contexts such as schools or day care centers are far from ideal environments for promoting literacy learning through child-initiated, meaningful participation in real—as opposed to contrived—literacy practices. Understanding how to use play to promote literacy learning may involve some stretching of the concept of play.

In what follows I hope to examine the notions of play and literacy learning used in the preceding chapters in this section. Then I step back and take a broader view of the ways in which educators, including parents and other caregivers, promote children's literacy learning. This requires some unpacking of the concept of teaching and seeing how different kinds of teaching can relate to different conceptions of literacy. It also means being clear about how home learning can differ from institutional learning. From a sociocultural standpoint I offer a framework for seeing how children's early literacy development can be facilitated and argue that it has implications for practical action, particularly in family literacy programs. Finally, I attempt to draw ideas together to identify where we might go from here in research and practice.

PLAY AND LITERACY LEARNING

The three chapters in this part, by Neuman, Hall, and Bodrova and Leong, all take a sociocultural view of young children's literacy learning, they all value play as a pathway to literacy, and they are all committed to identifying practical educational implications. However, they concern significantly different forms of play, and perhaps some of the examples stretch the concept of play to the limit. That is no bad thing, for we need a broad appreciation of literacy–play relationships if we are to optimize access to written language for young children in modern society, especially for those children from sections of society that tend to be excluded from educational opportunities.

Bodrova and Leong (chap. 11, this volume) provide an extensive and interesting theoretical justification, from a Vygotskyan perspective, for the importance of dramatic or make-believe play in children's literacy development. Their argument rests largely on the claim that such play develops children's capacity to engage in the kind of abstract thinking necessary for acquiring written language. They describe certain classroom practices developed, they say, to promote play and literacy development in preschool and kindergarten-aged children. The practices involved the children in writing plans to indicate in which of several available play activities they chose to engage in the classroom. The actual play activities did not necessarily include any literacy. The children's plans were, in true Vygotskian fashion, written in cooperation with teachers and with some well-thought-out scaffolding that fostered independence in the young writers. The plans were meaningful and had purposes (e.g., in clarifying who was allowed to play at what). Yet this is not so much an example of using literacy in play or playing with literacy as an example of using literacy to be allowed to play. It seems very probable that this classroom practice did promote children's literacy development (not least in developing children's self-regulation) but in itself it is hardly play. For the children it was definitely a means to an end. For the teacher, too, it appears to have been a means—for organizing the smooth running of play activities.

In the family literacy intervention program studied by Neuman (chap. 9, this volume), adolescent mothers were given high-quality, practical, individualized training, over 3 months, in interactive strategies to use with their children to promote language and literacy. The model of adult–child interaction informing the training reflected the concepts of guided participation (Rogoff, 1990) and scaffolding (Wood, Bruner, & Ross, 1976) but it was presented to the mothers more simply as four strategies: get set, give meaning, build bridges, and step back. The setting for the program was a day care center with provision for literacy-related sociodramatic play. There were three contexts for interaction: storybook reading, instructing the child in a goal-directed task, and facilitating sociodramatic play. Observational data on changes in mothers' interactions reported by Neuman are difficult to interpret, but she concludes that mothers' strategies tended to be governed by the context, a finding with implications for practice. In this study, however, it is not obvious where the play is and where the literacy is. One of the three contexts studied, storybook reading, was clearly literacy, but it is doubtful whether it was play. Neuman describes this context (and also the instructional context) as a "rather well- defined, goal-directed task." In the play context, mothers were encouraged to facilitate sociodramatic play and to get involved. That clearly counts as play but there is no report of there being literacy in the play (although the center environment had been reconstructed specifically to accommodate literacy-related activities). The play–literacy link in the study is rather indirect. Thus it is no surprise that, in her conclusions, Neuman rests her case for the contribution of play to literacy development on the general grounds that it promotes language, understanding of symbolic relationships, and feelings of competence and control.

In Hall's (chap. 10, this volume) compelling account of the classroom garage, the play–literacy link is more obvious. Five-year-olds in England were drawn into an extended, and cleverly supported, activity of setting up and operating an auto repair garage in their classroom. The garage was an area in the classroom set aside with suitable props, including such literacy items as notices, paper, and clipboards, for sociodramatic play. Hall describes how the teacher engaged the children in a number of activities outside the area, some even outside the school (visits to a real garage) including seeking planning permission to build the garage, advertising for staff, applying for jobs, providing an estimate for a repair, and dealing with objections from a neighbor. Rising to the challenges of these activities must have taught children about the purposes of written language and given them the opportunity and interest to acquire some specific skills. In addition, Hall reports that the activities influenced the quality of literacy-related sociodramatic play in the garage area. In this example we find the literacy in the activities outside the play area. The activities were teacher directed, but there is an element of make-believe about them (any of the children who thought they were going to get a real garage would have been sorely disappointed) so it could be argued that they constituted a form of play. There was also literacy in the freer sociodramatic play activities inside the garage, although it is difficult from the report to judge just how much.

There is no doubt that the examples of play and literacy in each of the three chapters offer much of interest to practitioners, many of whom would want to try out the ideas themselves, and to theorists who are struggling to work out the play–literacy connection. At this point I would like to offer three reflections.

First, these examples should encourage us to take a broad, inclusive view of what counts as play. If play is "behavior considered to be without direct function or purpose" or "a nonserious or exaggerated rendition of mature behavior and behavior in which the process of playing is more important than the end result" (Pellegrini & Galda, 2000, p. 67), then one could quibble about whether the activities described count as play. Some of them seem highly purposive, directed to meaningful ends. On the other hand, the activities are hardly the mature forms of literacy practiced by adults in the children's lives; neither do the activities involve children being drilled in meaningless skills. To that extent they are more play than nonplay. At the risk of overextending the concept of play, I suggest it would be profitable to count much—maybe most—emergent literacy behavior as play. Also, we should recognize that play is not an all-or-nothing activity. It is perfectly possible for an episode of play to have moments of very serious intent (as when a child struggles to form the letters of his or her name on a clipboard); and moments of playfulness can be interspersed in goal-directed activity (as when a child breaks off from sharing a storybook to imitate one of the characters). Perhaps one should think of play as a matter of degree; that children learn from a wide range of activities, some of which may be more or less like play. The main business is learning, and learning can sometimes have a high degree of play. Such a view would be consistent with that put forward by Pellegrini and Galda (2000) in their review of the function of play in cognitive development generally.

> There are many types of play, varied benefits that derive from play, and developmental influences on both type and benefits. There are also other experiences through which children learn and develop. Play may be important in children's development, but there are other routes to competence. Play is one of many. (Pellegrini & Galda, 2000, p. 74)

A second reflection is that, although the chapters introduce us to a range of literacy play activities, it is actually quite a narrow range. All the examples concern play and literacy in institutional—school or center—settings. (Even the family literacy example was restricted to an institutional setting although the goal, of course, was that parents transfer strategies to the home.) This is surprising, given that the power of the sociocultural perspective stems from recognizing that children learn literacy through involvement in literacy practices where they learn to participate through a combination of their own efforts at meaning making and others' readiness to involve them at an appropriate level. Literacy practices are likely to be more meaningful and more common outside institutional settings. Most of children's waking lives and therefore, arguably, most of their opportunities for learning literacy (including through play) take place in homes, communities, and noninstitutional settings. Given the theoretical position adopted by each of the chapter authors, I would be surprised if any of them took a different view. This is not to argue, of course, that institutional settings do not matter. On the contrary, in modern Western societies, they matter hugely. The point is that if we are concerned to promote children's literacy development, we must consider all the settings in which they can learn. We also need a realistic appreciation of the strengths and weakness of different settings. Table 12.1 suggests what these might be for schools and homes.

The suggested characteristics listed in Table 12.1 may be open to dispute. However, the list needs only be half right for us to see what a powerful learning setting the home can be in comparison with a school (or day care center) setting. In institutional settings literacy activities often have to be contrived. Perhaps that is why the idea of learning literacy from play is so attractive to educators. Play can be contrived and meaningful to children. Many of the activities described in the three chapters were contrived. They were creative—even inspired—attempts to compensate for the meaning deficit of the institutional setting as compared to the home setting. We arrive at a question: If the home setting is important for literacy learning, could a sociocultural perspective help us see how to influence it? I return to this later.

A third reflection concerns how best to describe what the adults do in the three examples. For example, in the family literacy programme, Neuman (chap. 9) refers to parents using strategies as they engaged in the verbal and nonverbal exchanges of everyday life, yet if one looks at the training that was given, and what was observed when they put the training into practice, it is very close to what one would expect of a good preschool teacher. Perhaps we should refer to what they were doing—and were later expected to do on their own with their children—as teaching. If not, what other word fits? In the other two examples there were teachers, but what they were doing was some way removed from formal instruction. It was teaching but not as many nonprofessionals know it.

To summarize, in reflecting on the insights afforded by chapters that have taken a sociocultural perspective, three needs are highlighted: a need to think of play as an integral, but varying, dimension of young children's tireless learning rather than something apart; the need to focus on home, as well as institutional, settings; and the need for an inclusive characterization of those adult actions that teach children literacy.

TABLE 12.1

Characteristics of Children's Learning at Home and at School

Home Learning	School Learning
Shaped by interest and need	Shaped by curricular objectives
Often seems effortless	Often seems to require effort
Rarely formally assessed	Often formally assessed
Often spontaneous	Timetabled
Flexible duration	Fixed duration
Extended conversations possible.	Limited opportunities for conversation
Natural problems	Contrived problems
May not encounter concepts in the easiest order for learning	Planned progression through subject matter
Special resources not usually available	Supported by special resources
Use of TV and print media often extensive and uncontrolled	Use of audio-visual and printed materials subordinated to teaching objectives
High adult-child ratio	Low adult-child ratio
Close and continuous relationships with few adults	Distant and discontinuous relationships with many adults
Adults as models	Adults as instructors
Recognition of children's achievements reflects many values	Recognition of children's achievements reflects school objectives
Vertical age group likely	Horizontal age group likely
Child sometimes in teaching role with younger children	Very few opportunities for child to act as a teacher
Opportunities vary with home background	Opportunities more equal
Accounts for much of the variation in school attainment	Only accounts for a fraction of the variation in school attainment

Note: Suggested by Hannon (1995), p. 39.

WAYS OF TEACHING LITERACY

Young children grow up in social groups composed of people—parents, older siblings, other family members, caregivers, visitors, professional teachers—who are ready to get involved in their learning. Most people are prepared to do something with children's learning. They may not do it reliably, they may not do it confidently, and they may not do it well, but many of them are prepared to do something. Hannon (2000) argued that there is a case for calling what they all do teaching. This is not as outrageous an extension of the term as it might first appear. The same word *teaching* is already used to refer to one-to-one teaching situations in a clinic or home or as well situations where there is one teacher to 30 or more learners in a classroom and where the learners may be as young as 5 or 6 years old. What the teacher does in these situations is very different. What is possible and desirable in one situation is impossible in another; what is a necessity in one is undesirable or unnecessary in the other. In relation to literacy teaching, in small groups such as families it is possible for learners to be initiated slowly and individually into literacy practices, whereas in large groups an emphasis on imparting discrete skills to all learners at the same time may be the only way teachers feel they can make progress. It would be naive to assume that family teaching methods could be transplanted unaltered into classrooms or vice versa. The theory of learning or the theory of literacy development most applicable to the teaching practice is likely to vary according to the setting, for example, in terms of the importance given to making learning activities meaningful versus learning by rote. There are also variations in terms of how far the teaching of reading is integrated with the teaching of writing. There are variations in the concept of literacy, which it is the aim of the teaching to impart. There is the issue of how deliberate is the teaching—at one extreme there can be systematic, planned instruction and at the other simply the provision of opportunities whereby learners can construct their own literacy in a social context.

Teaching approaches—professional and nonprofessional—also vary in which aspect or level of literacy they prioritize. We can conceptualize being literate as being able to deal with all the following levels of written language, usually simultaneously.

1. Purpose.
2. Text.
3. Sentence.
4. Word.
5. Subword.

Most teaching methods concentrate on teaching input in just one or two of these levels. For example, approaches that insist that children are taught phoneme awareness and phoneme–grapheme correspondences or knowing their letters before anything else are giving priority to Level 5. A sociocultural approach would focus on Levels 1 and 2, perhaps engaging with storybooks or scaffolding early writing. Few would dispute, however, that ultimately users of written language need competence at all levels.

When one considers how many permutations of all these variations are possible it becomes clear that simply to talk about the teaching of literacy is not adequate. Perhaps one needs to talk in plurals—about the teachings of literacies. Nevertheless what has happened in the development of teaching methods, and in the controversies they engender, is a tendency to focus narrowly on certain situations and certain levels of literacy to the exclusion of others. Sometimes this may be on the grounds that if one level is secured, the others can easily be added. Hence advocates of whole language teaching methods may focus on the upper levels in the belief that awareness and use of phonic regularities in reading and writing is something that will follow later as a result of the learner's own activity. Advocates of phonics often show little practical interest in whether children enjoy reading or appreciate the purposes of writing, believing that these are unproblematic once the basics are secured.

Turning now to the nature of teaching and how it relates to learning, we should note that teaching is not always necessary for learning to occur (and even when teaching seems to be necessary a very small amount can sometimes result in considerable learning). We know this from our own life experiences—outside as well as inside institutional educational settings—where we learn many things that no one has really taught us. Teachers with several years of experience, for example, usually feel that they have learned a considerable amount about their job but this is not because they have been taught everything (in fact they are often critical of how little they have ever been taught). Professional learning comes from having the right kind of opportunities, recognition of one's successes, stimulating interaction with colleagues, and teachers who serve as good models to emulate. Sociocultural perspectives on literacy learning show the value of this kind of learning by highlighting the capacity of young children to make sense of the world of print and its uses and thereby to learn literate aspects of culture without much obvious teaching. For example, Goodman (1986) argued that "the development of knowledge about print embedded in environmental settings is the beginning of reading development, which in most cases goes unnoticed" (p. 7). Ferreiro and Teberosky (1982), basing their investigations of children's literacy learning on Piagetian ideas, concluded, "In a field where it has been thought, in spite of a variety of viewpoints, that learning cannot take place without specific instruction, and where the learner's contribution has been thought to depend on and derive from the instructional methods, we have discovered a developmental line in which cognitive conflicts play an essential role" (p. 285). Meek's (1988) suggestion that children learn through active involvement in real literacy activities is summed up in the title of her monograph *How Texts Teach What Readers Learn*. From these perspectives there appears to be very little teaching going on. We might say that learning is the result of the individual's interaction with the environment. Of course, in the case of literacy, the environment is a social one in which others are producing and using written language for various purposes, sometimes in activities that involve the learner. Goodman, Ferreiro and Teberosky, and Meek share a strong implicit concern with social interaction in learning literacy. They take it for granted that those who are more proficient in the use of written language are often willing to help others—particularly children— who are still learning. Should we not call such help teaching? If there is teaching here—even if it is powerful—it is conducted in an intermittent and unobtrusive manner. I suggest that such teaching be termed *facilitation*. Providing, structuring, and supporting play is a case of facilitation. The three examples of using play, discussed earlier, are examples of facilitation.

Often, however, the word *teaching* implies a more deliberate and sustained attempt to shape another's learning. I suggest this be referred to as *instruction*—teaching that is explicit and planned, with clear aims and objectives and where experiences are provided for learners so as to maximize the probability of certain outcomes. Instruction can be carried out formally or informally but in either case it is purposive and governed by teaching aims. Instructional teaching episodes are likely to be time-tabled over a long period. Activities and experiences are organized for learners in such a way that they learn what is required as quickly and as efficiently as possible. The teacher decides on the optimum order for learning experiences and plans instruction accordingly. Irrelevant experiences are treated as distractions and excluded as far as possible. Instruction can be carried out with groups or individuals but is more common with groups, notably in class teaching where it is impractical for teachers to provide the individual interaction with learners characteristic of facilitation.

Compared to instruction, facilitation is a less intensive form of teaching and tends to be embedded in other (often everyday) activities. It is opportunistic—more patient and less urgent than instruction. It can still be deliberate, even if the teaching aims are at the edge of the teacher's consciousness. Teachers are aware of desirable learning outcomes even if they rarely plan teaching episodes to achieve specific objectives. The teacher, seeing the opportunity to impart some knowledge, might temporarily take on a teaching role before resuming an earlier one. Teaching episodes may be brief and relatively spontaneous. The teacher is open to unexpected learning and may be willing to follow the learner's interests. Facilitation can be very powerful for individual learners because it relates to their immediate concerns. For the same reason, it is less suitable for groups of learners.

Which is better, instruction or facilitation? Both have had their advocates. For example, in the 1970s Kohl argued that learning to read needed the kind of facilitation that works for learning to talk and that methods of teaching reading employed in schools were counterproductive. "Learning to read is no more difficult than learning to walk or talk. The skill can be acquired in a natural and informal manner and in a variety of settings ranging from school to home to streets" (Kohl, 1974).

In the 1980s, Meek (1982) expressed a similar view in these terms:

Reading is whole-task learning right from the start. From first to last the child should be invited to behave like a reader, and those who want to help him should assume that he can learn, and will learn, just as happened when he began to talk. ... Learning to read in the early stages, like everything else a child has come to know, is an approximation of adult behaviour with genuine meaningful function.

In the 1990s, however, opposite views of what kind of teaching is necessary have come to the fore. One example would be this claim:

Reading is skilled behaviour and, like all skills, it has to be taught from the bottom up, from the simple parts to the complex whole. No one would dream of asking a novice diver to attempt a difficult dive like a reverse jacknife. Nor would one teach a beginning piano student to use all ten fingers at the first piano lesson. All skilled learning builds piece by piece, through practice, until the skills are integrated. (McGuinness, 1998)

It is interesting to note the analogies chosen by these proponents. Meek and Kohl invite us to see the teaching of literacy as like the facilitation involved in helping a child learn to talk or walk; McGuinness prefers to compare it to the instruction involved in teaching high diving or piano playing.

How are we to decide between these different conceptions? Perhaps it is not a matter of opting for one or the other. We could entertain the possibility that there is some truth in both (however unwelcome such a thought might be to their advocates). We need to recognize that the phrase "teaching of literacy" refers to many aspects of literacy, to many different learners at different ages, and to many learning situations. Learning to walk or talk is perhaps an appropriate analogy for some learners, learning some aspects of literacy, at some times. At other times, in other contexts, at least some learners could benefit from instruction. Neither analogy has to be accepted as applicable to all cases all of the time. Second, instruction and facilitation need not be irreconcilable kinds of teaching. It might be more productive to think of mixing them in varying proportions according to need—of there being a *teaching spectrum* with instruction at one end and facilitation at the other. Literacy teaching in school (usually with one teacher to many learners) tends to be at the instruction end of the spectrum, whereas teaching at home (or in any context where learners do not greatly outnumber teachers) is likely to be closer to facilitation.

If literacy is seen as a social practice, and literacy teaching is seen as a matter of engaging children in those practices as meaningfully as possible with as much scaffolding as is required, then it is appropriate to turn to facilitation. This could include providing play experiences. Instruction fits more easily with a skills view of literacy. Yet, in principle, one could have instruction in literacy as a social practice or facilitation to learn skills. Figure 12.1 shows how views of literacy and views of teaching can relate. The literacy play examples discussed in the preceding three chapters fit most easily into the upper right quadrant of Figure 12.1. However, the figure shows there could be other possibilities (e.g., facilitation of skills learning) in the lower right quadrant. There is no need, surely, to restrict one's understanding of literacy teaching to any one quadrant. Figure 12.1 shows how play-based teaching approaches can fit into a larger educational space.

The teaching spectrum

Instruction --- Facilitation

Figure 12.1   Relating teaching possibilities to concepts of literacy.

A FRAMEWORK FOR THE FACILITATION OF LITERACY

Returning to a question posed earlier, let us consider whether sociocultural insights on literacy development can be used to enhance literacy learning in home settings. An attempt to do that, in the design of a family literacy program, has been the ORIM framework developed by Hannon (1995) and subsequently field tested by Hannon and Nutbrown (1997) and Nutbrown and Hannon (1997).

The framework starts from the premise that young children's literacy learning is facilitated by the social group in which they grow up; typically that is their family in a home setting. The children's interaction with family members is obviously of critical importance, and has been properly emphasized in the three chapters, but it is not the only way in which literacy learning is facilitated. First there must be opportunities for learning. In the case of literacy this could include opportunities to engage with environmental print; permission, materials, and space for writing and mark making; books in the home; and opportunities to develop oral language. As in oral language development, or indeed any aspect of their development, children's learning is facilitated by recognition of their learning achievements. A wide spectrum of interaction with others is necessary. Some interaction can be understood in Vygotskian terms, doing today in cooperation with others what will be done independently in the future and so on, but other forms of interaction, including instruction or playing, can also contribute to development. Finally, the social group can facilitate learning by providing models of users of written language who children may be motivated to emulate. The acronym ORIM summarizes the four aspects of facilitation: opportunities, recognition, interaction, and models.

The framework also identifies various strands of learning. In the case of early literacy learning, some obvious strands of experience are environmental print, books, writing, and oral language. There is some arbitrariness about picking out these particular strands. Literacy could be unpicked in other ways. These strands reflect current theoretical understandings and are also fairly obvious to parents and teachers. It is also possible to identify substrands. For example, substrands of oral language, known to be important in early literacy development, are engagement with stories, talk about written language, and phonological awareness.

The relation among the four aspects of facilitation and the strands of early literacy, within a single framework, is shown in Table 12.2. Each cell in the framework relates a particular aspect of facilitation to one of the literacy strands. The value of the framework is twofold. First, it can be used to map children's current literacy learning environment. This can be helpful, for example, in appreciating what families already provide for young children's literacy development or in auditing the quality of insititutional provision. Second, it can be used to structure an intervention (Nutbrown, Hannon, & Morgan, 2005). For example, work with parents in a family literacy program can be designed to cover certain cells, or all the cells, in the framework. Various activities for each of the 16 cells in the ORIM framework can be planned; for example, teachers working with families might ask, "How can we encourage parents to increase their interaction with their children around writing?" or "How could parents provide models of using environmental print?" Use of the framework is a check that there is input for each of the cells (up to 16) that have been targeted.

The ORIM framework has been used to design a low-intensity, long-duration (18-month) family literacy program offered to families with children aged 3 to 5 in disadvantaged areas of a city in the north of England (Nutbrown et al., 2005). A study of parents' experiences has found that the program had high take-up and participation, was welcomed by parents, and had affected family literacy practices (Hannon, Morgan, & Nutbrown, in press). A randomized control trial evaluation of the program has found gains in children's literacy development, particularly for children with the least educated parents, whose gains had persisted 2 years after the end of the program (Hannon, Nutbrown, & Morgan, 2005). Using the framework has therefore led to some practical effect.

Viewed through the lens of the ORIM framework, the classroom practices described by Bodrova and Leong (chap. 11, this volume) focused mainly on the writing strand and perhaps also to some extent on aspects of oral lan-

TABLE 12.2

The ORIM Framework

		Strands of Early Literacy Experience			
		Environment al Print	Books	Writing	Oral Language
	Opportunities				
Learning Facilitated by	Recognition				
	Interaction				
	Model				

guage. There was intent to enhance opportunities, recognition, and interaction. What, from the report, seems to have received less attention was providing children with models of literacy users. The most obvious literacy content in the program described by Neuman (chap. 9, this volume) concerned the book reading strand of early literacy and, within that, the focus was on parents providing opportunities, recognition, and interaction. There may have been more going on in the sociodramatic play area but that is not reported in any detail. Again, there appears to have been less concern about children having models. The garage initiative described by Hall (chap. 10, this volume) seems mainly to have concerned writing but there appears to have been some environmental print and perhaps some oral language (most likely in relation to talking about literacy). The children had opportunities, recognition, and interaction; there were also some interesting models of literacy users. Of course, there is no obligation to cover all the cells in the framework or to report everything that was done. Nevertheless, the framework serves to appreciate what educators are doing and may alert them to possibilities they may not have considered.

CONCLUSION

This commentary began with an appreciation of three thought-provoking studies of the play–literacy connection. Each study was animated by a sociocultural perspective that recognized literacy as a social practice in which children learn to participate through a combination of their own efforts at meaning making and the willingness of others in their social group to involve them. Each study involved a report of doing something involving play in educational settings to enhance young children's literacy development. For me, the three studies stimulated reflections about what play is, what literacy learning is, how learning is affected by setting, and what it is to teach literacy. I am perhaps less persuaded than some other contributors to this volume that "play's the thing"; certainly it is not the only thing. Play is an integral dimension of children's learning, including their literacy learning, and it should therefore be facilitated, in literacy as in other areas of development. It is particularly important in settings where opportunities are limited for meaningful engagement in genuine literacy practices and engagement has to be contrived. Our main goal in literacy education, however, should be to facilitate meaningful literacy learning. If we strive for meaningful literacy learning we will inevitably at some point be led also to value and support children's play.

REFERENCES

Ferreiro, E., & Teberosky, A. (1982). *Literacy before schooling.* Portsmouth, NH: Heinemann.

Goelman, H., Oberg, A. A., & Smith, F. (Eds.). (1984). *Awakening to literacy.* Portsmouth, NH: Heinemann.

Goodman, Y. M. (1986). Children coming to know literacy. In W. H. Teale & E. Sulzby (Eds.), *Emergent literacy: Writing and reading.* Norwood, NJ: Ablex.

Hall, N. (1987). *The emergence of literacy.* London: Hodder & Stoughton.

Hannon, P. (1995). *Literacy, home and school.* London: Falmer.

Hannon, P. (2000). *Reflecting on literacy in education.* London: Routledge-Falmer.

Hannon, P., Morgan, A., & Nutbrown, C. (in press). Parents' experiences of a family literacy programme. *Journal of Early Childhood Literacy, 1*(3), 19–44.

Hannon, P., & Nutbrown, C. (1997). Teachers' use of a conceptual framework for early literacy education involving parents. *Teacher Development, 1,* 405–420.

Hannon, P., Nutbrown, C., & Morgan, A. (2005). *Effects of a family literacy program on children and parents: Findings from the Raising Early Achievement in Literacy (REAL) project.* Paper presented at annual conference of the British Educational Research Association, Glamorgan, UK.

Heath, S. B. (1983). *Ways with words: Language, life and work in communities and classrooms.* Cambridge, UK: Cambridge University Press.

Kohl, H. (1974). *Reading, how to.* Harmondsworth, UK: Penguin.

McGuinness, D. (1998). *Why children can't read and what we can do about it.* London: Penguin.

Meek, M. (1982). *Learning to read.* London: The Bodley Head.

Meek, M. (1988). *How texts teach what readers learn.* Stoud, UK: Thimble Press.

Nutbrown, C., & Hannon, P. (Eds.). (1997). *Preparing for early literacy education with parents.* Sheffield/Nottingham, UK: NES Arnold/University of Sheffield REAL Project.

Nutbrown, C. E., Hannon, P., & Morgan, A. (2005). *Early literacy work with families.* London: Sage.

Pellegrini, A. D., & Galda, L. (2000). Cognitive development, play and literacy: Issues of definition and developmental function. In K. A. Roskos & J. F. Christie (Eds.), *Play and literacy in early childhood* (pp. 63–74). Mahwah, NJ: Lawrence Erlbaum Associates.

Rogoff, B. (1990). *Apprenticeship in thinking: Cognitive development in social context.* New York: Oxford University Press.

Roskos, K. A., & Christie, J. F. (Eds.). (2000). *Play and literacy in early childhood.* Mahwah, NJ: Lawrence Erlbaum Associates.

Teale, W. H., & Sulzby, E. (Eds.). (1986) *Emergent literacy: Writing and reading.* Norwood, NJ: Ablex.

Wood, D., Bruner, J., & Ross, G. (1976). The role of tutoring in problem solving. *Journal of Child Psychology and Psychiatry, 17,* 89–100.

Afterword

James F. Christie
Arizona State University

Kathleen A. Roskos
John Carroll University

The mix of old and new studies in this second edition brings us to a new place in our search for understanding of the play–literacy interface. We highlight what we have learned in this second "go-round" here, organizing our observations around what play does for the child's developing mind, how it contributes to the literacy learning environment, and its role as social activity that scaffolds literacy performances and mediates literacy practices. Our great hope, of course, is that we know more than when we started the compilation of the volume—and that we have laid the groundwork for further research so necessary for understanding the complex connections between play and literacy in early childhood. Before concluding our comments, we talk about our hopes in the context of this edition—those realized and those yet to be fulfilled.

THE PLAYFUL MIND

The three chapters in this part examine the play–literacy relationship from the perspective of what is going on the child's mind. They attempt to address this question: Does play promote cognitive growth that lays the foundations for literacy learning? Smith (chap. 1, this volume) starts the set off by examining the evidence that play makes important contributions to cognitive development in general. He cites three sources of evidence of play's role in cognitive growth: (a) the evolutionary history of play, which suggests that play may be a general-purpose learning mechanism; (b) cross-cultural evidence that pretend play is always present in young children and thus is likely to be useful; and (c) evidence on the extent to which play is designed to provide opportunities to develop specific cognitive skills, such as narrative skills and theory of mind, which in turn may promote literacy learning.

Smith examines the design research studies in more detail, focusing on evidence that pretend play contributes to the development of theory of mind, the awareness of one's own and other people's knowledge and beliefs. Positive results have been found in both correlational and experimental studies, suggesting that make-believe play may increase children's theory of mind, which may later help them with planning, guiding, and monitoring their own intellectual activity, including reading and writing (Flavell & Hartman, 2004). However, Smith points out a number of methodological limitations of both groups of research, such as the difficulties that third factors can create in correlational studies and a multitude of issues that can confound the findings of experimental research (e.g., inappropriate controls, experimenter bias, etc.).

Smith concludes that evidence supports that pretend play may help to bring about theory of mind and other cognitive skills, but the current evidence does not support the contention that make-believe play is necessary for their development. Make-believe play appears to be one avenue for developing the cognitive "equipment" that will lay the foundation for successful literacy acquisition, but these same skills can be also learned, perhaps more efficiently, through direct instruction. Smith does point out that play has one advantage over instruction: Play is highly motivating and enjoyable, giving it an important advantage with young children. However, little research has been done to explore this potential motivation advantage.

Sawyer and DeZutter's chapter (chap. 2, this volume) focuses on other design features of pretend play that may lead to the development of narrative competence, the ability to express and make sense of experiences through stories. Sawyer and DeZutter point out structural similarities between pretend play and narrative: They both (a) are framed as alternative worlds separate from everyday life, (b) have fictional characters, (c) involve decontextualized language, and (d) have plot elements (characters, goals, actions to attain goals, resolutions). When make-believe play becomes social and occurs in groups of children, an even more important parallel arises. Group pretend play and narrative both involve collaborative emergence in which "the outcome of the activity cannot be controlled by an individual; rather it emerges from the collective actions and contributions of each member." Sawyer and DeZutter propose that group make-believe provides children with experience at improvisation. When children collaborate in sociodramatic play, their contributions are evaluated and sometimes accepted by others. Each contribution builds on prior turns of others, resulting in the gradual emergence of a narrative. To successfully participate in group pretend play, children must negotiate with each other and coordinate their actions and symbolic transformation (e.g., everyone needs to know that the block of wood is a pretend hamburger). This negotiation draws children's attention to the features of narrative and also requires them to make judgments about what other players know and understand—the theory of mind discussed by Smith (chap. 1, this volume). Improvisation during group play also leads to collaborative learning in which children direct their playmates' attention to aspects of narrative that they might not attend to on their own. Finally, the collaborative nature of this improvisation creates "mutual enculturation" in which children learn to construct meaning in conventional ways that can be understood by others.

Rowe (chap. 3, this volume) concludes Playful Mind part with a thick, rich ethnographic description of very young children's book-related play. Data were collected in a 9-month naturalistic study of 2- and 3-year-old children's book-related play in a preschool classroom and in a case study of the author's child's literacy learning from ages 2 through 4. Results showed that the young children's book-related play involved (a) connecting books to concrete objects by playing with book-related toys (e.g., miniature dinosaurs), (b) personal responses to books (e.g., use toy to punish another toy that represents a "bad" character in the story), (c) participating in book-reading events through the persona of a pretend character (e.g., how a dinosaur feels about the story), (d) aesthetic reenactments in which children play out scenes from a book for the sheer enjoyment of the experience, (e) sorting out the author's meaning through play (e.g., how a steam engine works), (f) character studies (e.g., acting out characters that are only briefly mentioned in book—the brick seller in the *Three Little Pigs*), and (g) personal questions about the world (e.g., to learn more about smoking).

As Pellegrini and Van Ryzin (chap. 4, this volume) point out in their commentary, Rowe's research is exceptional in that it focuses on the play–literacy connection in toddlers who have just recently acquired the ability to engage in symbolic play. Rowe's studies provide a lens on book-related play as a satisfying, experiential means for very young children to interpret and make personal sense of books. Some of the children's story reenactments conformed with Rosenbatt's (1978) conception of aesthetic responses to literature "in which the reader selects out ideas, sensations, feelings, and images drawn from his past linguistic, literary, and life experience, and synthesizes them into a new experience" (p. 40). The book-related play also served other purposes, helping children to sort out an author's message, to explore the points of view of characters, and to conduct inquiries into matters of personal interest. This suggests that the "sense making" that occurs during early book-related play may set the stage for later comprehension strategies such as predicting, self-monitoring, and visual imagery.

In their commentary, Pellegrini and Van Ryzin examine all three chapters in the Playful Mind part from a design feature perspective. They point out that all three chapters do present evidence that play does have features that can be mapped onto the features of early literacy—links with theory of mind, narrative development, and comprehension—but play is defined very differently in each chapter. For example, in Sawyer and DeZutter's chapter, play is defined as group pretend in which children create their own stories in a improvisational manner, whereas in Rowe's chapter, play involves make-believe transformations of prefabricated stories contained in books. Pellegrini and Van Ryzin also point out some of the methodological problems with the research in the three chapters and encourage investigators to use longitudinal designs and modern statistical procedures to tease out subtle relationships between play and literacy and eliminate problems with third variables.

Taking all this into account, our view is that Smith's conclusion is right on target. It appears likely that the types of play examined in these chapters can lead to early literacy learning. However, it is also likely that these same early literacy skills can be learned just as well, if not more efficiently, through other means such as interactive storybook reading, shared writing, and age-appropriate forms of direct instruction. As Smith pointed out, play does appear to have some potential advantages as a learning medium for young children, such as high interest, engagement, and motivation. Yet these features of literacy-related play have not yet received much attention from researchers. We think back to the excitement that was initially generated by Sylva, Bruner, and Genova's (1976) finding that play has a facilitative effect on children's problem-solving abilities. In this study, children had to solve a problem that involved clamping sticks together to retrieve a marble or piece of chalk that was out of reach. Results showed that children who were allowed to play with the clamps and sticks did just as well at solving the problem as children who were directly trained to solve it. In addition, the play condition had an advantage. The children who got to play with materials were much more persistent in their attempts to solve the problem. Failed attempts did not appear to frustrate them because they were just playing around with the materials. Unfortunately for play advocates, these results may have been partially due to experimenter bias. When Simon and Smith (1983) tried to replicate the Sylva et al. (1976) study with double-blind assessments, the advantages for the play condition disappeared.

Our point is that, in this new era of early literacy basics, it is going to take more than design studies to show that play can result in children engaging in activities that are likely to promote early literacy. Research is needed to show that play experiences or curricula that have a strong play component are at least as effective, if not more so, than alternative means of instruction.

The Play–Literacy Instructional Environment

The focus of the chapters in this part shifts from matters of mind to the play–literacy instructional environment. The set begins at the curriculum level, with our own recent work focused on the concept of educational play and its role in helping children learn the new preschool academic basics. Next, the focus narrows to the instructional interactions that occur in literacy-enriched preschool classrooms. Han (chap. 7, this volume) reports on how individual differences in children's play predispositions appear to influence children's access to what the play environment has to offer. Finally, attention shifts to teacher education and professional development, which create the foundation for successful implementation of play–literacy curricula, instructional strategies, and classroom environments. Dunn and Beach (chap. 6, this volume) update their earlier chapter with new research findings on the state of typical early childhood literacy environments. In addition,

Dunn and Beach report on the impact of a large-scale, multi-year professional development project to increase teacher knowledge about effective early literacy environments and instruction.

In our chapter (Roskos & Christie, chap. 5, this volume), we begin by looking back at why play has been regarded as an essential component of developmentally appropriate, child-centered preschool programs. Next, we discuss the rise of three megatrends in early education: (a) the new "science-based" approach to early education, (b) the movement toward early childhood learning standards and standards-based education, and (c) the view that early literacy is the cornerstone of school readiness. All three of these trends put pressure on play's privileged status in early education programs and threaten to marginalize or eliminate playful learning opportunities from the curriculum.

We view the current situation as less dire than many play advocates, provided that early educators expand play's role to complement and enhance the new pre-K basics. In the past, play has functioned as a stand-alone activity, isolated from the rest of the curriculum. Play themes and materials were chosen on their own merit to elicit rich play, with little regard for how this play was connected to what went on during large-group circle time and small-group instruction. This needs to change. We believe that if play is to thrive in the current educational environment, a considerable amount of classroom play needs to be closely connected or networked with the academic curriculum. This can be accomplished by linking play environments and activities with the standards-based content taught in large- and small-group settings. In addition, teachers need to take an active role during play periods and guide children's play activities toward instructional goals. We use the Arizona Centers for Excellence in Early Education project as a model of this type of play–curriculum networking. Finally, we also recommend expanding the scope of the new basics to include self-regulation, an important prerequisite to academic success that has strong ties to play activity.

Previous research on literacy-enriched play environments has tended to be unidirectional, focusing on the effects of the environment and teacher scaffolding on children's play and literacy behavior. Han (chap. 7, this volume) examines these interactions from a bioecological perspective, looking at how child characteristics—play style and literacy ability—relate to children's access to play environment and supportive teacher interactions. Her findings support this multidirectional view. Children's play predispositions appeared to influence their choice of play setting, which, in turn, influenced their access to play materials and opportunities. Children's play predispositions also appeared to affect the amount and type of interaction that children had with teachers. Dramatists, who expressed a keen interest in people and sociodramatic play, spent more of their time in the dramatic play and art centers and were exposed to richer oral language, interactive storybook reading, and other supportive teacher interactions. Patterners, who were interested objects and their design possibilities, spent most of their time in the block and computer areas and received less attention from teachers. Han interpreted her results to indicate that the literacy-enriched play strategy, as it is commonly implemented, may be more effective for dramatists than for patterners. She pointed out the need to develop literacy play strategies that accommodate the interests and abilities of children with diverse play interests.

Dunn and Beach (chap. 6, this volume) update their chapter from the first edition, reporting on a series of studies that focus primarily on teacher preparation. The first set of studies examines the quality of literacy environments in child care settings. Their 1994 study revealed a situation that they describe as "far from the ideal." Classrooms contained minimal literacy materials (a library area and a few writing or drawing materials) and almost no support for literacy-related play. The larger scale 1999 study revealed slightly richer literacy environments than in the earlier study, but there was still much room for improvement. In addition, the 1999 study reported strong positive relationships between staff expertise and the quality of classroom environments. This latter finding, also supported by path analysis in the Early Steps to Literacy project (Beach et al., 2004), points out the crucial importance of preservice teacher education and inservice professional development. Finally, Dunn and Beach report on a long-term intervention project, Early Steps to Literacy, that used varying degrees of professional development to increase preschool teachers' knowledge of literacy learning and teaching. Two groups of teachers received nine full-day professional development sessions across an academic year. One of these groups received minimal support from mentors, whereas the other received sustained, ongoing assistance from mentors. There also was a control group that received no extra professional development. Results showed that, although both groups that participated in the professional development showed better literacy practices than the controls, the teachers who received extended in-class mentoring showed the largest gains. Dunn and Beach interpreted these findings to indicate the need for "sustained professional development that integrates instruction, application, reflection, and sustained support from a more knowledgeable other."

The commentary by Johnson (chap. 8, this volume) points out that the three chapters in the Instructional Environment part reflect a fundamental shift in early childhood education. In the past, emphasis has been placed on promoting all aspects of child development, whereas today the spotlight has been narrowed to academic skills and school readiness. Traditional play-based practices, such as lengthy free-play periods that are isolated from the main curriculum, do not fit well with the new emphasis on the basics. He gives guarded support to Roskos and Christie's notion of blended curriculum that network play activities and academic goals and standards. However, he also cautions against letting standards for content and basic skills learning lead to a neglect of the complex cognitive-affective processes that underlie learning. Johnson expresses hope that carefully planned play-based activities can be part of the pre-K–3 movement, aligning and coordinating early childhood education and primary-grade objectives and curricula.

The chapters in this section offer a ray of hope for the future of play in the current science-based early education environment. However, they also point out that there is difficult work to be done. The Roskos and Christie chapter points out the need for connecting many (but not all) play activities with the academic curriculum so that play directly supports standards-based educational outcomes. There is great need for carefully controlled experimental studies to compare this type of blended curriculum with programs that rely mainly on direct instruction and tiered interventions (i.e., skill-and-drill curricula). It is not enough to argue that play is beneficial for the whole child. We need evidence that play-based curricula are as effective, if not more so, than programs that do not include play. Our hunch is that, if given a fair test, programs that blend play and instruction will do just as well as instruction-only programs in terms of learning the basics. In addition, blended programs should produce some extra benefits in the areas of child engagement, motivation, and self-regulation.

Han (chap. 7, this volume) points out the importance of taking individual differences into account when designing curricula and doing evaluation studies. Effective curricula should include activities that appeal to the interests of genders, different cultural backgrounds, and basic personality characteristics such as play predisposition. For example, curricula that blend play and instruction should include literacy-enriched, theme-related activities in all centers—dramatic play, blocks, manipulatives, art, and computers. This will help ensure that all children get the academic, social, and emotional benefits of play activity. Evaluation research should always use designs that allow Subject × Treatment interactions to be examined.

Finally, Dunn and Beach (chap. 6, this volume) point out the necessity of improving professional development for early childhood educators. One-shot, short-term programs do not appear to be sufficient. Teachers need long-term, sustained professional development with opportunities to apply strategies in their own classrooms. They also need ongoing support, modeling, and feedback from experienced mentors and coaches. Without skilled, knowledgeable teachers, it will be impossible to effectively implement literacy-rich environments, blended curricula, and effective teaching strategies supported in the first two chapters in this part.

THE PLAY–LITERACY SOCIAL CONTEXT

Part III of the book includes three chapters that look at literacy–play relations through a sociocultural lens. Through their investigations, these researchers describe and interpret the influences of prevailing social and cultural systems on children's literacy experiences and development.

Neuman (chap. 9, this volume) describes an intervention program designed to help teenage mothers enhance the quality of their communicative interactions with their children during everyday home literacy activities and routines. This everyday literacy approach differs from previous family literacy programs that have attempted to train parents to provide school-like experiences for their children. Hall (chap. 10, this volume) approaches the in-school/ out-of-school dichotomy from a more critical perspective. Hall describes a play-based strategy in which teachers intentionally create obstacles to play. These play barriers nudge children to engage in ideological literacy experiences that are situated within the cultural values and practices of their community. Finally, Bodrova and Leong (chap. 11, this volume) provide a thorough explanation of the play–literacy connection from a Vygotskian perspective. Focusing on play and writing, they describe their research with a play planning procedure that integrates the development of mature play and writing.

Neuman (chap. 9, this volume) discusses a guided participation strategy, derived from Rogoff's (1990) work, that prods children to use their imaginations, make plans, and take personal responsibility for accomplishing everyday tasks. In short, they try their hand at the mental work that holds much in common with that of literacy. Mothers are taught a four-step strategy: (a) get set, in which the they adjust their level of involvement to match their children's abilities; (b) give meaning, in which they focus children's attention on certain aspects of activity through labeling, comparing, contrasting, or elaborating; (c) build bridges, in which she helps connect the current activity to her child's prior knowledge and experiences, and (d) step back, in which the mother phases out her support so that the child takes control of the task. Neuman investigated the effectiveness of this strategy in three contexts: storybook reading, instruction, and play. In general, the storybook reading context provided the most opportunities for mothers to give meaning to experience. In the play context, mothers were more likely to build bridges, helping children employ their imaginations. This can promote *distancing,* the ability to separate one's thinking from concrete here-and-now reality. Instruction appeared to provide a situation in which mothers could step back and hand over responsibility to their children.

Hall (chap. 10, this volume) draws heavily on a social literacy, a view that emanates from anthropology and sociology. Social literacy emphasizes how literacy is used in everyday life outside of school settings. Hall uses the distinction between ideological (everyday life) versus autonomous (school) literacy as the rationale for a new type of adult involvement in play. Hall recommends that teachers set up situations that require children to use ideological forms of literacy in connection with their play. This involves setting up problems or obstacles that children need to overcome before they can continue with their play (e.g., getting planning permission to build a play garage). This is quite different from the play facilitator role that is typically advocated in the play–literacy literature (Enz & Christie, 1997; Roskos & Neuman, 1993). Rather than simply assisting children's play efforts, Hall recommends that teachers stretch children's literacy skills by presenting them with challenges that link play with real life. Here the teacher acts as a "gadfly" or provocative stimulus, presenting children with situations and problems that link play with real-world ideological literacy activities. This strategy promises to expand the literacy learning potential of literacy-enriched play settings.

Bodrova and Leong (chap. 11, this volume) begin their chapter with a very detailed explanation of the relationship between play and literacy development in Vygotsky's cultural historical theory. According to Vygotsky, make-believe play creates its own zone of proximal development for acquiring the mental tools (e.g., symbolic representation, metalinguistic awareness, and self-regulation) that are needed to learn to read and write. Bodrova and Leong then describe their play planning strategy that promotes the acquisition of these mental tools. The teacher leads a 10-minute play planning period prior to center time in which each child makes his or her own plan for what he or she will do in centers. Teachers guide children to use these plans to manage their own behavior and to resolve conflicts with other players. Initially, children's play plans consist of meaningful scribbles. In time, the plans progress to drawings and then to emergent writing. When children are ready to use writing in their plans, teachers support the process with scaffolded writing. They teach children to write lines that serve as placeholders for the words the child wants to write. Initially, the child dictates words, and the teacher writes them on the child's lines. Soon, children begin writing their own words using invented spelling. Again, the teacher provides a support tool: picture alphabet charts. Eventually, children begin reading each other's writing, providing social motivation to use more conventional forms of spelling to represent words.

One theme that connects all three chapters in this part is the need to expand the definition of literacy beyond traditional academic boundaries and recognize that literacy is a social practice in which children create meaning with the help of others. In Neuman's chapter (chap. 9, this volume), the roots of literacy are embedded in everyday interactions between mother and child. Hall (chap. 10, this volume) focuses on ideological literacy, real-life literacy activities such as planning permits, help-wanted ads, and job applications. Literacy in the Bodrova and Leong chapter (chap. 11, this volume) involves meaning-laden scribbles, drawings, and scaffolded writing used to plan and manage play activities. Another common thread connecting the chapters in this part is the importance of adult scaffolding of children's play, language, and early literacy. Each chapter presents a scaffolding strategy: guided participation (Neuman), play challenges and hurdles (Hall), and play planning (Bodrova & Leong). In each of these strategies, the adult raises the bar while providing temporary assistance that helps children progress to the next level of development.

Hannon's (chap. 12, this volume) commentary points out an interesting limitation of these chapters: All deal with the play–literacy connection in institutional settings. He argues that more attention should to be given to play and literacy in home settings. In addition, he highlights the need for attention to be given to how play and teaching are defined, issues that we have also discussed in an earlier review of play–literacy research (Roskos & Christie, 2004).

CONCLUSION

So where are we now in this endeavor to understand the zone of convergence between play and literacy? Are we asking new, better questions or rephrasing old ones? Are we moving forward methodologically or standing still? Are we bringing forth new insights or going over old ground? We are optimists, but we are also realists in recognizing that research progress across the play–literacy interface is painfully slow.

Yes, across the studies herein we can see more clearly the cognitive processes that merge in play and literacy (e.g., using symbols to convey meaning), especially in the renewed emphasis on children's developing theory of mind. However, we lack the benefit of basic neuroscience research that goes to the core of the neural mechanisms that play and early literacy precursors may share (e.g., self-regulatory abilities). The developing mind, after all, is housed in a developing brain that organizes core processes at a neural level. Play arousal as a motivator, for example, may have implications for skill learning in media-rich early reading environments, such as an e-book. There is, in fact, some tantalizing evidence in this regard. In a recent study, Shamir and colleagues (2006) show the effectiveness of the play and read condition in an e-book reading environment for supporting children's learning of word meanings. Hence the possibility that the combination of play arousal in a highly interactive reading environment (print + audio + picture + animation) may heighten neural activity, thus affording sustained attention to words and their meanings. Basic research along these lines, vigorously pursued, adds a fascinating new dimension to our understanding of the playful mind.

The studies included in this volume show that we are gaining ground in learning about the external environments that support the transfer of play's processes and skills to the demands of literacy, both at individual and program levels. Environments differentially support individual play propensities with consequences for early literacy exposure. We are also making headway in understanding the role of instructional resources as capacity builders in the educational environment for linking play and literacy in more productive ways. Blended curricula and more knowledgeable teachers, for example, increase the potential of the learning environment for connecting play and literacy activities. As a result, the immediate educational environment affords proximal processes more supportive of early literacy development, which is a leading hypothesis from a bioecological perspective. Still, this bioecological agenda is only thinly addressed, probably because of the methodological challenges of examining the joint interactive effects of both individual child and environment resources (including human capital) on developing literacy. Han (chap. 7, this volume) takes a courageous step in this direction, but it is a hard road. Yet to more fully describe and explain the play–literacy interface in even an ecological sense, new studies that unbundle (and reassemble) the key components of instructional capacity in the classroom environment are very needed. Such studies need to address at least these general sets of capacity-building variables: the intellectual ability, knowledge, and skills of teachers and other staff; the quality and quantity of resources available for teaching, including time and support staff; and the social organization of instruction or instructional culture (Corcoran & Goertz, 1995).

Now to our progress from a social activity perspective, or more precisely that of situated cognition, which argues that learning is not only a matter of what goes in the head but is situated within a material, social, and cultural world. Literacy (and play for that matter) is not only individual mental work but also a social practice with built-in economic, historical, and political implications.

Suffice it to say we have not come too far in unraveling the play–literacy interface from this point of view. This is unfortunate in light of an exploding online world where images, symbols, graphs, diagrams, artifacts, and a plethora of visual symbols are significant. As a social practice, literacy is changing in the 21st century from reading (and writing) print-based texts to multimodal texts that intermix words and images, so much so that it is difficult at times to tell which is which. Text is a conglomeration of print, sound, and image that works synergistically to represent thoughts and ideas (Kress, 2003). From a very early age (late infancy), young children are exposed to play objects (e.g., *Baby Einstein*), multimodal texts (e-books), and video games on computer screens with which they interact and "play" in various ways (Wartella, 2006). Yet little attention has been paid to this digital turn at the play–literacy interface, which is amazing given the rapid expansion of new technologies in modern societies, such as televisions, DVDs, computers, handheld computers, cell phones, and computer games (Larson & Marsh, 2005). Clearly this is an area ripe for new studies that examine the links between play processes (e.g., engaging in semiotic activity) and new concepts of print involving nonlinear, nonsequential, multilayered negotiations of multimodal texts (Hassett, 2006). Early literacy learning in a new media age, in fact, may spur a resurgence of social play in early education because its demands for complex, abstract thinking (e.g., imagining, negotiating, improvising) are closely related to those needed for negotiating multimodal texts (navigating screens, interpreting images, parallel processing).

Drawing this edition to a close then, we have two synthesizing reflections. The first is that the periodic review with critical commentary of a sample of play–literacy studies is fruitful, because it allows for a kind of progress monitoring of the play–literacy interface as a domain of inquiry. It reveals the small steps forward (e.g., new concepts and approaches), and also the persistent theoretical and methodological problems that are barriers to scientific progress. In this volume we are made aware of just how slow progress can be and we are reminded again of scientific barriers, and that we must work more vigorously to overcome them. The second is that we are still very baffled by the complexity of connections between play and literacy, and even more so as we enter a new media age. A sense of bafflement requires some direction, and here we turn to the eminent play scholar, Sutton-Smith (1999), who at one point labored to overcome restrictive psychological definitions of play. He attempted a consilience of play definitions—consilience defined as "a jumping together of knowledge as a result of linking of facts, and fact-based theory, across disciplines to create a common framework of explanation (Wilson, 1998, p. 53, cited in Sutton-Smith, 1999). With Sutton-Smith, we seek consilience, and we urge you as colleagues at the play–literacy interface to do the same in creating a new generation of play–literacy research.

REFERENCES

Beach, S., Ball, R., Briscoe, B., Dunn, L., Han, M., & Kimmel, S. (2004). *Early steps to literacy: The impact of professional development on preschool teachers and children in their classrooms.* Symposium presented at the National Reading Conference, San Antonio, TX.

Corcoran, T., & Goertz, M. (1995). Instructional capacity and high performance schools. *Educational Researcher, 24*(9), 27–31.

Enz, B., & Christie, J. (1997). Teacher play interaction styles: Effects on play behavior and relationships with teacher training and experience. *International Journal of Early Childhood Education, 2,* 55–69.

Flavell, J., & Hartman, B. (2004). What children know about mental experiences. *Young Children, 59*(2), 102–109.

Hassett, D. (2006). Signs of the times: The governance of alphabetic print over "appropriate" and "natural" reading development. *Journal of Early Childhood Literacy, 6,* 77–104.

Kress, G. (2003). *Literacy and the new media age.* New York: Routledge.

Larson, J., & Marsh, J. (2005). *Making literacy real: Theories and practices for learning and teaching.* Thousand Oaks, CA: Sage.

Rogoff, B. (1990). *Apprenticeship in thinking: Cognitive development in social context.* New York: Oxford University Press.

Rosenblatt, L. (1978). *The reader, the text, the poem: The transactional theory of the literacy work.* Carbondale, IL: Southern Illinois University Press.

Roskos, K., & Christie, J. (2004). Examining the play–literacy interface: A critical review and future directions. In E. Zigler, D. Singer, & S. Bishop-Josef (Eds.), *Children's play: The roots of reading* (pp. 95–123). Washington, DC: Zero to Three Press.

Roskos, K., & Neuman, S. (1993). Descriptive observations of adults' facilitation of literacy in play. *Early Childhood Research Quarterly, 8,* 77–97.

Shamir, A. (2006, June). *Multimedia stories as a tool for supporting children's emergent literacy.* Paper presented at the KNAW Colloquium, How Media Can Contribute to Early Literacy, Amsterdam, The Netherlands.

Simon, T., & Smith, P. (1983). The study of play and problem solving in preschool children: Have experimenter effects been responsible for previous results? *British Journal of Developmental Psychology, 1,* 289–297.

Sutton-Smith, B. (1999). Evolving a consilience of play definitions: Playfully. In S. Reifel (Ed.), *Play and culture studies* (Vol. 1, pp. 239–256). Stamford, CT: Ablex.

Sylva, K., Bruner, J., & Genova, P. (1976). The role of play in the problem-solving of children 3–5 years old. In J. Bruner, A. Jolly, & K. Sylva (Eds.), *Play and its role in development and evolution* (pp. 244–257). New York: Basic Books.

Wartella, E. (2006, June). *Special audience; special concerns: Children and the media.* Paper presented at the KNAW Colloquium, How Media Can Contribute to Early Literacy, Amsterdam, The Netherlands.

Wilson, E. O. (1998, April). The biological basis of maturity. *The Atlantic Monthly, 281*(4), 53–70.

Author Index

A

Ageyev, V. S., 114, 116
Allen, J., 22, 34
Alward, K., 86
American Association of Colleges for
    Teacher Education, 142, 145
American Federation of Teachers, 91, 97
Anastasopoulos, L., 105, 110, 117
Anderson, A., 151, 164, 166
Androes, K., 39, 62
Anello, C., 45, 60
Angelillo, C., 7, 18
Ardila-Rey, A. E., 24, 33, 69, 75, 78
Arnett, J., 106, 115
Association for Childhood Education Inter-
    national, 142, 145
Astington, J. W., 11, 16
Attfield, J., 138, 147
Auerbach, E. R., 151, 166
Azmitia, M., 157, 166

B

Bakhtin, M. M., 28, 33
Ball, R. A., 105, 109, 112, 113, 115, 220, 226
Barnes, D., 60
Bartini, M., 79
Barton, D., 169, 172, 183
Bass, A. S., 41, 62
Bateson, G., 22, 33
Bateson, P. P. G., 69, 70, 75, 77, 78
Baughn, C. R., 23, 25, 27, 36
Baumer, S., 138, 139, 145
Beach, R., 57, 60, 62

Beach, S. A., 101, 103, 105, 108, 109, 110,
    112, 113, 115, 118, 137, 138, 142,
    145, 218, 220, 221, 226
Beals, D., 31, 33
Bearne, E., 139, 145
Benjamin, L. A., 151, 166
Bergen, D., 41, 60
Berk, L., 85, 95, 97, 98
Berlin, G., 156, 166
Bernstein, B., 69, 77
Berry, D., 113, 117
Biscoe, B., 105, 109, 112, 113, 115
Bishop-Josef, S., 3, 4, 19, 83, 100
Bjorklund, D. F., 75, 77
Blair, C., 95, 97
Blanchard, J., 93, 100
Blatchford, P., 4, 18
Bloome, D., 152, 166
Blurton Jones, N., 6, 16, 69, 77
Bock, J., 7, 16
Bodrova, E., 85, 90, 91, 97, 185, 192, 197,
    198, 199, 202, 212, 222, 223
Bogard, K., 133, 143, 146
Bowman, B., 91, 97, 113, 115, 142, 146
Branscombe, N. A., 22, 25, 33
Bransford, J., 95, 97
Bredekamp, S., 84, 97
Breier, M., 169, 184
Brennan, S. E., 31, 33
Bretherton, I., 9, 16
Briscoe, B., 220, 226
Bronfenbrenner, U., 90, 96, 97, 102, 115,
    120, 125, 130, 140, 146
Brooks-Gunn, J., 156, 166
Brown, A., 95, 96, 97

Subject Index